EXEMPLARY ENGLAND

Exemplary England

Historical Inquiry and Literary Recompense in Pope, Gray, and Richardson

Sarabeth Grant

UNIVERSITY OF VIRGINIA PRESS
CHARLOTTESVILLE AND LONDON

University of Virginia Press
© 2023 by the Rector and Visitors of the University of Virginia
All rights reserved
Printed in the United States of America on acid-free paper

First published 2023

1 3 5 7 9 8 6 4 2

Library of Congress Cataloging-in-Publication Data
Names: Grant, Sarabeth, author.
Title: Exemplary England : historical inquiry and literary recompense in Pope, Gray, and Richardson / Sarabeth Grant.
Description: Charlottesville : University of Virginia Press, 2023. | Includes bibliographical references and index.
Identifiers: LCCN 2022039156 (print) | LCCN 2022039157 (ebook) | ISBN 9780813948997 (hardcover) | ISBN 9780813949000 (paperback) | ISBN 9780813949017 (ebook)
Subjects: LCSH: Pope, Alexander, 1688–1744—Criticism and interpretation. | Gray, Thomas, 1716–1771—Criticism and interpretation. | Richardson, Samuel, 1689–1761—Criticism and interpretation. | National characteristics, English, in literature. | Literature and history—England—History—18th century. | LCGFT: Literary criticism.
Classification: LCC PR3634 .G73 2023 (print) | LCC PR3634 (ebook) | DDC 820.9/005—dc23/eng/20221021
LC record available at https://lccn.loc.gov/2022039156
LC ebook record available at https://lccn.loc.gov/2022039157

Cover art: *The Death of General Wolfe*, Benjamin West, 1770. Oil on canvas, 152.6 x 214.5 cm. (National Gallery of Canada, Ottawa; gift of the 2nd Duke of Westminster to the Canadian War Memorials, 1918; transfer from the Canadian War Memorials, 1921; photo: NGC)

CONTENTS

Preface	vii
Introduction: "Such Labor'd Nothings," Rhetorical Showmen, and the Study of History	1
1 "Another Phoebus, Thy Own Phoebus": Verse Satire and Class in *The Dunciad*	35
2 "Their Artless Tale Relate": Pastoral Elegy and Geography in "Elegy Written in a Country Churchyard"	91
3 "She Has Now a Tale to Tell": The Epistolary Novel and Gender in *Clarissa*	150
Coda: "Building a Monument, or Burying the Dead"	209
Notes	221
Bibliography	241
Index	251

PREFACE

I FIRST met Alexander Pope, as many probably have, as an undergraduate, when I was forced to take an Age of Satire class to fulfill the pre-1800 requirement for English majors. Going into that class, I knew nothing about Pope, the Hanoverians, the Restoration, or even satire itself. By the time I completed my degree two years later, I had written my honors thesis on *The Dunciad*.

I often wonder how it happened that I fell for Pope so quickly and so ardently. After all, he certainly never exuded the rakish swagger of a Lord Rochester or Byron, the type of devilish ease long capturing the imaginations of readers (and Hollywood). I could say it was Pope's profound respect for the heroic couplet that amazed me, or perhaps his steadfast commitment to a life of letters despite the manifold physical, religious, and political disadvantages aimed at disabling him. But, truth be told, it was those moments of painful, poignant, and grotesque bathos that captured my attention: the coronation of Bays, the vapid king of the dunces; the heroic games where participants chase after excrement and shadows; the "Universal Darkness" that "buries all," inevitably and ruthlessly.[1]

There have been many scholars who have written on Pope's work, a few who have attempted comprehensive biographies, and countless readers who have either condemned his work as possessing "something infernal in it" or have reified him as "a master of style."[2] From these I soon located Pope's relentless commitment to articulating eighteenth-century England, both as he experienced it and as he imagined it could be. *The Dunciad*, the culmination of decades of Pope's study and engagement with society, archives the clash of conflicting ideologies orbiting the tension between nostalgic yearning for the past and hopeful anticipation for future innovations. His is both a guidebook to eighteenth-century culture and people as well as a fantasized version of English nationhood.

First and foremost, this is a book about historical inquiry and nation building. For Pope, deciding what meaning the past can hold for the present forms the cornerstone of national identity. He uses his work to consider what constitutes history—physical objects that one can hold, or the ethos and actions of specific individuals verifiable to historical record, or the recitation of facts, dates, numbers? He deliberates how those various meanings impact the current religious, political, and social landscape and, finally, how those choices construct the nation.

Yet he is not alone. Curiously, the publication of three mid-century masterpieces occurred within less than a decade: Pope's *The Dunciad* (the four-book version of 1743), Thomas Gray's "Elegy Written in a Country Churchyard" (1751), and Samuel Richardson's *Clarissa* (1748). Despite this temporal proximity, we tend to isolate each of these men and their respective texts from shared conversations, privileging their differences in genre and subject. If we look for interconnectedness, though, we find the astonishing. For instance, in a letter dated September 1725 written to Jonathan Swift, Pope affirms his investment in studying history: "I mean no more translations, but something domestic, fit for my own country, and for my own time."[3] Curiously, Gray pens a letter to Richard West circa December 1735 that bears a striking resemblance to Pope's letter to Swift: "I believe I must not send you the history of my own time, till I can send you that also of the reformation."[4] The phrase "my own time" emergent from both Pope's and Gray's letters reflects a shared concern with articulating history and constituting time—in particular, with recording, preserving, and representing the complexities of extant and inward events.

From this, we begin to see further connections. Lord Bolingbroke, in the second letter of his *Letters on the Study and Use of History* (1755), states, "We are fond of preserving, as far as it is in our frail power, the memory of our own adventures, of those of our own time, and of those that preceded it."[5] Again the phrase "own time" appears, specifically in terms of commemoration. Likewise, when writing of his endeavor to assemble his correspondence to Lady Bradshaigh in May 1758, Richardson writes, "All I shall trouble myself about, with regard to my Collections, is, as Time and Ability shall be lent to me, to run them over cursorily, and scratch out great Numbers of them, by way of saving Survivors Trouble."[6] Here, too, we find the acknowledgment of the present moment (my own time) as itself historical, just as the past is historical. Such an awareness suggests that one's own consciousness is historical, both historically situated and able to reflect on its situatedness. In being historical, individual consciousness invests historical inquiry with a deeply personal quality, one that fuses the individual citizen to the nation in the shared endeavor for articulation.

But there's more connecting Pope, Gray, and Richardson: the use of the creative imagination to conjure alternatives—and correctives—to historical realities of the present day. *The Dunciad* offers Pope's apocalyptic view of eighteenth-century England, but in so doing he presents multiple versions of England, the one he refuses and the one he desires. Likewise, the "Elegy" imagines an encounter between an unnamed individual and a rural hamlet, a happenstance that allows Gray to attempt to placate real-world class divisions, offering an idyllic rendering of English rural life and of English solidarity. Lastly, Richardson's *Clarissa* represents conflicting versions of events as understood by Clarissa and Lovelace, as well as a myriad of other individuals. The desires and intentions informing the actions of the characters are types of fantasies, the imagined constructions shaping and manipulating the outcome of the historical recording. As in Pope and Gray, the disparate voices competing for articulation suggest that Englishness is a compilation of fantastic and fantasized versions of potential narratives.

Perhaps I perform a risky move in aligning Pope with Gray and Richardson. Perhaps I should continue to segregate them based on the disparities in genre and subject: a verse satire aimed primarily at the elite, a pastoral elegy considering the lives of the rustic poor, and an epistolary novel taking arranged marriage, rape, and the possession of women as its subject. But I believe the benefits outweigh the dangers here. We should view these writers as historians, invested in the efficacy of narrative and non-narrative modes of history writing, attempting to use literary genres to establish a relationship between the past and present so that a more capacious view of historical knowledge may emerge, one that avoids the all-consuming "Universal Darkness" frightening Pope.

Bringing Pope, Gray, and Richardson together illuminates the 1740s as a privileged ideological space allowing for the potentialities of an expansive Englishness, potentialities later eradicated with the contentions arising after the 1750s. Englishness in the latter eighteenth century points to the changing conditions of subjectivity and nationhood brought on by the American Revolution, the French Revolution, and both internal and empiric political developments. Critical theories on the 1740s typically focus on class or gender oppositions, yet I propose that the Englishness offered by the works of Pope, Gray, and Richardson provide an aesthetic suturing together of loss and innovation, discontinuity and continuity, capable of forging an English nation and of ensuring a viable English futurity. We begin to see the risks these writers took by considering that England could be defined by more than its elite white men. In so doing, historical inquiry and Englishness potentially expands, available to more than the enfranchised privileged few. As other voices emerge, a more inclusive England becomes possible, even if not comprehensively democratic as we might consider today.

As I write this book, I am drawn outside of eighteenth-century England to my own country and to my own times, and I find the same restless need for decoding the past and its relationship to the present moment. Pope, Gray, and Richardson continue to fascinate me because their struggles poignantly reflect our own twenty-first-century attempts at defining our national identity, shockingly evident by the riot on the U.S. Capitol, on January 6, 2021, the continued inefficacy of the numerous calls for justice by the disenfranchised and brutalized, and the heated, often violent, assessments of national historic monuments. In these times, we look to literature to explicate that relationship and to assuage the pain endured. I hope this book can help: while the wounds may be old, they are indeed still raw.

This book's journey began with Pope and that first Age of Satire class I took, and so do my acknowledgments. To Professor Mark Blackwell at the University of Hartford, I owe a great debt of gratitude. Without his insatiable enthusiasm for eighteenth-century studies and his indefatigable teaching style, I doubt I would have appreciated the dynamism of Pope and his contemporaries. From my undergraduate honors thesis to my dissertation, Professor Blackwell's unfaltering belief in the strength of my ideas and the integrity of my academic career consistently rejuvenated me—and still does.

I sincerely thank the English Department of Brandeis University for its sustained support of my work, first as a graduate student and then as an alumna. Foremost, this book would not have been possible without the careful and frequent feedback provided by Professor Emerita Susan S. Lanser and Associate Professor Thomas A. King. Professor Lanser's sharp eye for detail polished the articulation of my arguments and encouraged me to move beyond my comforts, to challenge the perceived limits of my goals and abilities. Likewise, Professor King's gracious investment in the scope and nuance of my interpretations invited many of this book's readings, expanding the boundaries of my scholarly sensitivity. Long after I ceased to be their official student, Professors Lanser and King continue to offer their knowledge generously and thanklessly. I also wish to acknowledge the importance of Associate Professor David Sherman to this book, particularly, the graduate courses he offered that introduced me to works of literature that deliberate temporality and its intelligibility in narrative forms.

Many thanks to all those individuals at the University of Hartford who so willingly and thoroughly read drafts of this manuscript: Assistant Professor Beth Richards of the Writing Program; Professors Bryan Sinche and William Major of the English Department; and Assistant Professor Rachel Walker of the History Department. Thank you for sharing your expertise enthusiastically and competely.

To Angie Hogan of the University of Virginia Press and the anonymous peer reviewers of this book, I thank you for seeing the potential of this project and helping it to be realized. The suggestions for improvement provided by the peer review reports directed the final version of this book, pointing me to alternative scholarship while also validating my own ideas. The impact of this input on this project is immense. Additionally, thank you to all the editors whose keen eyes carefully reviewed this work on its journey to becoming a book.

I now turn to those dearest to me, whose unshakeable faith carried me through years of long commutes, paper-grading, independent scholarship, and the negotiation of bus stop routes. To my husband, I cannot repay the myriad ways you have made this book possible. Together, we viewed Pope's grave, studied in England, and watched every Jane Austen movie. To my children, you are the reasons I continue my academic journey. Lastly, countless thanks to my parents and family, who are always eager to cheer me on.

Finally, to the readers of this book: thank you for taking the time to consider Pope, Gray, and Richardson from the perspective of historical inquiry and literary recompense. I hope the ideas in this book prove productive of new ways of interpreting the meaning the past holds for your own present moment, generative of fresh modes for discerning and articulating your own historicalness and that of your own time.

EXEMPLARY ENGLAND

INTRODUCTION
"Such Labor'd Nothings," Rhetorical Showmen, and the Study of History

BOLINGBROKE, WRITING in 1755, confidently declares that "history is philosophy teaching by examples."[1] Of great concern to Bolingbroke, as evidenced by the title of his *Letters on the Study and Use of History*, is the misuse of historical knowledge by readers. In his first letter, he sketches caricatures of individuals who access historical data (facts about past people, cultures, and customs) for amusement only, "just as they play a game at cards," or, much worse in Bolingbroke's estimation, "those who read to talk, to shine in conversation, and to impose in company: who having few ideas to vend of their own growth, store their minds with crude unruminated facts and sentences; and hope to supply, by bare memory, the want of imagination and judgment."[2] The misappropriation of historical data, and the debasement of historical inquiry by such rhetorical showmen, haunts the *Letters*.

Usually, Bolingbroke is joined with David Hume and Edward Gibbon to form the great trifecta of male eighteenth-century history writers. However, I draw on Bolingbroke because of his positioning of historical inquiry beyond the provenance of the transparently historical or the officially historical tome. Bolingbroke situates the historical in the public and the social, as interwoven into the witty banter of polite conversations. As the excerpt above from the *Letters* shows, Bolingbroke's philosophy of historical example is not limited to those texts the twenty-first century might categorize as "historical." Bolingbroke is deeply interested in the everyday wit, the individual who dons the role of "the historian," solely to provide entertainment and to aggrandize his/her own vanity. Historical knowledge becomes debased into trivia, a trove of amusing tidbits to be mined for caddy statements, sacrificed on the altar of wit. Indeed, Bolingbroke's vignette of the rhetorical showman recalls to mind Pope's earlier caricature of the wit in his *An Essay on Criticism* (1711):

> Such labored nothings, in so strange a style,
> Amaze the unlearn'd, and make the learned smile;
> Unlucky as Fungoso in the play,
> These sparks with awkward vanity display
> What the fine gentleman wore yesterday;
> And but so mimic ancient wits at best,
> As apes our grandsires in their doublets dressed.[3]

Pope's sense of the "labored nothings" of conversation comes from the same distaste for rhetorical showmen that haunts the *Letters*, those "sparks" who cull from history petty details in order to "display"—entertain, amuse, showcase—their own "awkward vanity."

Bolingbroke's disgust for rhetorical showmen grounds the *Letters*, providing the foundation for his famous assertion in letter 2 that "history is philosophy teaching by examples." This oft-quoted precept articulates the moral-didactic imperative of Bolingbroke's view of historical knowledge, pointedly shifting it away from the witty repartee of the drawing room and positioning it as the cornerstone of citizenship. For Bolingbroke, "the true and proper object of" history writing "is a constant improvement in private and public virtue" aimed at forming "better men and better citizens."[4] Although not to be used as a parlor trick at dinner parties and in ballrooms, Bolingbroke nonetheless understands historical inquiry as essential to the good breeding necessary to form the private individual and the public citizen. There is a redemptive quality to Bolingbroke's efforts as he offers his defense of the utility of historical study, acknowledging the social settings that should allow for the imitation of those individuals of moral and civic virtue.

Bolingbroke's *Letters* clearly advocate for a backward-looking gaze, wherein past examples instruct and structure current activities for the betterment of the nation. In Bolingbroke's philosophy, the historical data most essential for modern use comes from narratives of exemplars, the "great men" of history who provide a criterion of ethos suitable for guiding individuals to be useful citizens.[5] The ceremonial verse of the epideictic form described by Aristotle in *The Art of Rhetoric* typically narrates the lives of such individuals, commemorating them as either beacons of virtue or types of vice. Homeric heroes of antiquity and the great men of past centuries constitute an ideological link between ancient civilizations (regarded as a storehouse of maxims applicable to any situation) and eighteenth-century England.[6] Reflecting the nexus of power, exemplars engage with great councils of war, sovereign dilemmas, and large-scale issues of strife.[7] Roughly contemporaneous with the *Letters*, Hume's monumental multivolume *History of England* (1754–61) and Catharine Macaulay's *History of England* (1763–83) rely on such extraordinary figures as motivating historical change in England, such as monarchs, generals, and philosophers.[8]

Consider, too, Benjamin West's circa 1770 painting *The Death of General Wolfe* commemorating the 1759 death of one of England's famed military heroes. Mortally wounded at the Battle of Quebec while defending his country against the French, the exemplary Wolfe—legend attests—refused to die until he learned that the English would indeed win the battle. As the British flag flies in the background of the painting, West intimates that Wolfe is divinely recompensed for his sacrifice. In addition, a cursory glance at many of the canonical literary texts spanning the seventeenth and eighteenth centuries show the propensity of writers to invoke, likewise, the exemplar as the individual assigned responsibility for the dissemination of moral and civic lessons. Although not overt historical documents, prose and poetry often employ the exemplar as described by Bolingbroke, including the references to Elizabeth I in Edmund Spenser's *The Faerie Queene*, to specific civil war figures in John Milton's *Paradise Lost*, and to notable politicians in Henry Fielding's novels.[9]

I suggest that pausing on Bolingbroke's description of the "crude" attempts at historical wit in the *Letters* proves fruitful, forcing us to recall that, for the eighteenth century, history was not considered a discrete field of study as it appears to us today; rather, historical inquiry permeated other such discussions as natural philosophy, letters, and sociability. Not until the later nineteenth century does history as a formal study emerge, along with other disciplines: zoology, geology, and political philosophy.[10] However, the intellectual curiosity and examination of the past that drives historical inquiry appears much earlier. It is appropriate, then, to consider Bolingbroke's comments on exemplars outside of the genre of history writing as represented by Hume, Macaulay, and Gibbon. We can use Bolingbroke's conception of the exemplar in a more pedestrian sense, as the cornerstone of the good breeding allowing for the making of the virtuous individual and citizen. Indeed, his emphasis on the rhetorical showman in drawing rooms supports a reading of the exemplar beyond the strictly "historical" genre.

Consider, for instance, that one of the most enduring examples Bolingbroke provides for his philosophy comes from a domestic scene. Bolingbroke argues that paintings or sculpture of exemplary figures constantly remind individuals of past feats of greatness, providing a connection between past events and present circumstances. To illustrate, he specifically mentions the Roman predilection for ornamenting the vestibules of their homes with busts of the deceased that "recalled the glorious actions of the dead, to fire the living, to excite them to imitate and even to emulate their great forefathers."[11] In narrating this tendency of Roman households, Bolingbroke forges the connection between the private and the public and locates historical inquiry in the familial rather than the properly historical as we might define it today. In so doing, Bolingbroke provides a starting point for considering historical inquiry and exemplars in alternative locations.

Bolingbroke seems confident in his assessment that history is a series of events shaped by individual valor, and that history writing—and, by extension, civic participation—is the narration of an exemplar's capacity to shape events. Yet in this book I will argue that the problem with deriving historical knowledge from such exemplars as Bolingbroke advocates is the exclusionary nature of the exemplar. The exemplar model recognizes historical change as dictated by the actions and decisions of specific individuals, typically elite white men. As such, the exemplar model resists a heterogeneous history, refusing to commemorate the nonelite, and denying historical status to a variety of individuals, events, and actions. Samuel Johnson, writing in 1750, expresses dissatisfaction with exemplary models for this reason. Meditating on biography as a literary form in the *Rambler*, no. 60, Johnson bemoans the lack of similitude between the "mistakes and miscarriages, escapes and expedients" that mark his life, and the general impulse of exemplary narratives that "never descend below the consultation of senates, the motions of armies, and the schemes of conspirators."[12] By privileging the elite over the common, and by restricting historical visibility to upper-class men connected to the court, men engaged in significant martial action, and men with recognized achievements in the arts and sciences, exemplary narratives severely limit historical knowledge.

In the following chapters, I perform a sustained reading of three canonical eighteenth-century texts whose authors write history through literary genres. Literature provides these authors the freedom to challenge traditional conventions employed by writers more explicitly engaged in the writing of history, such as Hume and Gibbon. Pope's verse satire *The Dunciad* (four books of 1743), Gray's pastoral elegy "Elegy Written in a Country Churchyard" (1751), and Richardson's epistolary novel *Clarissa* (1748) demonstrate that historical knowledge can involve alternative classes, geographies, genders, and genres than those typically associated with the exemplar. These writers meditate the constitution of history: history as a series of unrelated but interwoven factors of impersonal causation; history as economic, political, or religious institutional superstructures; history as the cultures and traditions embedded in the *longue durée*; history as traumatic rupture, significant memories recurrent and unresolved; or history as an archive of tangible objects, both natural and manmade, that can be categorized by visual characteristics.

Pope, Gray, and Richardson shift the focus of history writing away from specific named individuals and its narrative focus, consequently adjusting the representation of England thus afforded. If historical knowledge does not come from heroic examples of moral didacticism, does that mean that *anyone* can become part of a historical record, recognized as an agent of historical change and national value? Should civic concerns (public political, economic, and religious regulations) dominate our conception of history, or can history also explicate private meditations and customs? Does history emerge only in cosmopolitan locations, or also in rural landscapes where agricultural and preindustrial platforms inform patterns of life? Should the historical subject still be culled from the elite of society and assumed to be male, or can those disenfranchised from the nexus of power achieve historical status, including women, non-English, colonial subjects, nonwhites, and non-Anglicans?

Concerns about temporality and historical knowledge are deeply connected to the nascent origins of nationalism in the period. Karen O'Brien explains that "the reading of history imparted practical, useful knowledge, but it was also a cognitive activity allowing the individual to connect him- or herself to collective experience."[13] I will expand O'Brien's point to consider literary texts as markers of this change in historical inquiry. As Pope, Gray, and Richardson considered how to access and interpret the English past, they considered how to write that past adequately so that it might be intelligible and meaningful for sculpting the present and, eventually, the future. *The Dunciad*, the "Elegy," and *Clarissa* suggest that a narrative of English history may be accessible to the disparate groups competing for membership as English citizens, a national narrative that either includes or does not include certain categories of person as a function of gender, geographical origin, status, trade, or profession.

Rather than focusing on the externals of political history, the writers explored in this book chart an inward, subjective, historical consciousness. The literary text commemorates the inadequacies of the exemplar while it offers a new model of writing history, one that provides future readers with the moral-didactic frame once granted by the exemplar. What links these texts together, despite differences in genre convention, is the shared understanding that when experiencing and reflecting subjects recognize the inadequacy of the available modes of representing their individual experiences, new literary techniques for expressing historical subjectivity arise. The aesthetic process of narrating historical consciousness depends not on excluding the available modes of representation but on revitalizing, extending, and renewing them.

Why Pope, Gray, and Richardson?

Choosing these three canonical writers may seem at odds with this book's aim of challenging exemplary narratives, since Pope, Gray, and Richardson appear to embody the exemplary status of elite white males, and certainly their biographies reveal their personal prejudices. Oddly enough, this is one of the primary reasons why I have selected them for study. By choosing these canonical—and hence exemplary—writers and their texts, we can perform the same critique of the exemplary category as they do. This book asks its readers to reconsider these writers as confronting historical, literary, and social labels rather than affirming them as privileged exemplars. After all, in their own ways, Pope, Gray, and Richardson each occupied a liminal position, excluded from true gentlemanly status due to religion, social rank, or profession.

Curiously, Pope, Gray, and Richardson all donned the vestiges of the coveted gentlemanly status primarily through geographic affinity to landed estate: Pope at Twickenham, Richardson at North End, and Gray by residing frequently with his landed friends. Despite these aspirations at estate possession, however, all three enjoyed their privileges from a peripheral position in society. Each of these writers experienced the effects of marginality and exclusion in their historical identities, details that the legacies of their canonical status might obscure—Pope through the limitations placed on him by his Catholicism and his physical deformities; Gray through his favoring of seclusion over profession as gentleman-poet; and Richardson through his trade as printer. I propose that by reading these writers' engagements with eighteenth-century historical inquiry, we can position Pope, Gray, and Richardson as both inside the canonical history they helped to create and outside of that history. In the following chapters, I will show that the texts, correspondence, and meditations of these three writers are steeped in historical inquiry and questions of nation building that refine contemporary notions of the exemplar.

In contrast to many of the earlier canonical writers, Pope, Gray, and Richardson are not connected to centers of power in a traditional exemplar sense. Unlike the aristocratic writers in the coterie of Henrietta Maria during the reign of Charles I, the court wits under Charles II, or the inner Tory circle at the court of Anne (such as Swift and John Arbuthnot), Pope, Gray, and Richardson are not members of the most privileged class. Instead, they are in a position of dependency on patronage and are outside of (or at best adjacent to) the court—and, later, the ministry. Like John Dryden (who lost his capacity to "speak" for the public as poet laureate after his reconversion to Catholicism) and Milton (whose critical views of the parliamentary establishment during the Commonwealth and whose puritanism and blindness during the Restoration positioned him on the periphery, despite his canonical standing as the poet of *Paradise Lost*), Pope, Gray, and Richardson utilize their marginality as the means of reinventing access to historical knowledge.

Moreover, each of these writers invokes in his texts other groups consistently disenfranchised from a hegemonic rendering of Englishness. Pope, despite his fame as a misogynist, recognizes the discerning taste of women readers, albeit of the higher class, as well as the increasing visibility of nonelite writers. Gray, by emphasizing rural locales in his famous "Elegy," considers laborers' placement in historical narratives. Richardson interests himself in domestic concerns—specifically, the experience of female suffering. These three writers look beyond the traditional exemplar to find alternative events and individuals valuable for historical study; in so doing, they imply that such endeavors are necessary to rectify the inadequate modes of representation currently available.

The same, of course, could be said about many eighteenth-century writers: the novelists Henry Fielding and Charlotte Lennox, the essayists Joseph Addison and Eliza Haywood, and the poets Lady Mary Wortley

Montagu and Hannah More. Yet I have chosen Pope, Gray, and Richardson for three specific reasons, in the hope that this book can provide the springboard for other scholars to broaden the discussion to additional period writers and thinkers:

First, Pope, Gray, and Richardson are canonical white male writers. I hope that by reading them as critiquing exemplary narratives we can learn more about the inclusion and exclusion inherent to the literary canon and its enduring legacies. I offer three writers, coming from three different backgrounds, whose lives embodied such differing circumstances, yet their work reveals surprising moments of interconnectedness.

Second, these writers clearly constitute historical inquiry beyond exemplary narratives, perhaps in more direct ways than their contemporaries. Their texts are perched on the cusp of changes occurring in the long trajectory of their individual genres, looking both backward and forward when considering genre convention. Pope, Gray, and Richardson use their historical imaginations to insert themselves into situations and voices not their own so that they may critique exemplary restrictions.

Third, the three focal texts of this book were published in less than a decade. This fact gnaws at me, drawing me to these specific writers and their works, suggesting that differences in genre and subject should be minimized in order to gain a more capacious view of eighteenth-century England. These three works offer the 1740s as a privileged decade, one open to the possibility of discussion about English identity and historical recording, past the age of Milton and Dryden and preceding revolutionary and Romantic sentiments. This is why I have selected *The Dunciad*, the "Elegy," and *Clarissa* out of the respective oeuvres of Pope, Gray, and Richardson. I believe that there is a kinship existent among these three writers, one built on both personal and intertextual connections. It is striking that each of these works, all published in less than a decade, were subjected to intense revision and pressure by the reading audience. The revisionary histories of *The Dunciad*, the "Elegy," and *Clarissa* speak to the ongoing commitment of the writers to their texts, and of the relationship between literary revision, historical knowledge, and nation building. These revisions suggest that the nation is not a static object, but one that evolves, generative and adaptive, necessitating new articulation in new genre forms.

The publication and reception histories of *The Dunciad*, the "Elegy," and *Clarissa* show—more profoundly than the other works by their respective writers—the deep investment of readers in their evolutions, demonstrating that historical inquiry is an ongoing process of writing and revision. Correspondence between writer and audience encouraged many of the editorial decisions associated with the various versions of these texts, such as font style, prefatory apparatus, and cover design, as well as issues related to plot, character development, and resolution. The texts invite eighteenth-century and future readers to empathize with the struggles described, offering a means of forging a literary community invested in scripting a legitimate history. History writing opens up in these texts, becoming the provenance of the scrutinizing demands of the reading public, rather than the product of a privileged Muse or reclusive intellect. As espoused by Francis Bacon and Walter Raleigh, to be a historical thinker "one had to be a man of experience, education, high birth, and public life."[14] Yet Pope, Gray, and Richardson challenge such an exemplary rendering, troubling the exemplar as the singular caretaker of historical memory, imagining alternative means of disseminating historical knowledge. The public's active role in constructing a text upsets the assumption that the reader of history is simply a passive recipient, beneficiary of the didactic instruction provided by an exemplar.

Connections with readers conferred celebrity status on these texts and their writers, providing the opportunity for a wide readership to participate in reimagining both the nation and the inscription of its history. This relationship entailed the wide dissemination of the ideas explored in these texts, inviting inclusion into an imagined English identity, stitching together disparate classes and genders through the shared experience of reading and reflecting on them. Such aesthetic suturing acts as recompense for what I read as the shocking experience of self-alienation depicted by each of the three core texts.

Recompense as an Interpretative Frame

This book insists that eighteenth-century historical inquiry in Pope, Gray, and Richardson can best be understood when viewed through the interpretative frame I am calling "recompense." According to the *Oxford English Dictionary*, the first known use of "recompense" as a verb appears in 1422, meaning "to reward, requite, or repay (a person) for something done or given." In 1425 appears the first known use of "recompense" as a noun, invoked in John Lydgate's retelling of Trojan history, defined as "reparation made for a wrong done; atonement or satisfaction for a misdeed or offence." The foundation for recompense, as evidenced by both definitions, is reparation, compensation, retribution, or repayment.

More significantly, an ethical exchange seems inherent to the term as well, with the act of recompense outlined in the second definition functioning as the means of absolving an individual of guilt after they have inflicted damage upon another person. Recompense, therefore, is predicated upon this damage, a violence or injury to property or person that necessitates the attempt to repair that which has been torn. These fifteenth-century uses of recompense outlined in the OED seem to position it under tort law, in which the primary aim of bringing a legal claim against another is not imprisonment but the allocation of relief through awards for damages, and the deterrence of others from committing similar injuries. In this model, recompense involves reconciling the individual interest to the public good; that is, the public interest in power, and the attribution of guilt and innocence falls to particular personages as a result of particular events—the same way that the exemplary-didactic mode aims to reconcile the individual consciousness to the extraindividual ethical good. Tort, then, because of its specificity, allows for adjudication and resolution, and centers on private disputes, such as the theft of farm animals or the stolen honor of a daughter.[15] Traditionally, recompense involves a linear causal relationship: a wound, a trauma, or an invasion occurs to the individual, and, subsequently, the individual incorporates that wound and moves forward.

What is immensely attractive about recompense is its trajectory: in order for the act of recompense to occur, a violence must first be committed, a trauma endured, and a desire for reparation voiced. Thus predicated on an act that is in itself a violence because it strays beyond the boundaries of cultural norms, the possibility of recompense cannot be separated from conversations about collective and individual identity, from philosophies of knowing and becoming, and from narratives of identity and self as they engage with differing valuations of history. This linearity, steeped as it is in the language of legality and process, offers, I argue, a promising interpretative frame by which to view *The Dunciad*, the "Elegy," and *Clarissa*. Recompense articulates the origin of a crime and the reparation made for the infliction of that crime. It is a process of adjudication involving an infraction and a punishment of specific individuals associated with a particular event. Yet how can the performance of recompense occur when there is an absence of specificity, of attribution? The negotiation of recompense falters when discrete, named individuals cannot be distinguished as either guilty or innocent. The *OED*'s definitions and tort law seemingly suggest that upon requital, the offended individual is indeed satisfactorily healed of the initial wound. Gestures of repair may be more complex, though, when events do not progress in a linear fashion. Moreover, recompense relies on origins to determine outcome: What is the originating event that ultimately leads to a compensatory gesture?

Such questions gain importance when we consider them in terms of eighteenth-century nation building. In so doing, we move away from a private dispute between two named individuals to a relationship between a nation and its populace. The nation, as an abstract albeit geographic entity, provides structures by which the self is constructed and regulated. In turn, the individuals comprising the populace mutually sustain the nation by providing the support and stability (economic, cultural, social) upon which the nation is built. The interpretative frame of recompense provides the language of wound and restitution, begging the question: Of what wound could the abstract nation inflict on the multitude? Exemplary narratives would attribute the actions of a nation to specific figures possessing power and authority, reinforcing history writing as political propaganda. In the eighteenth century, these figures include the prime minister Robert Walpole and the series of King Georges. Yet if we use recompense as an interpretative frame, thus searching for origins, we might be left wondering what crime these particular politicians committed and against whom. Clearly, the answer depends on the political, economic, and social affiliation of the person responding. And who indeed has the *right* to respond, to claim injury? Do great men acknowledge the complaints of the nonelite or the nonmale? Are such encounters worth recording and thus remembering? Can all wounds be traced to a single act of aggression?

Moving from recompense as a legal term to an interpretative frame illuminates the intersection of trauma, nationhood, and historical recording as expressed by Pope, Gray, and Richardson. Tort law proves inapplicable to the literary situations explored by these writers because of the *anonymity* fundamental to national violations, injuries, and ruptures. The investigations into recompense articulated by Pope, Gray, and Richardson demonstrate the difficulty of producing such a compensatory transaction when attributions of guilt and innocence crumble or when the binary labels of victim and aggressor blur. *The Dunciad*, the "Elegy," and *Clarissa* suggest that recompense involving the nation is not a straightforward transaction at all, lacking a clear originating event from which a gesture of repair may stem. These texts offer a new view of historical time in which chronological development interweaves with discontinuity and where temporal distinctions between past, present, and future collapse.

The breakdown of chronology is how this book will constitute and explore trauma. Rather than embracing the enormity of literature devoted to studying trauma, its origins and manifestations, this book relies solely on Cathy Caruth's definition as she articulates it in *Unclaimed Experience: Trauma, Narrative, and History*. I have chosen to invoke Caruth because her definition of trauma as "a break in the mind's experience of time" pairs so well with other conceptions of history as breakage explored in this book, such as Walter Benjamin's emphasis on rupture as constitutive of historical temporality and knowledge.[16] Although this definition of trauma may be restrictive, certainly ignoring the huge body of scholarship devoted to investigating the complexities of the subject, my approach nonetheless offers a focused method by which to appreciate the struggles depicted in *The Dunciad*, the "Elegy," and *Clarissa*. Trauma, as explicated here, underscores the horrifying psychological and emotional repercussions involved in processes of recompense when wounds assume national and historical import yet lose their connection to specific individuals or actions. In so doing, these texts represent, in a more nuanced way, the complexities of eighteenth-century historical people and events than traditional exemplary narratives.[17] Therefore, recompense, not trauma, is the overarching frame of this book.

The interpretative frame of recompense that I am advancing might seem most appropriately related to the purposes conventionally associated with elegy. Indeed, the idea of recompense is hinted at in the very nature of elegiac lament, since both involve the trajectory from wound to repair. As potentially best seen in Milton's *Lycidas* (1638), the convention of mourning for the elegiac speaker serves as the basis for scripting a spiritual restitution for the loss endured, as Michele Sharp indicates: "Elegy's central concern is securing the continued life of the poet as a living voice in the face of death."[18] As we find in *Lycidas*, elegy involves the cosmic reckoning of individual grief in order to prompt a new understanding of one's relationship to historical memory, historical subjectivity, and historical time:

> Now, Lycidas, the shepherds weep no more:
> Henceforth thou art the Genius of the shore,
> In thy large recompense, and shalt be good
> To all that wander in that perilous flood.[19]

Milton's speaker successfully utilizes his private grief to script a narrative beneficial to the collective reading audience. The recompense achieved by the poem atones for the loss of Lycidas through the emphasis on the instructional underpinnings of the event: Lycidas as poetic "Genius," fulfills, after death, a moral-didactic purpose. Here, the traditional rendering of recompense and exemplary narrative converge: the ongoing utility of Lycidas as muse offers compensatory repair for the wound inflicted by his death. Moreover, such recompense creates a commemorative artifact; that is, both the poem and the ocean that at once buried Lycidas and precipitated his continuity in historical knowledge and temporality.

Likewise, although not an elegy, the speaker of William Wordsworth's "Lines Written a Few Miles above Tintern Abbey" (1798) articulates a wound, incorporates it into his selfhood, and moves forward animated by the knowledge that he has gained. Despite mourning the loss of his youthful "joys," he welcomes the wisdom such a loss provides. "Tintern Abbey" celebrates his new awareness of the emotive energies of humankind, "the still, sad music of humanity."[20] He specifically frames such an experience as "recompense":

> That time is past,
> And all its aching joys are now no more,
> And all its dizzy raptures. Not for this
> Faint I, nor mourn nor murmur; other gifts
> Have followed, for such loss, I would believe,
> Abundant *recompense*.[21]

Significantly, Wordsworth's articulation of recompense involves the commemoration of a consciousness aware of temporal collapse. As Wordsworth's speaker revisits Tintern Abbey, chronological history unravels over the course of the poem through memory and memorial—a temporality that also confronts the speaker of Gray's "Ode on a Distant Prospect of Eton College" (1747) discussed in chapter 2.[22] Similar to *Lycidas*, Wordsworth's speaker finds solace from the connection he imagines between himself and the larger reading audience. The affinity of his circumstance with that experienced by others, the progression from youth to adulthood, gives him pleasure much like Milton's speaker feels when imagining Lycidas as poetic genius.

Milton and Wordsworth both describe the movement from an individual to a national consciousness that involves the loss or submersion of the individual in the national, but this is not the only way to imagine recompense. Pope, Gray, and Richardson imagine a recompense that retains individual consciousness even as it emotively binds the individual to the national and vice versa. By reading Pope, Gray, and Richardson using the framework of recompense, we can better read the wound inflicted by the nation as the sense of disparity and disconnect arising because of the myriad political, economic, and cultural changes occurring. As already seen in *Lycidas*, the individual is placed in relation to collective identity, rather than to a particular person; thus, although the individual could sustain some form of injury (as in *Clarissa*), the injuries sustained are not interpersonal, as in tort law, but collective, wherein the individual is innocent of but implicated in the rupture occurred.

Gray's "Elegy," as an elegy, most clearly benefits from recompense as an interpretative frame, meditating on the type of individual traditionally memorialized in verse. The speaker, in mulling over the rural hamlet and its graveyard, considers the relationship between the anonymous peasant and the wealthy elite. Ultimately concluding that both have a place in national historical records, the speaker attempts to imagine his own grave among the rustics. He intends to close the gap between the rich and poor by permanently fixing his own memorial. The poem stands as recompense for the suffering experienced by the speaker throughout the course of the poem, as well as recompense for the disparaging attitude of the elite toward the rustics. Yet, in the process, Gray's speaker meditates on the crime that originated the necessity for such recompense, realizing that a single event cannot be identified because the victim and aggressor involve entire communities. Poverty and disenfranchisement, as habits of living and as categories of selfhood, are not discrete crimes able to be ameliorated decisively. Traditions and patterns of behavior spanning generations point to the fruitlessness of the speaker's endeavor and challenge the recompense he imagines.

Likewise, Richardson's *Clarissa* purposefully muddles the trajectory of recompense through the experiences of Clarissa. The originating crime that Lovelace commits, the rape, is indirectly scattered across Clarissa's "mad papers" and alluded to in her will—not sufficient evidence to convict Lovelace under the law. Moreover, Clarissa's escape from Harlowe Place with Lovelace complicates the novel's understanding of "victim" and "aggressor," no matter how successfully Lovelace tricks her. Lovelace boasts that he could easily manipulate the court system by using its respect for his social rank and the attendant assumptions regarding his honor. His attitude points to the inapplicability of tort law in a metropolitan and fashionable society, one where crime and punishment is often dictated by wealth and sociopolitical consequence, rather than authentic renderings of right and wrong. Although Richardson offers us specific, named individuals as motivating the action of the novel—Clarissa and Lovelace—the many manipulations of identity and stratagems employed by Lovelace compromise the trustworthiness suggested by their appellations.

The connection between Pope and recompense might seem the most tenuous out of the three writers discussed in this book, considering that *The Dunciad* is one of literature's foremost satiric attacks. If traditional recompense as understood by tort law attempts to trace a specific crime to a definitive punishment, then certainly *The Dunciad* does not fall under this formula. *The Dunciad*, as verse satire, thrives on an immersion into dullness built on bathos, vice, and folly—the types of crimes, although perhaps ridiculous, that are not punishable by law. The catalogue of crimes *The Dunciad* memorializes stem primarily from insults directed against Pope personally by named individuals and are thus identifiable according to tort law, but the injustices they represent are indicative of larger moral degeneration occurring in England itself for which there can be no sufficient recompense.

Pope writes to John Gay in a letter written in 1730 that *The Dunciad* "may stand for a *publick* Epitaph."[23] Notice that Pope marks the poem as a public possession rather than as a list of personal grievances experienced, a text offered as an "epitaph"—an elegiac gesture I read as steeped in conversations regarding recompense. Consider, too, that Pope, Gray, and Richardson all end their respective texts with some form of commemorative artifact that seeks to outlive the temporal constraints of mortality, inserted into historical time so that future readers may be edified by the past in the present moment, thus creating a more stable futurity for other anonymous readers. Burial practices perform a commemorative function aimed at narrating English national identity and literary recompense in *The Dunciad*, the "Elegy," and *Clarissa*.

Recompense as explored by Pope, Gray, and Richardson sutures nostalgia and modernity, continuity and rupture, offered by the literary text as evidence of the mid-eighteenth century's resiliency and innovation. This recompense consists in the formation of a national literature, accessible to the expanding reading public and capable of offering an affinity of ideas and emotions between disparate individuals, as well as effecting unity between the writer, the speaker, and the reader. I argue that Pope,

Gray, and Richardson figure the aesthetic imagination as the means by which each member of the English populace can envision his or her own relationship to the English national identity, bridging the people with the nation in ways not supported by exemplar narratives.

Nation Building in Pope, Gray, and Richardson

The main deterrent to defining a coherent English national identity in the period is, of course, the fractured nature of England at the time. The 1707 Act of Union, integrating England, Scotland, and Wales into the monolith titled "Great Britain," certainly speaks to the period's interest in nation building. Yet the apparent stability promised by Great Britain did not prevent disputes arising from sectional and regional differences—disputes that undermined, and at times threatened, a cohesive England, in both geography and ideology. The establishment of a Great Britain had consequences for a narrowly defined English nationhood. For instance, Krishan Kumar explores the elusive nature of English identity, particularly in contrast to that of Scotland and Wales, by tracing the usage of terms such as "British," "English," and "Anglo-Saxon" across literary texts, pamphlets, and treatises. Like Linda Colley, Gerald Newman, and Leslie Ellen Brown, I see a national English identity emerging, albeit a fragile and, at times, contradictory object. Rather than grounding this identity in unity around patriotism and a shared national antagonism against France as does Colley, or as a response to the internal pressures caused by the Hanoverian ascension in 1714 as do Newman and Brown, I find Englishness emergent in the possibilities offered by literary genre.[24] This writing narrates the past in order to inform and potentially influence the unfolding of present (and hence future) activities.

Writing history and nationhood converge with a shared focus on subjectivity: who is remembered in history writing reflects national ideologies concerning representation and inclusion in citizenship. Englishness, as manifested by the three focal texts of this book, is comprised of various individual groups or nations—a political nation, a literary nation, an economic nation—that compete for recognition by the English cultural elite, the traditional purveyors of an English historical record. Each of these groups proposes differing accounts for membership in an English nation, espousing various definitions of historical subjectivity, such as political acumen, leadership in letters, education, taste, reason, or, most basically, citizenship.

Despite the very real segregation, prejudices, and limitations existing in eighteenth-century England, the idea of England becomes the rallying cry around which the diverse populace may unite and find meaning. However, it would be difficult to compress each eighteenth-century conflict (such as debates over women's access to public voice, slavery, capitalism) into a universal notion of Englishness, as that would require the general leveling of all individuals and events into an abstract formula for national uniformity. Such an intense variety prevents a homogeneous categorization of national characteristics and values. Instead, I posit viewing the national collective as an imagined historical object, a fantasy offering the stability once granted by exemplar narratives.[25] Viewing Englishness thus offers cohesion "regardless of the actual inequality and exploitation that may prevail . . . [in] this fraternity."[26] The imagined nation and its attendant historical record represents the desirability of historical subjectivity for integrating the individual into the collective, desirable because of its ability to present the disenfranchised with the illusion of historical status, as well as its promise of solidarity. Englishness becomes general enough to attract the disparate social, political, and economic groups, while seemingly providing a concrete ideological entity.

I start this book with Bolingbroke because his philosophy reminds us that historical inquiry in the eighteenth century is diffused in many arenas, not restricted to what we might consider properly "historical" circumstances. If we agree with this premise, then it makes sense to find in Pope, Gray, and Richardson evidence of the pervasive nature of historical thinking, especially when viewing their texts as acts of recompense. *The Dunciad*, the "Elegy," and *Clarissa* welcome the disparities of eighteenth-century England, reimagine them as valid and valuable literary subjects, and cast them as beacons of hope. Rather than acting nefariously, as offering false promise to the multitude of disenfranchised individuals residing in England, the recompense presented by these texts stems from a more inclusionary impulse than that motivating traditional "great men" writing. The literary genres invoked by Pope, Gray, and Richardson are fundamentally more expansive than exemplary narratives, drawing on the imaginative potentials of literary writing rather than the extant, verifiable data of history. Englishness does not possess a discrete identity but is an open-ended categorization; *The Dunciad*, the "Elegy," and *Clarissa* open up the possibilities for what Englishness *could* entail, rather than espousing a single metanarrative of English identity, thereby offering literary recompense to the nation.

I will now offer a brief overview of the historical inquiry existent in Pope, Gray, and Richardson as I understand it, as well as in their three respective texts. In so doing, I risk losing the structural integrity of this introduction, but I think it is necessary that we assess the historicalness of these three men individually before viewing them together again. Just as important as reading these three together, we need to appreciate each writer as part of his own literary context in order to discern his exemplarity *and* his challenges to exemplarity. Once we situate the discrete text in the general trajectory of its respective genre, then we can start asking surprising questions. Afterward, I will return to consider the connective tissue binding Pope, Gray, and Richardson and *The Dunciad*, the "Elegy," and *Clarissa*.

Historical Inquiry in Pope

Perhaps there are no two eighteenth-century poets more diametrically opposed than Pope and Gray. Pope, the poet of the city, of the satiric, and of the ridiculous, seems to bear little resemblance to Gray, the contemplative, pensive, and melancholic poet of rural and spiritual concerns. Pope, even from his pseudogentleman's residence in Twickenham, brandishes his satiric weapon toward the concrete historical figures and events of the day: Walpole, the Whigs, financial speculation, and other evidence of cultural degradation. Such a rendering appears at odds with Gray's retreat at Cambridge, isolated in his chambers, donning the Regius Professorship of Modern History. The differences between the poets suggest an almost innate or natural separation between the earlier "Augustan" period and the mid-century "graveyard" school, and, indeed, for years university survey courses typically fostered such a conception of the century, one as organically moving away from the neoclassicism of Pope and toward the emotive, inward-focused meditations closing the period.

Thanks to scholars such as David Fairer, scholarship has challenged this trajectory, but one needs only to glance at a research database to conclude that criticism acknowledges Pope as a poet of history, immersed in extant historical data, while likewise placing Gray as a poet removed from history, with no interest in recording the actions and decisions of specific, verifiable individuals immanent to cultural activities.[27] Certainly, Pope embraced a life of visibility and controversy, refusing to retreat into obscurity despite his manifold disabilities brought on by physical, religious, and political limitations. Never one to avoid conflict, Pope's work and letters not only foster but also thrive off contentious debate, insulting caricatures, and barely masked innuendo. His canon offers a stockpile of eighteenth-century vignettes, sketching the period in forceful, nuanced prose and verse.

In a 1725 letter written to Swift, quoted briefly in the preface to this book, Pope affirms his investment in studying history: "Your Travels I hear much of; my own, I promise you, shall never more be in a strange land, but a diligent, I hope useful, investigation of my own territories. I mean no more translations, but something domestic, fit for my own country, and for my own time."[28] Pope's declaration to Swift showcases a restlessness and dissatisfaction with current aesthetic values, ultimately instigating a new period in Pope's poetic career, one that disengages from the subjects that had characterized his early work, donning instead those of historical inquiry. Indeed, the "re-articulation" of Pope's poetry from his early pastorals and translations to the biting, often vengeful, satire of his later career is striking, although hardly celebrated by his contemporary detractors and Romantic successors.[29]

Pope's awareness of the necessity for a new poetics, a form capable of authentically representing the dilemmas, contradictions, and problems of early eighteenth-century England, certainly positions his poetry as interested in historical thinking. The chronology of Pope's career showcases his shifting interest from the heroes of antiquity and the shepherds of pastoral landscapes to the extant historical events of the period. Pope's 1725 thoughts to Swift precede the composition of many of his significant canonical texts, such as the *Moral Essays* of the 1730s and the various versions of *The Dunciad* beginning in 1728—texts that committed the "unpardonable sin," according to Elizabeth Rowe, a writer of devotional and moral poetry, of rejecting the "tender sentiments of nature so far as deliberately to give Anguish and Confusion to Beings of his own kind."[30] Such criticism lacks attentiveness to the potency of Pope's decision to abandon "those romantically-minded readers who turned reluctantly from him to Thomson and Shenstone and Young."[31] His 1725 thoughts reveal the capaciousness of his poetic intuition, the sensitivity that prompts his mindfulness of the inadequacies of current aesthetic expectations, and demands he turn his gaze domestically, inwardly, to England and to his own period. Indeed, names, events, dates, and descriptions dominate Pope's later canon, infusing the reader with the desperation to "rummage in footnotes for the references we require."[32]

Nowhere is this better seen than in Pope's four-book *The Dunciad*. Pope crafts *The Dunciad* as a curious blend of mythic history and contemporary detail cataloging eighteenth-century figures, events, and data. On the one hand, the poem invests in a mythic time, hearkening back to literary precedents that presuppose a particular historical model based on elucidating the actions of exemplary figures, those he once translated, such as found in *The Iliad* or *The Odyssey*. The opening lines of *The Dunciad* gesture toward Queen Dulness's greatness through references to past literary formulations of greatness; therefore, she is "the Mighty Mother," the "Goddess," the "Daughter of Chaos and Eternal Night" who possesses the "ancient right" to rule. On the other hand, the poem invokes "the Smithfield Muses" alongside of "Dunce the Second" and "Dunce the first" (book I, ll. 1–8) as it begins its tirade against the Hanoverians, the Whigs, and anyone else Pope gleefully decided to ridicule. From this collision of the mythic with the contemporary, Pope creates more than simply verse satire; Pope scripts a temporal interweave between past and present and the futurity that will one day become the present. In so doing, Pope makes a claim on what counts as legitimate sources of history, the way that history is written, and the type of knowledge disseminated.

Pope's satiric practice of naming points to a larger historical project: "Increasingly in Pope's later poetry the historical role impresses with more urgency; the decision to name names becomes not only a matter of satiric strategy but a determination to leave a record—the true record—for posterity, a record often spilling over into footnotes meant to outlast the pseudohistories of Walpole's propagandists."[33] From Pope's first appearance in print in 1709 leading up to the publication of his collected *Works* in 1717—and indeed through the publication of his translations of *The Iliad* in 1720 and *The Odyssey* in 1726, and his edition of Shakespeare in 1725—the poetic practice of imitating ancient poets and invoking the pastoral dominated Pope's early verse.[34] Certainly, Pope's *Works* of 1735 represent different poetic interests from those represented by the *Works* of 1717. The final 1743 version of *The Dunciad*, which I rely on in this book, embodies Pope's interest in historical inquiry since its inception in 1728, spanning two decades of critical cultural insights and historical recording, its publication history and series of revisions enacting the problem of articulating and writing history.

Historical Inquiry in Gray

In sharp distinction to Pope's investment in city life, polite manners, and in exposing the follies and vanities of specific individuals, Gray's association with the so-called graveyard poets has traditionally positioned his interest with the melancholic, the rural, and the meditative. Lacking "implicit social engagement" and characterized by a marked disinterest in extant recordable events, John Sitter claims that poets writing from the mid-1740s onward apparently embrace "a lyric flight from immediate history," a "retreat" from the "crushing presence" of high politics, great men, and religious strife.[35] Enshrined as "the pensive poet," concerned only with otherworldly ideas, poets such as Gray seem removed from the concerns of Pope, distanced from him as much by content as by style.[36]

Indeed, traditional readings of the "Elegy" praise Gray's stylistic mastery of form and the poem's rendering of commonplace emotions, readings that persist from the Victorians through the late twentieth century. Amy Louise Reed, writing in 1924, and Harold Bloom, writing in 1987, both celebrate Gray's ability to capture the emotive qualities of a generic readership, due in part to his invocation of literary precursors. Not until the early 1980s do historical concerns become important to discussions of the "Elegy," with Sitter arguing in 1982 for an abstract, nonreferential model, and Henry Weinfield in 1991 and Suvir Kaul in 1992 reading the poem in terms of class struggle and economics.[37]

Certainly, other poems of Gray, particularly the Pindaric odes, have proven more attractive for critics who read him as responding to public and national historical issues, simply because these poems clearly utilize the formula of exemplary attribution found in Pope. In "The Bard" (1757), which Sitter calls "the best example of such a collision between the poet-speaker and the hostile force of history," Gray draws on his knowledge of medieval history to retell Edward I's conquest of Wales and to envision prophetically the literary accomplishments of Spenser, Shakespeare, and Milton through the last surviving Welsh minstrel.[38] Gray attributes to the heroic bard the role of exemplary caretaker of civic and poetic virtue, who, "with a master's hand, and prophet's fire," solidifies temporal continuity between ancient and modern writers.[39] Charles Hinnant invokes the language of the exemplar when he writes, "By making the dramatic climax of his poem the suicide of his Welsh harper, [Gray] sought to transfer to the bard something of the emotions of admiration and respect which were accorded to the dying heroes of classical antiquity."[40] Consider, for example, the Homeric figure of Odysseus or Virgil's Aeneas, exemplars who display their moral integrity through similar acts of defiance and strength. Another of Gray's 1757 Pindaric odes, "The Progress of Poesy," also offers easy readings of the relationship between literary and national histories as it explores the heroic transport of liberty and poetic genius from the ancients to Britain.

Both "The Bard" and "The Progress of Poesy" invoke the long association between poetry and the exemplary usually found in the ceremonial verse of the epideictic form. Such an association easily lends itself to reading Gray's Pindaric odes as interested in exemplary historical individuals and events, as scholars have indeed done. Paul Odney, in his discussion of Gray's self-reflective manipulation of style in "The Progress of Poesy" and "The Bard," convincingly shows Gray's poetic control over the representation of his historical data. Odney argues that Gray "makes conspicuous the artificial nature of 'origins' and of their forging power" by purposefully uniting two different historiographies into his verse, one classical and one British.[41] Bringing together two disparate historical strains undermines, for Odney, any sense of a "natural" or "transparent" quality of history, showcasing instead Gray's rhetorical mastery of form. The historiographic quality of Gray's Pindaric odes arises not only from the "self-consciously fictive elements" with which he manipulates the presentation of history in his writing, but this rhetoric "dramatizes a choice between versions of the past."[42] Gray understands the multitude of perspectives that furnish a historical account and the myriad of emphases that ground a historical retelling.

Gray's interest in literary and historical origins emergent in his Pindaric odes fails to find critical reception in his other, earlier, meditative poems. The standard reading of Gray's canon typically disassociates his historical odes from a text such as the "Elegy." However, by reconfiguring historical subjectivity beyond the exemplar model and its attribution of responsibility to specific, recordable individuals (such as the conquest of Wales in "The Bard"), the "Elegy" clearly enters into conversation with Gray's larger interest in writing history and rescues the poem from its "stock responses" and "commonplaces."[43] Odney locates in the Pindaric odes the same reflection on genre and complication of the exemplar that I find in Gray's "Elegy," where the exemplar exists as a construct of the speaker rather than an inevitable datum, a point that begins to undermine the transparency of exemplar narratives as a mode of history writing.

In Gray there is a decided commemorative impulse joined with an emphasis on historical inquiry that reveals an interest in a specifically English nationality, an attribute often lacking in other graveyard poets. Even William Collins's "Ode on the Poetical Character," which interests itself in the creative imagination as offered through a restricted view of English literary history, lacks reflection on the historical position of the poet and the historical determination of poetry. Edward Young's *Night Thoughts*, similarly, offers a spectacular, at times theatrical, encomium to the meditative, the nocturnal, and the dead without Gray's attending historical concerns or awareness of historical consciousness.[44] Instead, like Pope who writes to Swift of finding the proper subject for his own particular milieu, Gray is attuned to the same specificity of his period when he writes to West that "the language of the age is never the language of poetry," a sentiment that, as M. H. Abrams points out, "earned him the harsh criticism of Wordsworth in his Preface to *Lyrical Ballads*."[45] Often, scholars read Gray's sentiment regarding "the language of the age" as evidence of his aloofness from his historical moment, since he appears to choose a language of the past as opposed to the language of the present. Yet such an evaluation follows too linear an understanding of both Gray's poetry and his handling of historical knowledge, consigning him to historical avoidance while attesting to Enlightenment ideals of progress.

Both Pope and Gray express a dissatisfaction with the disjunction they perceive between the period's aesthetics and the history from which those aesthetics arise, as well as a desire for a poetic counterpart to the novelty of eighteenth-century culture, politics, and society. Thus, the artificial diction and distorted word order that often characterizes Gray's work, such as the opening stanzas of "Eton College," gesture toward an affinity with Pope rather than with the Romantics, as Wordsworth's derisive comments on Gray's "Sonnet on the Death of Richard West" substantiate.[46] Gray's sense of "the language of the age" necessarily includes rather than rejects the language of the past, incorporating that language instead of privileging a chronology in which progress can only be expressed through novelty.

Indeed, evidence of Gray's fascination with historical processes abounds in areas beyond his overtly historical verse. In personal meditations, as in his Pindaric odes, Gray feels the pressure of historical urgency, never disassociated from worldly and immanent concerns, as he elaborates to West (excerpted briefly in the preface to this book):

> When you have seen one of my days, you have seen a whole year of my life; they go round and round like the blind horse in the mill, only he has the satisfaction of fancying he makes a progress, and gets some ground; my eyes are open enough to see the same dull prospect, and to know that having made four-and-twenty steps more, I shall be just where I was; I may, better than most people, say my life is but a span, were I not afraid lest you should not believe that a person so short-lived could write even so long a letter as this; in short, I believe I must not send you the history of my own time, till I can send you that also of the reformation.[47]

Gray's comments certainly register with his persona as "the pensive poet," given to melancholia and solitary musings, disliking publication and the public presentation of his work.[48] Always painfully aware of the limited quantity of his endeavors, here Gray weaves together his lack of poetic production with the lack of his era's "reformation." His self-deprecating humor, regarding himself as "short-lived," runs alongside of his ability to write in a way that suggests an awareness of the interplay of temporalities and histories, of the connection between himself, cloistered at the university, and larger worldly developments. Not only is he as "the blind horse in the mill" within his academic pursuits, the unceasing repetition of his individual days pressing upon him, but he is also cognizant of that role as deeply implicated in and emblematic of "the history of my own time." In this brief passage to West, Gray surely reveals his own melancholia but, significantly, also locates the connectivity between private and public histories, between past, present, and future times, and between articulating history and aesthetic imaginings, links that emerge as central forces in the "Elegy."

Gray's attempt, ultimately abandoned, to write a history of poetry (including translations) further contributes to an understanding of Gray as thoroughly invested in historical inquiry across the body of his work and not solely in his Pindaric odes. As Herbert W. Starr notes, Gray's wide breadth of knowledge in multiple fields, including natural history, foreign languages, philosophy, the arts, and even cooking, equipped him well to write authoritatively on many subjects and to provide a historical overview of his period. Joseph Wood Krutch similarly elaborates on Gray's capabilities, particularly emphasizing the use of his marginalia in commonplace books on a myriad of topics.[49] Both Starr and Krutch locate Gray's talents in his insatiable curiosity for detailing and recording.

Although turning aside from writing a history of poetry, Gray's methodology and erudition certainly position him as deeply invested in cultural awareness, historiography, and strategies of recording—all of which he then maps onto literary production.

Historical Inquiry in Richardson

Richardson entered the world of literary fame rather late in life, certainly not claiming to be, as Pope asserted of himself, a child prodigy. Having already established a successful career as a printer, Richardson turned towards writing. His first novel, written at the age of fifty-one, turned out to be a success, with readers completely infatuated with the story of *Pamela* (1740). The tale of Pamela's threatened virtue became an iconic example of moral-didactic instruction and granted Richardson celebrity status.

As a master printer, Richardson was well acquainted with the trends and developments in eighteenth-century historical events, maintaining connections to leading thinkers such as Johnson and William Law and to centers of power through his work for the House of Commons. As Louise Curran shows, Richardson was never the reclusive writer; instead, he was highly aware of his work's reception: "In his voluminous correspondence Richardson elicited criticism of his novels, as well as other printed works, and theorised about the role of fiction as a public form of self-expression. An understated feature of this corpus is Richardson's interest in the minutiae of his correspondents' lives and in their histories."[50] Not only his profession as a printer, which brought him into contact with the major historical events and figures of the period, but also his avid interest in connecting with his audience places Richardson as a writer immersed in historical inquiry.

Richardson's literary career showcases the general eighteenth-century enthusiasm for experimentation, particularly, as Curran notes, at the intersection between "fiction, autobiography, and other forms of creative impersonation."[51] Indeed, Richardson was not content to create lives for his imaginary characters; he also took pleasure in learning the private details of his correspondents. In a letter dated February 1755, Richardson writes to Mary Watts, "Your little Stories, as you call them: Your Histories: Your Descriptions, are indeed charming, Never avoid interspersing them into your kind letters."[52] Curran shows how this often led Richardson into trouble with his readers, such as Lady Bradshaigh, when he requested private details too freely and without apology. Regardless, Richardson's relationship with his audience and his use of the epistolary style speak to his love of invention, and his desire to push the boundaries between the fictive and the verifiable. As Peter Sabor notes, "On numerous occasions, Richardson urged his readers to tell him what they found 'objectible' in his novels: the word recurs throughout his massive correspondence."[53] In turn, Richardson offered his readers "strange reworkings of his own" texts, participating good-humorously with readerly endeavors to imagine alternative endings to his works, such as joining Lady Bradshaigh and her sister Lady Echlin in rewriting (although not appearing as the conclusion to the printed form) the original tragic ending of *Clarissa*.[54]

Richardson's investment in correspondence with his readers establishes him as vastly concerned with the people and events of his milieu. Teri Doerksen, for instance, in her study of Anna Meades's *Sir William Harrington* (1771) notes the intimacy Richardson cultivated with his correspondents. Using Meades's fiction, Doerksen argues that "there are three levels at which the novel performs public identification with Richardson and his celebrity status, associating itself with Richardson's thoughts and words as if they were relics to be treasured by readers."[55] These three levels involve intertextual and interpersonal relationships and "the multilayered Richardsonian influence on the plot and character" of Meades's novel.[56] Doerksen concludes that "each level offers different means for the novel to manifest public intimacy with Richardson and to offer the reader the synthetic experience of being part of a literary conversation with Richardson, even after his death."[57] The influence of Richardson diffuses into many different forms of writing in the period: epistles, prefaces, annotations, pamphlets, and novels. Richardson's openness to conversation with his readers, as evidenced by his assistance with Meades's novel, is reflected by the frontispiece for the 1804 posthumous publication of the six-volume *Correspondence of Samuel Richardson*. Sören Hammerschmidt, in his study of this text, emphasizes the affability conveyed by the engraving: "Before readers ever encountered as much as the first volume's title page, they were confronted with Richardson's author portrait. Book in hand and quill at his back, he faces readers with an open, friendly mien and looks as if they had just encountered him rereading (or maybe re-editing yet again) his morally elevating didactic fiction."[58] Richardson welcomes his readership, opening himself up to the scrutiny and desires of his audience, encouraging the imaginings and responses of other people to his novels. Significantly, the revisions and fantasies penned by others form a crucial part of the histories of his novels, providing a view of history writing that is more inclusive and accessible to general readers than that offered by traditional exemplar narratives.

In addition, corresponding with his readers granted Richardson the opportunities to test the limits and potentials of his historical voice. More than simply a pleasurable exercise or a leisurely way to pass time, "the mediations that constitute the core of and define the conditions for correspondence also generate its greatest power, since it is only by virtue of the letter's mediations that correspondents—acting at a distance and across time—may communicate refined versions of themselves."[59] Richardson's avid experimentation with his characters, his correspondents, and his texts reveal his attempt to appropriate a historical identity, one that maintains the liveliness of individual personality with the morality he embraced. His reworkings of his novels, combined with the ideas proposed by his readers, suggests that he realized the impact such decisions would have on himself in perpetuity. He seems hyperaware of the significance of his opinion on his readership. Epistles act as a playground for Richardson's imagination, allowing him to try the alternatives that he would never condone for the official printed editions of his novels. Epistles offered Richardson the chance to live vicariously, entertaining, for instance, the conversion and repentance of Lovelace, something that his own moral certitude would never permit.[60] One possibility he mentioned to Lady Echlin involved transporting Lovelace to the American colonies and setting him up as a governor.[61]

His interest in the "refined versions" offered by the epistle, though, suggests concerns about the existence of an accurate self, one that maintains its integrity across time, despite refinements, or if there is only a series of performances akin to what Judith Butler has described in her theory of gender identity. Although Richardson might have read the refinement offered by the epistle as positive, encouraging the "best" appearances of ourselves, I argue that *Clarissa* recognizes the deception inherent to epistolary writing rather than its potentials. At the start of the novel, Clarissa assumes that her epistolary correspondence with her family will grant her the freedom to express her deference, humility, and virtue—that is, the qualities that constitute the "best" version of her exemplary self. Instead, Clarissa's attempts to write an accurate history of her involvement with Lovelace are frustrated by the epistle. The other letter writers in the novel often edit and refine their letters, but such actions are intended to mask their schemes for securing her as Lovelace's prize.

Richardson challenges the assumption that historical knowledge exists only in static exemplars. Instead, his writing suggests that individuals possess complex emotive and philosophical frames, private impulses that structure behavior and decision-making processes, and that these frames often change over time. These frequently conflict with other people's intentions and motivations, leading to cacophony rather than illumination. Richardson's correspondence and the epistolary troubles Clarissa encounters in the novel offer a view of history writing more complete when seen alongside of *The Dunciad* and the "Elegy."

Chapter Overview and Interconnectedness

Pope, Gray, and Richardson draw on differing conceptions of history and pose varying narrative dilemmas but appropriating an intelligible historical voice becomes the burden of each individual seeking to negotiate space within the collective imagined by their texts. Pope's *The Dunciad* offers a vision of apocalypse and chaos, while Gray's "Elegy" deliberates the friction arising from the intrusion of an elite force upon a rural hamlet. Richardson's *Clarissa* presents female violation and the dissolution of domestic stability. In the following chapters, I will trace the engagement of these writers with history: their awareness of historical events, deployment of historical consciousness, and sensitivity to collective memory. I will show the enfolding of multiple temporalities that most horrifies the speakers of the three texts, and the necessity to utilize both a forward and backward gaze in order to apprehend fully the continuity and discontinuity inherent to history.

Chapter 1 reads Pope's *The Dunciad* as challenging the assumption that historical change emerges from the decisions and choices of specific, named, extraordinary individuals, usually born into the higher class. Although focusing on the traditional "great men" of exemplar history, such as the members of the Hanoverian monarchy and the Walpole ministry, Pope undermines exemplary notions of greatness. In the poem, the "great" are great because they continue to perpetuate dullness, stagnation, and ineptitude—not because they possess a superior moral code or elite education. Moreover, Pope's verse satire inserts into history writing those private aspects of humanity not necessarily found in exemplar renderings, such as scatological references to bodily needs. Emphases on the folly and the disgusting habits present in those closest to the nexus of power evacuates the exemplar of inherent class-based privilege and didactic traits.

The chapter also considers access to the historical past through virtuosic endeavors aimed at collecting historical objects and the archival impulse of newly founded libraries and museums. These non-narrative methods prove equally distressing to Pope, who finds that most collectors foster an incomplete view of the past, misusing the knowledge they have and misinterpreting the past to others.

Focusing on Gray's "Elegy," chapter 2 critiques the geography usually associated with exemplar narratives, those places connected to public expressions of power and the institutional superstructures of society, such as the court, Parliament, councils, urban spaces, and religious edifices. The "Elegy" positions a rural graveyard and an isolated country hamlet as viable sources of historical knowledge. Gray uses the form of pastoral elegy to focus on unnamed individuals, figures who cannot be verified by historical research, a poetic decision that refuses to rely on an exemplar as motivating historical action. Such anonymity emphasizes the private and the familial, rather than the public and the civic, as cornerstones of English national identity. Like Pope's *The Dunciad*, Gray's "Elegy" thwarts the assumption that outward signs of exemplary status indelibly mark an individual as worth preserving in historical knowledge, here, rendered through elite burial rituals: large tombs, elaborate monuments, ornate statues, and lengthy inscriptions. Gray argues that even the rural graveyard, with its unimpressive headstones, houses individuals worth preserving in historical memory, individuals whose lives narrated moral-didactic lessons and whose actions continue to serve as models of imitation for both the rural and the elite.

Chapter 3, on Richardson's *Clarissa*, challenges the gender usually associated with the exemplar. Richardson positions the white gentlewoman as the exemplary figure of his novel, a domestic woman unlike the scandalous females of Aphra Behn and Daniel Defoe. Richardson turns away from the public ceremonial events usually commemorated in historical knowledge to consider domestic and female concerns. Moreover, the exemplar typically possesses no moral ambiguity, or even a complex inner life substantially explored by the text. Yet, although Clarissa is clearly set up as a feminine ideal, Richardson also exposes Clarissa's moral incertitude as vital to her story. In privileging intentionality, Richardson challenges the substance of historical recording, suggesting that inner (private) meditations may hold more historical value than the outer (public) demonstrations of acquiescence, fortitude, compromise, or valor commemorated by exemplar narratives. The polyvocal method of Richardson's epistolary form allows him to explore the ambiguous nature of intentionality as something usually hidden from public exposure and, therefore, difficult to identify and assess. As a result, Clarissa learns that she must diversify her voice, articulating it in multiple discursive forms. She develops many other ways of recording her history outside of the epistle, such as through the legal discourse of her will and the visual images of her coffin. Richardson's epistolary style critiques the exemplary emphasis on the single, stable voice as motivating historical change and as the sole arbitrator of moral integrity.

Although Pope, Gray, and Richardson do not explicitly claim to be writing or refuting exemplar history, using the interpretative frame of recompense allows us to see that their texts do indeed provide valuable insight into historical inquiry. I see a turn toward inwardness, away from the external divisions of social class or political party, as central to imagining and articulating a new, more expansive, model of national identity. These texts thus chart a movement away from the externalized political events embodied in the great accomplishments of exemplary great men, and toward an emotive, inward consciousness that ponders the role of moral intentionality in decision-making, the relationship of the domestic setting to the public sphere, and the power of memory to bend temporal distinctions between past, present, and future. *The Dunciad*, the "Elegy," and *Clarissa* all attempt to broaden membership in the English nation by incorporating individuals and events into historical knowledge that the exemplar model typically excludes, particularly by encouraging the capacity for self-reflection that crosses political, economic, social, cultural, and gender divisions.

I have concluded my chapter on Pope with a glance at his "Eloisa to Abelard" (1717) because I see it as exhibiting the same historical inquiry as Gray's "Elegy," which follows. Similarly, I end my chapter on Gray with a look at his "Epitaph on Mrs. Clarke" as it forms a connective tissue with *Clarissa*. These concluding reflections to the chapters further showcase the importance of burial rituals to constituting history as understood by Pope, Gray, and Richardson, particularly as they, like *Clarissa*, offer male-authored female voices attempting to reimagine historical visibility for those individuals and situations typically disassociated from exemplar narratives.

Genre Conventions and Historical Knowledge

Perhaps it would be useful to turn for a moment to Gay's dramatic satire *The Beggar's Opera* before moving on to the more sustained examination of Pope's use of satire in *The Dunciad* that comprises chapter 1. Although written in 1728 and therefore slightly earlier than the three core texts of this book, the first performance date of *The Beggar's Opera* coincides with the beginnings of Pope's scripting of the first version of *The Dunciad*. One scene from *The Beggar's Opera* illustrates the problem of the dissemination of historical knowledge when that dissemination depends on the conventions of genre. Issues of genre are tied to historical inquiry in the eighteenth century; we cannot understand Pope, Gray, and Richardson's challenges to the exemplar unless we notice the way that genre conventions shape the expectations of readers *and* the volition of poetic speakers and fictional characters.

At the conclusion of *The Beggar's Opera,* the Beggar returns to the stage along with the Player to decide on Macheath's fate. Finally captured, the gallant hero-highwayman awaits his sentence while the Beggar and the Player discuss options. Although the Beggar favors hanging Macheath in order to bring "poetical justice" to the drama, the Player insists that such a scripting is inconsistent with the happy ending expected of an opera: "Why then, friend, this is a downright deep tragedy. The catastrophe is manifestly wrong, for an opera must end happily."[62] The Player regards the Beggar as a dim-witted fool, unable to comprehend that an opera "must" follow certain conventions; indeed, the Player prioritizes the integrity of the genre over an ethical rendering of Macheath's crimes. Under the pressure of this objection, the Beggar readily agrees to alter the ending, leaving Macheath safe from hanging and, instead, married to Polly.

The Beggar's decision to alter his conclusion positions him, momentarily, outside of the celebratory ending expected by the genre as understood by the Player. The Beggar insists that his original ending contains a strategy for edification wherein those disassociated from public domains of power, such as governmental or legal authorities, suffer punishment for their crimes, even if those crimes mimic those of the traditional great men: "Through the whole piece you may observe such a similitude of manners in high and low life, that it is difficult to determine whether (in the fashionable vices) the fine gentlemen imitate the gentlemen of the road, or the gentlemen of the road the fine gentlemen. Had the play remained, as

I at first intended, it would have carried a most excellent moral. 'Twould have shown that the lower sort of people have their vices in a degree as well as the rich: and that they are punished for them."[63] In direct counter to the philosophy espoused by Bolingbroke, the didactic here rests with condemning the disenfranchised for imitating the exemplary figures of society. The play would grant criminals historical status but only so that they may be held accountable for the collective avarice and folly created by the great. However, in denying this ending to the Beggar, the Player eliminates such moral edification from the conclusion, instead fixing an ending appropriate to both the genre and the tastes of the audience. Such a concern satirizes the lack of control experienced by playwrights when confronted with the demands of theatrical managers looking to secure a three-night performance run. Moreover, the emphasis on genre privileges sentimental tastes over critical reflection on the national consciousness.

By sparing Macheath's life, the Beggar suggests his own historiographic dexterity, his ability to reconceive the narrative so that it better fits the financial demands of the production and the expectations of the audience. Yet this dexterity indicates a larger problem. The need for revision, and the corollary need to appease an audience, shifts the focus away from the ethos of the exemplar to the mode of representation—that is, the genre through which the historical knowledge is disseminated. Rather than condemning Macheath for his inconstancy to women and his villainous lifestyle, the play ends as it begins: by casting him as the attractive rogue, the epitome of manliness. The success of *The Beggar's Opera* suggests that the Beggar made the right choice in sparing Macheath's life. As with *The Dunciad*, the "Elegy," and *Clarissa*, *The Beggar's Opera* certainly achieved celebrity status in the eighteenth century, spawning the production of such commemorative souvenirs as playing cards and engravings.

The Beggar readily agrees to alter his conclusion, but Gay ensures that the specifics of the original ending remain included. Inserted into the historical record, then, is not just the rewritten outcome but the history of how that outcome came to exist. To Gay, the intended ending occupies a place of historiographic value equal to that possessed by the actual ending, important enough to remain as part of the performance. Such a choice seems to suggest that it is the Player, rather than the Beggar, who is the fool, because of his blind obedience to what he conceives as the rules of the genre, placing him, perhaps, on par with Bolingbroke's rhetorical showmen and Pope's "labour'd nothings." Reading the conclusion of *The Beggar's Opera* in this manner showcases a dependence on form, a strict reliance on rules rather than on the moral-didactic purpose of history writing. If historical knowledge about the past is given to us through genre, then, as *The Beggar's Opera* shows, that information is shaped by the conventions of that genre.

Like *The Beggar's Opera*, *The Dunciad*, the "Elegy," and *Clarissa* deliberate the genre forms capable of rendering Englishness adequately by examining various ways of articulating history and constituting time available to eighteenth-century thinkers. They consider historical knowledge as public expressions of moral-didactic power, as an introspective examination of an individual's relationship to historical narration, and as accessed by empirical methods for the observation and categorization of objects thought to hold historical significance. In challenging the assumptions of exemplar narratives and in considering the conventions of genre, Pope, Gray, and Richardson offer three different representations of, and possibilities for inclusion in, an English national identity.

1

"Another Phoebus, Thy Own Phoebus"

Verse Satire and Class in *The Dunciad*

The *Dunciad*'s satiric inversion of exemplarity marks its relationship to the exemplar model of history writing, perhaps in a more straightforward manner than either the "Elegy" or *Clarissa*. After all, Augustan verse satire as a literary form powerfully expresses the eighteenth-century theory of history as exemplary attribution, as a project embodied in the proper names of people, places, and events. Founded on pointing fingers and naming names—allusively or blatantly—it exposes (whether fairly or not) the assumed vices envisioned by the poet. As Andrew M. Wilkinson expresses, "The social importance of Satire had usually been accepted in the Augustan Age, when it was ranged with the Law and the Church as one of the three guardians of the moral order."[1] Overtly mimetic, satiric poems represent and record persons, acts, and events that already have public visibility, authority, and power. Along exemplar lines, these poems explore the role of the City in the formation of a national identity, the expression of urbanity, and the high political concerns related to governance, such as economics, empire, warfare, religion, and the arts.

The formal verse satirists of the early eighteenth century—Dryden, Swift, Pope, and Johnson—advocated for the "informing purpose" of satire, believing in the instructional use of their poetry to identify ills in society and attempt to reform them.[2] In *Professional Imaginative Writing in England, 1670–1740*, Brean S. Hammond identifies "conservative reaction against and anxiety over proliferating print, and its apparent corollary declining literary standards" as "an important determinant of [the] satiric 'voice.'"[3] Hammond shows how the satiric "energy" of Pope and his friends "is energy primordially generated by" their antipathy toward those individuals forced to use writing as a means of survival—that is, hack writers.[4] Indeed, Augustan verse satire thrives off the distinction between leisurely and professional writing, intersecting with many other cultural issues of the period, such as new forms of commerce, political divides, and the growing reading public. Augustans such as Pope invest their verse satire with the moral-didactic spirit of exemplar narratives, using their poetic lines as weapons aimed at dismantling vice and folly.

The "pattern of praise and blame" invoked in early verse satire provided examples of both the ridiculous and the sensible so that readers could acquire lessons on proper actions to be imitated.[5] John Brown's *Essay on Satire, Occasion'd by the Death of Mr. Pope* (1745) emphasizes the satirist's method: "By turns bid vice and virtue strike our eyes."[6] Likewise, Aaron Hill commends Pope's pairing of "vice" and "virtue" in his assessment of Pope's poem "Seventeen Hundred and Thirty Eight," remarking on its marriage of what Wilkinson terms "Juvenalian acrimony and Horatian ease."[7] Augustan verse satire locates and remedies social degradation by educating the audience on the depravity and merits of named individuals, recognizable to and available for imitation by readers, harkening to exemplary models.

From its initial publication in 1728, *The Dunciad* uses verse satire to represent Pope's widespread depiction of eighteenth-century England, providing subsequent generations of readers with an introduction to the extant historical culture, politics, and ideology of the period. The opening lines of *The Dunciad* mark its vital investment in satirizing specific individuals in order to deliver Pope's apocalyptic vision of the devolution of society:

> The Mighty Mother, and her Son who brings
> The Smithfield Muses to the ear of Kings,
> I sing. Say you, her instruments the Great!
> Call'd to this work by Dulness, Jove, and Fate;
> You by whose care, in vain decried and cursed
> Still Dunce the second reigns like Dunce the first
> Say how the Goddess bade Britannia sleep
> And poured her spirit o'er the land and deep. (ll. 1–8)

History, as it emerges from this passage, manifests in the decisions of specific individuals who can be documented by the poem. Colin Nicholson's critical terminology when discussing *The Dunciad* channels the methodology of exemplar narrative history where the actions and ethos of named individuals motivate historical change over time. He writes that the fall of Walpole in 1742 "had brought forth a satire ... of unparalleled specificity and boldness, attributing to the Hanoverian court and its former first minister primary responsibility for a general moral and cultural decay."[8] Nicholson showcases the interconnectedness of genre and subject in *The Dunciad*, with Pope's reliance on verse satire as the means of lambasting the elite.

Critical scholarship has successfully documented those individuals and events satirized by Pope in *The Dunciad*, such as the two Georges.[9] When reflecting on Pope and history, readers usually consider his engagement with specific historical events or individuals. For instance, scholars have copiously documented Pope's contribution to the ancient versus modern debate, his relationship to the mass expansion of print and commercialization of letters, his use of technology, and his interaction with the economic developments of the period. Hammond elucidates that "Pope established himself as a conduit of opposition to some of the major cultural tendencies that he saw as prevalent in his period: professionalization of writing, increasing literary production, literary production undertaken by socially inappropriate individuals."[10] Others have also pinpointed specific historic moments that proved significant to Pope's development, such as his betrayal by Joseph Addison after the 1714 Hanoverian succession.[11] All of these various readings of *The Dunciad* follow what Russell West-Pavlov terms "the fundamental sequentiality of history," where history follows direct causal patterns, here linked to Pope's personal vendettas.[12]

Yet the opening passage of *The Dunciad* suggests that the poem provides more than mere biographical gossip. Through the vilification of specific individuals and events, *The Dunciad* participates in and contributes to eighteenth-century debates on the efficacy of knowing history through the narratives of exemplary great men. While the particular individuals satirized indeed stand as personal targets for Pope's revenge (political, literary, or personal), their inclusion also indicates the poem's destabilization of easy mappings of historical knowledge, as well as the compensatory gestures of repair involved in recompense. The poem, because of its satiric form, upsets the apparent linear understanding of time found in exemplary narratives as elucidated by Bolingbroke's adage that "so Selim emulated Caesar ... so Caesar emulated Alexander; and Alexander, Achilles."[13] Bolingbroke traces the ancient lineage of exemplars to show that imitation and repetition of historical ancestors fosters a stable futurity.

From the outset of *The Dunciad*, though, Pope strategically derides those individuals usually commemorated by historical recording, the Caesars and Alexanders of whom Bolingbroke writes.[14] The satiric object of Pope's ridicule is the government under the rule of George I and George II whose inability to care properly for Britain has allowed "the Mighty Mother," Dulness, and her heir, Bays, to overwhelm the nation. This opening passage signals the poem's interest in rethinking the assumption that historical change emerges from the choices of specific, named, extraordinary individuals, usually of the higher class. Although focusing on the traditional great men of exemplar history—such as the members of the Hanoverian monarchy and the Walpole ministry, those whom Nicholson identifies as central to Pope's verse satire—Pope undermines exemplary notions of greatness. "The Great," those possessing access to the public nexus of power, subsequently possess historical subjectivity in the exemplar model: by virtue of their connection to governmental authority and their direct influence on the individuals and events of the period, the Great (such as aristocrats, parliamentarians, members of the prime minister's regime) represent those acknowledged as historical subjects, worthy objects for imitation and commemoration. Greatness in *The Dunciad* emerges satirically—not from heroic courage or virtue, but from the magnitude of lethargy and folly an individual commands, ultimately sustaining the kingdom of dullness.

In the opening lines, the speaker boldly calls attention to the trace of the father to the son, the king to the prince, the "Dunce the second" and the "Dunce the first," emphasizing the public, royal succession that indelibly affects the collective experience of "Britannia" and her general populace occupying her "land and deep." The poem begins with a promise of the stability inherent to a linear model of history, with both the perpetuation of Dulness and the seamless royal succession, where specific people (and bloodlines) motivate stability. However, the single word "still" of line 6—"still Dunce the second reigns like Dunce the first"—records a history of continuity based on stagnation, the ongoing transmission of dullness from one generation to the next and the refusal to alter the narrative scripted by "the Goddess."

In having the privilege of public access, the Great are entrusted with the "care" of "Britannia," a task, according to the speaker, in which they have failed. Yet these exemplars continue to lead the nation, preventing the nation from disentangling itself from inadequate models. Continuity, in this opening passage, proves destructive to civic security and responsibility, rather than acting as its foundation. Pope's satiric inversion of exemplarity argues that the Great are great precisely because they continue to perpetuate inadequate forms of historical knowledge. The poem asks, then, who, if not the Great, should history represent if those assumed to possess proper "historical" qualities—the traditional exemplars—are found grievously lacking? Moreover, who should recompense the damage inflicted on the nation by such acts of ineptitude and folly?

By asking these questions, *The Dunciad* appears to fulfil the "informing purpose" of Augustan verse satire. Through its examination of historical figures and events, the poem reveals its moral-didactic use, its investment in reforming society by depicting the virtues and vices of the Great. However, if we consider *The Dunciad* as part of the longer trajectory of verse satire over the course of the eighteenth century, then, surprisingly, we can view the poem as teetering on the cusp between Augustan verse satire and, later, more self-doubting and introspective writing. According to Wilkinson, verse satire was "falling off in the 1740s," precipitated, Thomas Lockwood claims, by an "identity crisis" built on uncertainties stemming from the genre's ability to live up to its pretensions.[15] Lockwood identifies the movement "away from the impersonal point of view of heroic satire," marked by a "much mellower and more indulgent" tone indicative of the satirist's "conspicuously self-conscious" attitude.[16] In many post-Augustan poems, the speaker directly questions the efficacy of satire to rectify social problems or institute meaningful changes in behavior or viewpoints. Consider, for instance, William Cowper's *The Task* (1785):

> Yet what can satire, either grave or gay?
> It may correct a foible, may chastise
> The freaks of fashion, regulate the dress,
> Retrench a sword-blade, or displace a patch;
> But where are its sublimer trophies found?
> What vice has it subdued? whose heart reclaim'd
> By rigour, or whom laugh'd into reform?[17]

Notice that Cowper purposefully identifies satire's pattern of pairing vice with virtue in his invocation of the "grave" or the "gay" tones of Augustan verse. Such balancing, though, succeeds only in critiquing the frivolous or the vain, not the "sublimer trophies" of moral and civic "reform."

Cowper's doubts seem particularly provocative if we read them alongside of Pope's defense of satire in his 1738 *Epilogue to the Satires, Dialogue II*:

> Praise cannot stoop, like Satire, to the Ground;
> The Number may be hang'd, but not be Crown'd.
> Enough for half the Greatest of these days
> To 'scape my Censure, nor expect my Praise:
> Are they not rich? what more can they pretend?
> Dare they hope a Poet for their Friend?[18]

From these lines we can discern an inverted conversation about the purpose of satire, even though Pope crafts them as a discussion about praise instead. Through his contrast between praise and satire, Pope affirms satire's position as the modern equivalent to "in the trenches," literally in battle at ground zero. He insists that although satire "stoop[s]," it is never concerned with the "Number," defined by John Butt as "those who count as population and nothing beyond."[19] Because the vast majority of common individuals "escape" Pope's "Censure," he considers them "rich." His haughty tone in the concluding line reveals his incredulity that they might "dare" to suggest that satire could be concerned with anything other than those who are "Crown'd" with greatness. While Cowper positions verse satire as only effective in combating minor and frivolous ills, Pope explicates an unshakeable belief in the "sublimer" purpose of the genre, concerned with misdeeds truly sinful—exemplary—in their enormity.

Although I offer here only two examples of period discussions on verse satire, this pairing would seem to suggest that Pope adheres to formal Augustan satire wholeheartedly in his oeuvre, a dedication that crumbles in others as the century moves onward. Yet if we look at one more snippet from Pope, from his slightly earlier *Epistle to Dr. Arbuthnot* (1735), then perhaps, unexpectedly, we can begin to dislodge Pope from such exemplary commitment. This epistle sets up an imagined dialogue between Pope and Arbuthnot (anticipatory of the style in *Epilogue to the Satires*) that reveals and then justifies Pope's insistence on identifying specific individuals as crucial to verse satire:

> Whom have I hurt? has Poet yet, or Peer,
> Lost the arch'd eye-brow, or *Parnassian* sneer?
> And has not *Colly* still his Lord, and Whore?
> His Butchers *Henley*, his Free-masons *Moor*?
> Does not one Table *Bavius* still admit?
> Still to one Bishop *Philips* seem a Wit?
> Still *Sapho*—"Hold! for God-sake—you'll offend:

No Names—be calm—learn Prudence of a Friend:
I too could write, and I am twice as tall,
But Foes like these!"—One Flatt'rer's worse than all.[20]

These lines certainly reveal Pope's pride that he possesses knowledge of the foolery of human behavior and his ability to use satire as the means of exposing it (humorously, despite his short stature). To do so, he blatantly names specific individuals. In keeping with exemplary narratives, he attributes virtue and vice to named figures, a practice that Arbuthnot desires him to stop, out of fear for his safety and his reputation. Arbuthnot views Pope's "foes" as the elite, those capable, because of their wealth, power, and visibility, of inflicting damage on Pope, despite Pope's dismissal of them. Curiously, though, Pope begins these lines by wondering, "Whom have I hurt?" Although his haughty and abrasive tone eliminates any real concern that Pope might have felt for those he attacks, the question itself indicates a doubt, a slight proviso to Pope's apparent unshakeable belief in verse satire's pretensions to instruction. The lines that follow this question provide evidence of the failure of satire to enact that meaningful and lasting change of which Cowper later writes. The practices of folly are still existent in the world—ribaldry, debauchery, and deceit—despite Pope's satiric verse productions.

Certainly, this is not a comprehensive overview of eighteenth-century verse satire or poetry more generally. However, we can nonetheless appreciate the "generic confusion" ensuing from such moments and the exciting possibilities that they offer for a reading of *The Dunciad*.[21] This loose trajectory of the movement of verse satire over the long eighteenth century is fascinating because we have at least three scholars pinpointing the decline of the genre to the 1740s, as well as to the death of Pope himself. Both Wilkinson and Lockwood, writing in the mid-twentieth century, identify the decade in which Pope, Gray, and Richardson all published their signature texts as a moment of change. More recently, Jennifer Snead pinpoints the publication of Colley Cibber's *Apology for the Life of Colley Cibber* in 1740 and its connection to the Theater Licensing Act of 1737 as vital to the development of *The Dunciad*. Sitter, writing three decades after Wilkinson and almost a full decade after Lockwood, also gestures toward the 1740s as a privileged decade and Pope's death as an event instigating significant change.[22] Again, Hammond acknowledges that the dates bookending his project, 1670–1740, "correspond roughly to the lifetime of Alexander Pope" and the "long shadow" that he "cast[s]" over the eighteenth century.²³ The especial quality of the 1740s, and Pope's role in it, I argue, is not only motivated by literary, political, or philosophical shifts but also indicates a moment of serious historical inquiry.

Keeping these scholarly assessments in mind, limited in number as they may be, allows us to consider Pope's deployment of verse satire and *The Dunciad* in new ways. For example, J. Paul Hunter, in his discussion of the attractiveness of the novel as a genre to eighteenth-century readers, performs a traditional view of Pope's exemplary status:

> After Dryden, the turn-of-the-century writers largely felt that they had to choose a loyalty, as philosophers and scientists had already had to do. Either they looked back to a past with authority, dignity, and a clear set of guidelines for subsequent ages, or they looked toward a future that might be unlimited but certainly was unknown.... It is not difficult to pin badges of "ancient" or "modern" on almost anyone at the beginning of the eighteenth century, and—as if there could be doubts—Pope's catalogue of the damned in *The Dunciad* provides a permanent, nearly infallible record. Dunces espoused the present and sought the values of the future. Heroes looked backward.²⁴

Hunter explicates one of the main debates informing the early eighteenth century: the relationship of the past to the future. For Hunter, this relationship is inherently binary, with the past and the future representing two separate temporalities, and, subsequently, two different ideologies. He claims that "Dryden, poised as he was on the border of two centuries and even more delicately balanced between old and new values, gives a much fairer sense of what contemporaries saw when they looked forward than does Swift or Pope" because Pope relies on the exemplar method of "record[ing]" people, places, and dates.²⁵ Hunter's study does a remarkable job of justifying the rise of the novel, particularly in examining the reasons why period readers would embrace it based on the types of texts they encountered before it emerged. However, I ask that we challenge the assumption articulated by Hunter: that Pope, loudly and voraciously, claimed affinity with the ancient past because that past is peopled with heroes—and that the past is indelibly distinct from the present.

The complete *Dunciad* of 1743 is poised on the outskirts of verse satire's past *and* on the brink of its future, a tribute to the high didactic ideals governing the formal Augustans and anticipating the uncertainties and unease characterizing the verse satires of the later century (most notably,

Cowper and Crabbe of the 1780s). Certainly, we can read *The Dunciad*'s celebrity status as arising from its dependency on the commercial developments it bemoans, as not only meditative of those developments but generative of them: "Pope has a fair claim to be the first great professional writer in English letters: the first writer to make a fortune by applying extraordinary commercial acumen to the exploiting of his literary talents."[26] His aptitude with marketing, subscriptions, and product design is probably the most obvious way that we can read *The Dunciad* and Pope as on the cusp between an older literary world and the new.

Yet I believe there is still another way to see Pope as marking a tipping point, one that exists beyond the commercial, arising from the larger trajectory of eighteenth-century verse satire as a genre. By satirically critiquing exemplary narratives in *The Dunciad*, I wonder if Pope completely believes in the integrity of verse satire, despite his avowals in the *Epilogue to the Satires* in its pretensions to rectifying social ills through "acrimony" and "ease." Is it possible that *The Dunciad* contains the same crippling self-doubt that plagues the verse satires of the later eighteenth century, those written alongside of melancholic, sentimental and Romantic ideologies? Should we read the overwhelming despair at the end of book 4, combined with the long revisionary history of the poem, as acknowledgments of Pope's reservations? Doing so allows us to position Pope as both epitomizing Augustan verse satire and critiquing it, further validating the work of those scholars who seek to bridge the divide between the Augustans and the Romantics, as well as offering further connective tissue linking Pope, Gray, and Richardson.[27] I would propose that the especial circumstances of the 1740s allows Pope to engage in a process of historical inquiry that challenges the assumptions engrained in exemplary models and that ultimately reveal him to be a more complicated exemplar than his canonical legacy—and commitment to verse satire—might suggest.

The Problem of Naming and Linear Recompense

In a letter to Swift written April 20, 1733, Pope iterates his commitment to Augustan verse satire even at the sacrifice of audience approval: "I will not render them [his satires] less important or interesting, by sparing Vice and Folly, or by betraying the cause of Truth and Virtue. I will take care they shall be such as no man can be angry at but the persons I would have angry."[28] In this letter, Pope fashions himself as attorney and judge, imparting justice for crimes committed, thus inviting readings of

The Dunciad that position its satiric attacks as recompense for personal injuries Pope sustained. True to his word, the prefatory material to *The Dunciad* includes quotations from Pope's enemies, who, in order to denigrate his poetics, explicate various principles of satire. As Valerie Rumbold writes, "By citing his victims' own defences of satire on bad writers, Pope has made them 'justify' the satire he will turn against them," or, as Pope concludes this section of the prefatory material, "*Out of thine own Mouth will I judge thee, wicked Scribler!,*" echoing the words from Luke 19:22, wherein a master chastises his servant for misusing his talents.[29] An extract from Lewis Theobald published in *Mist's Weekly Journal* in 1728 states, "ATTACKS may be levelled, either against *Failures* in *Genius,* or against the *Pretensions* of *writing without one.*"[30] By including this line as a preface to *The Dunciad,* Pope clearly implies that his satiric attack against Theobald, the initial king of the dunces, is warranted because of Theobald's "failure in genius" and for his preposterous "pretensions" of assuming he writes well. Pope uses Theobald's logic against him as a satiric weapon for illuminating Theobald's—not Pope's—literary deficiencies.

The Dunciad uses verse satire to make visible those qualities that may not be fully disclosed in specific individuals, acts, or events possessing public visibility. Although "much history of the period was designed to serve a present political polemical purpose," historian Jeremy Black explicates, and although "the past [remained] a source of legitimacy," as in exemplar models, "both modern and ancient history . . . were plundered to make political points."[31] Black's use of the term "plundering" seems particularly apt, as it describes *The Dunciad*'s satiric impulse for exposing what might not be readily apparent, or what may be hidden, or what may be denied representation in public visibility. Dryden's *A Discourse Concerning the Original and Progress of Satire* (1693) describes the efficacy of "plundering" an individual's identity in order to represent it satirically: "How easy it is to call rogue and villain, and that wittily! But how hard to make a man appear a fool, a blockhead, or a knave, without using any of those opprobrious terms! To spare the grossness of the names, and to do the thing yet more severely, is to draw a full face."[32] Dryden emphasizes the finesse of satiric attacks, displacing the satiric force from "grossness," simple name calling, and positioning it as a techne. As Dryden goes on to write, "There is a vast difference betwixt the slovenly butchering of a man, and the fineness of a stroke that separates the head from the body, and leaves it standing in its place."[33] Verse satire is a craft capable of undermining an individual's integrity, perhaps without that individual's even comprehending it. Verse satire's probing into and depiction of vice fosters the scripting of a historical record based on illuminating human folly, vanity, and avarice.

Dryden's use of the term "grossness" is telling of another element of verse satire that Pope embraces in *The Dunciad*. Invoking excrement, impolite bodily parts, and base human appetites, verse satire commemorates the disreputable in the individuals charged with producing and promoting a historical narrative. Reflecting upon the relationship between eighteenth-century satire and its literary precedents, Peter Thorpe writes, "Satire is a hostile sort of art, and perhaps it can be said that the verbal hostility of the Augustans replaced the physical hostility that agonized so much of the seventeenth century."[34] To expand on Thorpe, the "hostile" of verse satire often arises from scatological references that aim, firstly, to humiliate the individual satirized with evidence of his own bodily functions, and, secondly, to perform an act of leveling in which the body stands as the common human element effacing the particularity of the individual satirized. In both instances, this hostility satirically recasts the type of knowledge typically gained from exemplar narratives.

The pissing contest between Curll and Chetwood in book 2 of *The Dunciad* clearly offers a depiction of such satiric hostility. Part of the heroic games, the contest involves two named figures clearly immanent to history writing: Curll and Chetwood competed against each other in the publishing trade. Pope reworks the exemplar model, though, by positioning their heroic feat as a urination contest. Dulness will declare victory to "Who best can send on high / The salient spout, far-streaming to the sky" (ll. 161–62). The scatological design of the endeavor certainly eliminates the didactic function of the exemplar, especially with the insinuation of Curll's venereal disease: "Thro' half the heav'ns he pours th' exalted urn; / His rapid waters in their passage burn" (ll. 183–84). The exemplar model of history "advocated the imitation of the actions of great men in history for the current, reading man's political life," with the assumption that those valorized in the historical record—the Great—offered valuable moral and civic lessons applicable to contemporary individuals and events.[35] Pope vacates history writing of such ethos, replacing moral imitation with gross entertainment. His verse satire undermines the accepted correlative between historical visibility and a moral-didactic code, initiating conversations on the proper details to be included in a historical record.

It might be helpful to think of *The Dunciad* in terms of what Daniel Woolf identifies as the transition occurring in late seventeenth-century history writing toward the adaption of "the Procopian genre, previously underutilized in Britain, of the 'Secret History', purporting to lay open in public the *arcana imperii* and the private scandals of great men."[36] Certainly, *The Dunciad* exposes the imagined "secrets" and "scandals" of those purported "great," damaging the public reputations of those visible in government offices. If we push the concept of "secrets" further, broadening it to include processes of self-examination and introspection, then we find further connections existing between Pope, Gray, and Richardson.[37] All three writers gesture toward the hidden as inherent to all individuals and as taboo, or at least adjacent to cultural standards of normativity: Pope vilifies concealment as key to upsetting exemplary assumptions about greatness; Gray's speaker valorizes the crimes and passions buried in the graveyard in order to imbue the poor with worth on par with the rich; Richardson presents Clarissa as cognizant of her secrets as emotive and important through her reflective writings. In *The Dunciad*, the "Elegy," and *Clarissa*, the exposure of secrets reveals the humanity, not the exemplarity, of individuals, and suggest that this humanity, common as it may be, might still hold historical value.[38] Visibility in Pope's verse satire, as in Gray's pastoral elegy and Richardson's epistolary novel, collapses distinctions between public and private by thrusting into publicness—history writing—those aspects of humanity typically assigned to personal spaces, upsetting assumptions about what historical knowledge entails and records.[39]

That is not to say that contentions did not arise among writers of Augustan verse satire about the degree to which such exposure should occur. The differences between the satiric practices of Pope and Swift, especially their use of naming, demonstrate such disagreements. In *Epilogue to the Satires,* Pope depicts an imagined conversation between himself and a "friend" in which the friend argues against naming in satire. Pope boasts of his ability to preserve in verse all contemporary scandal and vice:

> Vice with such giant strides comes on amain,
> Invention strives to be before in vain;
> Feign what I will, and paint it e'er so strong,
> Some rising genius sins up to my song.[40]

In response, the friend scolds Pope's enthusiasm for identifying the particular authors of the "sins," separating Pope from other writers who also reflect on period degradation: "Yet none but you by name the guilty lash; / Ev'n Guthrie saves half Newgate by a dash. / Spare then the person, and expose the vice."[41] The friend attempts to distinguish between "the person" and "the vice," thus dismantling the link between name and action. Horrified at such a suggestion, Pope mocks his friend's implication that such assignation be kept a "secret," since, he argues, it is only fair that the proper individual be blamed for the vice they committed.[42] Note, again, the emphasis on making visible the secret histories of those commemorated in order that they may be punished.

Also published in 1738, Swift's "Verses on the Death of Dr. Swift" align with the thoughts of the friend in the *Epilogue*:

> Perhaps I may allow the Dean
> Had too much satire in his vein;
> And seemed determined not to starve it,
> Because no age could more deserve it.
> Yet malice never was his aim;
> He lashed the vice, but spared the name;
> No individual could resent,
> Where thousands equally were meant;
> His satire points at no defect,
> But what all mortals may correct.[43]

Both Pope and Swift, in their respective works, deliberate the distinction between attacking general vice, thus claiming that the whole "age"—all ranks, all professions—participates in it, and attributing to specific individuals the proliferation of vices. Swift's poem contains a glimmer of hope that satire potentially offers the means of correction, made possible by the general sense of calamity contained in his satire. Swift follows Dryden's prescription to "spare the grossness of the names" as outlined in his *Discourse on Satire*.

Pope, though, positions verse satire as a means of punishment, where specific individuals are condemned for explicit offenses. He imagines recompense emerging from the assignation of labels indicating criminal and victim, as well as guilt and innocence, with poetry as the means of offering reparation for injury. James McLaverty points out that in 1726 Pope and Swift shared "a negative view of the role of naming in satire, but they responded to the social and political pressures on their writing in the following years in different ways," so that by 1738 they clearly occupied opposing camps.[44] Such an insight should seem curious when we consider this book's claim that the 1740s represents an ideological space welcoming the consideration of alternative modes of constituting historical subjectivity. Pope's pride in satirically judging and condemning individuals—the triumphant tone of "yet none but you"—motivates the relish with which he names (and convicts) in his satires. Pope's "uncompromising direct claims of moral and philosophical absolutism in satiric poems," David Nokes argues, "simultaneously require us to uncover the devious motives of his enemies."[45]

Similar to Swift, Arbuthnot in the *Epistle* declares against Pope's invocation of names, instigating Pope's horrified reaction:

> Good friend forbear! you deal in dang'rous things,
> I'd never name Queens, Ministers, or Kings;
> Keep close to Ears, and those let Asses prick,
> 'Tis nothing—Nothing? if they bite and kick?
> Out with it, *Dunciad!* let the secret pass,
> That Secret to each Fool, that he's an Ass.[46]

Pope justifies his method by emphasizing the treatment he himself has endured, the "bite and kick" of the derogatory comments of his detractors. He asks Arbuthnot, "You think this cruel?" but refuses to acknowledge any cruelty in his satiric practice, offering *The Dunciad* as recompense for his personal sufferings.[47] Notice that Pope uses the word "secret" twice in the last couplet of this passage, emphasizing the didactic use of verse satire in schooling his audience in the private issues that would typically not be commemorated by exemplar narratives.

Pope's motivation seems to uphold the integrity of causality in recompense that moves from offense to wound to reparation. The difference between Pope and Swift, and between Pope and Arbuthnot in the *Epistle*, indicates two distinct ways of viewing the history of the period—and how to write that history. Swift attributes historical change to the whole age, but Pope continues to attribute vice to specific, recognizable individuals. Swift's method points to vice as a widespread epidemic, whereas Pope places blame on designated figures, fostering, albeit satirically, the impulse of exemplar history with knowledge and action motivated through discrete people. Likewise, Arbuthnot recognizes the elite as a class of individuals that have the power and resources of typical exemplars, but Pope does not stand in awe of this wealth or the actions it excuses.

The problem arising from Pope's use of these specific, named individuals is the easy attribution of personal revenge to Pope. Reading *The Dunciad*'s attacks as the direct result of Pope's personal grievances confines the poem to a formula of causality; in this understanding of cause and effect, *The Dunciad* is the result of abuse Pope suffered from his detractors, thus reinforcing historical knowledge as derived from biography. The temporal infrastructure of *The Dunciad* is not built on such linearity, though; the satiric project of the poem moves beyond solely vilifying those who had wounded Pope. When removed from this temporal insularity, these attacks indicate a more complicated interweave of personal histories manifesting from various points in Pope's life, in his mentors' lives, and in England's life: "There is a strangely belated quality about many of Pope's most heartfelt loyalties: as a young man he tended to adopt as mentors distinguished men whose active careers were largely behind them; and their quarrels often became his quarrels, to be pursued with the intensity that marked his commitment to friendship as an ideal. This is highly relevant to the values espoused with such passion in the *Dunciads*, values which in important ways hark back to issues debated in the late seventeenth century, long before Pope was of an age to be directly involved."[48] The ability to attribute *to Pope* specifically the force of the satiric attack is marred by his own personal interconnectedness to others, interpersonal relationships that manipulate temporality through their gestures to the past.

Linear causality does not propel *The Dunciad* forward; instead, a tangled web of injustices and offenses emerge that cannot be traced sequentially. The issue of "belatedness" speaks to the same problem concerning memory expressed by philosopher Maurice Halbawchs: "We preserve memories of each epoch in our lives, and these are continually reproduced; through them, as by a continual relationship, a sense of our identity is perpetuated. But precisely because these memories are repetitions, because they are successively engaged in very different systems of notions, at different periods of our lives, they have lost the form and the appearance they once had. They are not intact vertebrae of fossil animals which would in themselves permit reconstruction of the entities of which they were once a part."[49] Memory collapses strict boundaries between past, present, and future, eliminating the possibility for certitude or linearity.[50]

Pope details the vices and follies of nameable individuals, but the so-called crimes of these individuals may not have occurred in Pope's historical present moment—and indeed may not have been committed against him directly. Instead, these individuals are held accountable for crimes that occurred in past conversations in which Pope was not involved (but to which he became privy through his later friendship with a participant), or for crimes whose import have degenerated into anachronistic or residual aesthetic insults that have lost connection to their original impetus. Pope's vendettas and their inclusion in *The Dunciad* showcase the problem of recompense as a straightforward transaction involving the binary assignation of victim and aggressor, as well as the incontrovertible attribution of innocence and guilt. The injuries sustained and thence documented by the poem are interpersonal but often arise from conversations excluding the direct engagement of Pope, yet Pope feels the need to rectify them. His desire to offer a compensatory gesture for wounds inflicted by others in situations external to his own historical past complicates the trajectory of recompense when the origins of historical data are obscured by the cacophony of competing and perhaps contradictory renditions of events.

Moreover, opened up to the gaze of the reading public, the narration of injuries in *The Dunciad* creates a historical record that, like Halbawchs's thoughts on memory, is dependent on the personal emotive, cultural, and philosophical values of the reader who must interpret the evidence preserved by the literary text and cast their own judgements on the crimes. Both Wilkinson and Lockwood emphasize verse satire's serious "informing purpose," the didacticism marking it as a genre. In this spirit, Pope might transpose Theobald's own words into the prefatory material of *The Dunciad*, but, although he intends that readers will interpret those words as opprobriously as he did, he cannot guarantee it. Tort law adjudicates local crimes where the parties involved and those responsible for their settlement are, if not intimate, at least familiar, bearing geographic, social, or economic ties. In eighteenth-century England, however, Pope's readers were potentially strangers, alienated from his own values, disadvantages, and perspectives. This estrangement possibly eliminates empathy for Pope's suffering in his dealings with Theobald and others. Will this unknown public read the recompense of *The Dunciad* as necessary or as extraneous? As poetic justice for a legitimate act of aggression or as a mere temper tantrum preserved by poetry?

The act of naming, ostensibly pointing toward an explicit presence in *The Dunciad*'s history and reinforcing linear recompense, instead troubles the significance attached to a referent.[51] The poem relies on the absence of particular individualism beneath the weight of all-consuming dullness. Indeed, even the heir, Bays, has no determinate identity, only what Michael Seidel refers to as the "hero's nonstatus."[52] The various characters existing in the kingdom of dullness live in the shadow of "the cloud-compelling Queen" (book 2, ll. 79), bound to the kingdom that they help to perpetuate: "None of Dulness' creations ever really breaks free from her maternal adherence, as none ever really wishes to."[53] Their unique identities are swallowed by the expanse of her lethargic influence so that their character descriptions provide little more than faint, blurred outlines of grotesque phantoms that feed on the very boredom they help to sustain and produce. Queen Dulness, too, is ultimately only a pawn of the greater force, dullness. Book 4 obscures the distinction between queen and kingdom when Queen Dulness ascends her throne, "her head a cloud concealed" (l. 17), as well as when she is addressed by her subjects as their "dusky queen" (l. 80). The awfulness of her presence is created not by her own strength and power, but by the strength and power of the force she serves: "Her ample presence fills up all the place; / A veil of fogs dilates her awful face" (book 1, ll. 261–62). She is both "ample" and "veiled"; like her subjects, she, too, is poetically visible—endowed with subjectivity—only to be vacated of it, made invisible, through her characterization. In this way, Pope manipulates the assumption that specific names indicate discrete individuals, as in exemplar writing, and that those possessing names in exemplar history represent clear moral-didactic types, further complicating the ability to assign labels indicating guilt or innocence, or criminal and victim.

The heroic games of book 2 further demonstrate the inadequacy of naming as proof of possessing historical value according to an exemplar model. Pope describes the specific individuals who participate in the diving contest into the mud of the Thames. For 39 lines (ll. 269–308) Pope lists with great enthusiasm the endeavors of the various dunces associated with weekly journals, such as Oldmixon (l. 283), Smedley (l. 291), and Concanen (l. 299). Abruptly, though, Pope rejects the listing procedure he has just relied upon, refusing to go any further in his diatribe, declaring, "Ask ye their names? I could as soon disclose / The names of these blind puppies as of those" (ll. 309–10). The poet seems unconcerned with his inability to stipulate names at a moment when naming has been crucial to the satiric force of the heroic game; indeed, the poet's inability (or undesirability) to specify rests on the lack of individuating features in the participants. Pope's refusal to continue naming deemphasizes the value of those he does name, inverting standard commemorative practices by disavowing identity and dissolving visibility of particularity: names have no meaning when there is no moral-didactic instruction involved. This moment in *The Dunciad* must seem striking when we consider it alongside of Pope's earlier enthusiasm for naming as professed in the *Epilogue to the Satires*, and especially if we continue to view Pope as the exemplar of Augustan verse satire—and hence a poet trained to reify specificity.

As conceived by *The Dunciad*, the exemplar is perpetually at odds with anonymity, as attribution relies on referential specificity. Generic catalogs or general practices common to all people ignore the exemplar's insistence on infusing names with discrete values, tests of strength, and epistemological lessons. Gray's rude forefathers in the "Elegy," discussed in the next chapter, refuses the naming strategy of the exemplar model, meditating, instead, upon the anonymous individuals buried in the rural hamlet. Richardson's Lovelace manipulates the names and stations of other people multiple times in *Clarissa*, indicating a name's untrustworthiness. Pope, who locates history in high political, externalized events, chooses, like Gray and Richardson, to turn his back on naming during this section of the heroic games.

In so doing, Pope's *The Dunciad* demands a rereading of accepted historical processes, challenging assumptions about whom and what constitutes proper objects of historical thinking, and how those subjects are written into history. In *The Dunciad*, the corrective impulse of Augustan verse satire leads not to imitation, as with the lessons of exemplar history to be incorporated by succeeding generations into their culture, but to alteration, the enactment of change in order to avoid the repetition of the actions and decisions of those blamed for the period's devolution. Pope performs this change himself during those moments when *The Dunciad* refuses to adhere to formal Augustan satiric practices, such as his rejection of naming in book 2.[54] These moments of refusal are, importantly, instances of self-consciousness, usually involving a direct question posed, such as Pope's "Ask ye their names?" directed to the reader above. Here, we see Pope interweaving verse satire with the type of introspection we might expect from a text like Gray's "Elegy" or Richardson's *Clarissa*, one that uses its hyperawareness of itself as an expression of genre to critique our assumptions about the possibilities and limitations of that genre, especially what that genre can offer historical inquiry. As performed by *The Dunciad*, possessing satiric subjectivity publicly commemorates the individual, thus granting that individual historical status, while simultaneously devaluing the individual as unworthy of transcription into the historical record. This devaluing forces the poet to turn his critical gaze inward, to examine closely both his genre and his self; this process, for Pope, generates the hostile and reactionary quality that we typically associate with verse satire—and with Pope. Certainly, written as verse satire, the exemplary in history becomes, instead, the infamous.

Misusing the Past

The Dunciad's hostility toward the infamous emerges less from the umbrage Pope might have felt against his named detractors than the crushing sense of bathos he perceives as crippling the entire nation. In a letter to Gay dated October 23, 1730, Pope writes, "I can tell you of no one thing worth reading, or seeing; the whole age seems resolv'd to justify the *Dunciad*, and it may stand for a publick Epitaph or monumental Inscription. . . . There may indeed be a Wooden image or two of Poetry set up, to preserve the memory that there once were bards in Britain."[55] Here, Pope's distaste for current literary values and forms is obvious; less obvious—and what I intimate in the introduction—is Pope's vision of his aesthetic creation as an act of commemoration, a specifically "publick" act of commemoration. The poetic composition of *The Dunciad* is rooted in "the whole age," a recognition of the deep tie between poetic depiction and historical reality. Commemoration, for Pope, involves the preservation of national historical memory, just as much as the quality of poetry itself—and that memory is indelibly tied to England's historical past, the "bards" that came before. The poetic process, for Pope, emerges from his desire to determine what constitutes Englishness when the bards of the past seem incapable of representing contemporary England. Structurally, the inefficacy of the past reveals itself through *The Dunciad*'s satiric perversion of traditional literary forms and expectations.

Pope's *The Dunciad* predates Bolingbroke's *Letters* that articulate disgust for the misuse of historical data by aspiring wits, but, like Bolingbroke, in his verse satire Pope claims that the contemporary milieu misappropriates—and thus deforms—past terminology because it does not know what that terminology truly means. A break in epistemology exists as the present cannot translate past figures, events, and individuals properly, transforming that data into rhetorical playthings. Recompense involves a clear relationship between the past and the present, wherein the past serves as the model for present generations: open, accessible, and didactic. Oddly enough, we might best understand the interweave between past and present in Pope if we turn to Percy Bysshe Shelley's circa 1820 *Satire upon Satire*. Shelley writes,

> If Satire's scourge could wake the slumbering hounds
> Of Conscience, or erase the deeper wounds,
> The leprous scars of callous infamy;
> If it could make the present not to be,
> Or charm the dark past never to have been,
> Or turn regret to hope.[56]

Like Cowper's earlier critique of verse satire, the repetition of the "if" statements in these lines magnify Shelley's disillusionment, his disappointment in the capability of verse satire to enact meaningful and lasting change.

More than this, as Wilkinson perceives, Shelley's words indicate the importance of historical time to Augustan verse satire: "The Augustans would not have seen the point of dispensing with the present, because they accepted the present; and the dark past had been a necessary preliminary to it."[57] This relationship bears resemblance to exemplar narratives, wherein the past (ancient troves of philosophy and examples of virtue) contains the lessons needed for current generations to thrive. Pope rehearses this viewpoint in his preface to his collected *Works* of 1717:

> All that is left us is to recommend our productions by the imitation of the Ancients; and it will be found true, that in every age, the highest character for sense and learning has been obtain'd by those who have been most indebted to them. For to say truth, whatever is very good sense must have been common sense in all times; and what we call Learning, is but the knowledge of the sense of our predecessors. Therefore they who say our thoughts are not our own because they resemble the Ancients, may as well say our faces are not our own, because they are like our Fathers: And indeed it is very unreasonable, that people should expect us to be Scholars, and yet be angry to find us so.[58]

Curiously, Pope both enshrines the ancients as purveyors of "sense and learning" and as family members, physically etched onto the faces of their progeny. Earlier, in his 1709 *A Discourse on Pastoral Poetry*, Pope also reifies the ancients, writing, "But after all, if they [his pastorals] have any merit, it is to be attributed to some good old Authors, whose works as I had leisure to study, so I hope I have not wanted care to imitate."[59] Pope clearly advocates for a backward-looking gaze and reliance on the ancients as worthy of imitation. For him, verse satire's purpose rests not in making "the present not to be" or "the dark past never to have been," but in immersion into the potentialities offered by the interweave of past, present, and future.

However, if we treat Pope's assertions more carefully—if we agree with Hammond that "Pope does not quite mean what he is ostensibly saying"—then we can see that for Pope the past cannot be straightforwardly replicated in the present moment.[60] Despite Pope's earlier claims in 1709 and 1717, *The Dunciad* demonstrates a more robust relationship to the historical past, one that is built on his recognition of the differences between ancient Rome and eighteenth-century England. Traces of what Wilkinson terms "tragic regret" and "bitter remorse" runs through *The Dunciad*, not in terms of individual loss, as you might find in Shelley or other Romantics, but loss for society as a whole. The past is "dark" not because it is full of committed wrongs but because it recedes from our collective grasp, battered and abused by those rhetorical showmen who misuse historical knowledge.[61] Walter Benjamin in "On the Concept of History" seems to resonate with this discussion, particularly his claim that "the historian turns his back on his own time, and his seer's gaze is kindled by the peaks of earlier generations as they sink further and further into the past," beyond our reach.[62]

The Dunciad attempts to anchor its history in references to the past (past literary figures, past historical examples), but present circumstances (Grub Street, new literary practices) interfere, preventing the ubiquitous mapping of the old onto the contemporary and the straightforward performance of linear recompense. For instance, Grub Street and the "battle of the books" between hack and elitist writers—that is, contentions over the value of aesthetic assumptions and practices—forms a central concern in *The Dunciad*.[63] Elitist writers, approaching literature with "polite" standards, privileged tenets established by ancient philosophers. "Such humanistically-educated men believed that values derived from Greek and Roman literature provided authoritative standards of virtue, rationality and aesthetic taste" in contradistinction to practices espoused by contemporary writers utilizing new methods of printing, publishing, and selling texts.[64] To writers like Pope (despite his very own use of modern technologies), those profiting from the new forms of literary production were merely hack writers, members of Grub Street, who could script nothing of literary legitimacy.

The significance of Grub Street and the attendant ancient/modern quarrel is the degree to which the past would be privileged as the authoritative demarcation of not only taste in the eighteenth century but also of historical subjectivity. Rumbold rehearses the standard reading of Pope's denigration of Grub Street as "a powerful image of shabbiness of way of life, morals and literary standards: it may overlap, in strictly factual terms, with only a small minority of the careers cited as evidence for the triumph of Dulness, but it retains the figurative capacity to smear even the successful with the connotations of their complicity in a new system of literary production which Pope—and others—resented as a betrayal of traditional values."[65] Pope's "Martinus Scriblerus of the Poem," affixed as a component of the prefatory material to *The Dunciad* beginning in 1729, describes the effect of mass printing on the growth of Grub Street: "Paper also became so cheap, and Printers so numerous, that a deluge of Authors covered the land."[66] This "deluge" obviously negates the singularity inherent to exemplary worth, thus altering the relationship between historical visibility and value.

Indeed, book 1 describes the danger that Grub Street poses to the exemplary status of the past:

> With less reading than makes felons scape,
> Less human genius than God gives an ape,
> Small thanks to France, and none to Rome or Greece,
> A past, vamp'd, future, old, reviv'd, new piece. (ll. 281–84)

The dangerous talent of Grub Street lies in its ability to mingle "past" with "future" work through processes of revival and vamping (patching together to appear new) that suggest the appropriateness of reworking past texts. Exemplary narratives, though, by definition, should stand outside of correction because of their "sublimer trophies." Grub Street's literary practice relies not solely on imitation of the ancients, but, more significantly, as Pope posits, on the rescripting of the ancients for contemporary self-aggrandizement. Pope expressively charges Grub Street with mishandling exemplary formulas and thus mangling historiographic preservation and the knowledge received. By treating past models as sources of literary piecework, Grub Street disrupts a linear understanding of history wherein the past is transposed without alteration onto the present.

Pope strategically invokes individuals who misappropriate past exemplary models. Barrett Kalter explains that "the Ancients emphasized the importance of taking from the past lessons directly applicable to the present, whether for the practical instruction of the politician or the moral cultivation of the polite reader."⁶⁷ However, Pope challenges the assumption that the moral-didactic lessons of exemplar writing are intelligible to all—especially to members of the elite class. For instance, one of the politicians that Pope scorns in the poem is Sir Thomas Hanmer, "a high-bred politician who became Speaker of the Commons and then attempted a showy edition of Shakespeare in 1743–4."⁶⁸ Attending the coronation of Bays, Hanmer represents one of the great men of exemplar history, eliciting deference from others: "Courtiers and patriots in two ranks divide, / Through both he passed, and bowed from side to side" (book 4, ll. 105–9). Hanmer evidently possesses the named visibility typically understood as historical subjectivity. However, Hanmer's pompous movements, his "superior air" (l. 105), dominates Pope's depiction, not an epic catalog of his achievements and virtues. Playing on Hanmer's aristocratic title, the use of "knight" simultaneously reinforces his ridiculousness and the discrepancy between what he professes to be and the historical ideal of the past. When a rebel captive tries to push him out of the way, "the decent knight retired with sober rage" (l. 113). The force of the satire lies not simply in the comic figure Hanmer presents as he continually bows from one side of the crowd to the other, but in its reliance on juxtaposing the supposedly dashing Hanmer with the chivalrous knights of the past. Hanmer proves to be no knight, as he is unable to spring heroically to action in defense of his title, retreating from the poem. His anger does not transform into inspiring motivation but simmers soberly in the background of the coronation. Hanmer, rather than reflecting the past appropriately, turns the past into a charade.

The description of Queen Dulness's administrative headquarters in book 1 further illustrates the inadequacy of past models. Her palace is called "her own Guildhall" (l. 270), which, as Rumbold notes, points to the London Guildhall, the "ceremonious and administrative centre of the City of London."⁶⁹ In this reading, the Guildhall represents the movement of those who begin writing for the lord mayor of London and then travel west to the court, seeking patronage from the monarchy, in a move that signals their growing confidence in themselves as legitimate writers. "In the *Dunciads*, which from the beginning featured a kind of progress from the plebeian and mercantile City of London towards the royal and aristocratic Westminster," Rumbold writes, Pope "signals an overarching allusion to the action of Virgil's *Aeneid*, in which Aeneas leaves the ruins of Troy and sails westward to found the new and greater city of Rome.... Just as Aeneas has for his mother the powerful goddess Venus, so Pope's hero has Dulness."⁷⁰ Scholars such as Rumbold and Aubrey Williams have sufficiently traced the relationship between *The Aeneid* and *The Dunciad*, and the invocation of the Guildhall in this sense absolutely plays on this relationship.⁷¹ Of course, Pope denigrates this epic connection by associating the dunces of the Guildhall with "the clubs of Quidnuncs" (l. 270), those obsessed with insignificant trivia and gossip.

Moreover, the description of the Guildhall contains two further interpretations. "Guildhall" alludes to the glory of the heroic mead halls in medieval times where the pomp and wealth of the lord would be displayed (consider the importance of the mead hall in *Beowulf*, for instance). Or, as in the case of a guild or corporation, access would be permitted to those possessing membership. Pope's satiric play, though, undermines the grandeur of this privileged association, since the membership celebrated here is one of dullness, and the heroic mead hall serves as the seat of "opium" and "owls" (book 1, l. 271), owls being "emblems of pompous and boring stupidity."⁷² The suggestive possibilities within the term "Guildhall" manipulate a straightforward association of past meanings with current situations, indicating a disjointed relationship to the past in which the past loses efficacy when mapped onto eighteenth-century concerns.

Crucially, though, *The Dunciad* denies any estrangement from the past. Fundamental to the poetic vision of the poem is the literary history with which Pope engages: the reliance on past texts to illuminate the subtleties of his own verse satire. As with the great epics of his predecessors (such as the works of Homer, Spenser's *The Faerie Queene*, or Milton's *Paradise Lost*), the poem is broken into a series of books. Indeed, Pope flaunts the poem's affiliation with the classics, as Joel Weinsheimer suggests.⁷³ Epic diction is used from the very beginning of the poem, such as in stanza 2 when "Pallas" and "the Thunderer" (book 1, l. 10) are invoked to establish the long history of Dulness. "Chaos" and "Night" (l. 12) hearken back to the creation stories of Genesis in the Old Testament and that of Mount Olympus in Greek history in order to establish the noble ancestry of Dulness's "ancient right" (l. 11) to rule. Line 18—"For, born a Goddess, Dulness never dies"—reinforces the immortality of Queen Dulness. The title of the poem mirrors the grand titles used by Homer in *The Iliad* and Virgil in *The Aeneid*.

The Dunciad's connection to its literary precedents has been well documented by scholars; here, I want to show that its manipulation of epic conventions and allusions to past literary works continue the poem's interest in dislodging past models as sources of legitimate authority and national identity. Dryden's verse satires stand foremost as points of reference for Pope's work. Not only was Dryden "the inventor of the Augustan satire in English" and, as poet laureate to both Charles II and James II, celebrated for his poetic skill, but, as Howard Erskine-Hill emphasizes, as a convert to Catholicism, and thus subsequently suffering the deprivation of his offices, Dryden "was a most important forebear: The greatest poet of the last age, and a fellow Catholic."[74] Pope certainly borrows sentiments from Dryden's *MacFlecknoe* (1682), a succession satire similar to *The Dunciad* in which a dunce inherits the throne of his parent. In both *MacFlecknoe* and *The Dunciad*, scatological language mocks the seriousness of the act of coronation and reinforces the offensiveness that the reigns of the new rulers bring to the kingdoms. Dryden's *Absalom and Achitophel* (1681), though, forms the key literary backdrop for the historical inquiry that Pope performs in *The Dunciad*. Not only do Dryden and Pope both seek to create poetic spaces that encourage links between past, present, and future, primarily through their shared anxiety over succession, but they also both invoke specific individuals, events, and concerns as emblematic of the collective English identity—an attribution of historical subjectivity typical to an exemplar model of history. Although recognizing the connections between Dryden and Pope already established by scholars, I emphasize instead the crucial distinction between them: Pope's dismissal of past historical models as legitimate forms of eighteenth-century representation.

Dryden's political satire connects the past with the present by drawing parallels between the contemporary and the ancient; the poem enfolds multiple temporalities upon each other rather than isolating them as exclusive demarcations of time. *Absalom and Achitophel* seeks to wind this thread from the Genesis story of Adam and Eve to the Old Testament story of Absalom and Achitophel and, finally, to the seventeenth-century England of Charles, Monmouth, and Shaftesbury. The typology between God, David, and Charles; between Adam, Absalom, and Monmouth; between the Serpent, Achitophel, and Shaftesbury; and between Michal and Catherine are intended to shock the reader into realizing that actions are not confined to an immediate milieu but reach outward in ways that can only be imagined through the poetic process. As Fredric Bogel explicates, the "play of sameness and difference," or the assimilation of the events of the past with the present while acknowledging their separation, enacts the tension between that which remains stagnant and that which is innovative across time periods.[75]

Like *MacFlecknoe* and *Absalom and Achitophel*, Pope draws on the literary precedent established by Milton in *Paradise Lost*. *The Dunciad* is "like *Paradise Lost* because Pope allusively draws on establishing the dunces' London as a species of Hell and in enclosing all his poem's acts and persons, however commonplace, in a great religious metaphor."[76] Book 2 mirrors the opening of book 2 of *Paradise Lost*. Milton describes Satan's throne in Hell using language that conveys its splendor, as well as the fallen angel's high rank in his kingdom:

> High on a Throne of Royal State, which far
> Outshone the wealth of Ormus and of Ind,
> Or where the gorgeous East with richest hand
> Show'rs on her Kings Barbaric Pearl and Gold,
> Satan exalted sat, by merit rais'd
> To that bad eminence; and from despair
> Thus high uplifted beyond hope.[77]

The mixed references to politics, imperialism, and philosophy anchor the seat of Satan's government, depicting the center of Hell's power in blinding rays of light. In contrast to the degradation of Satan's status from Heaven, this description ironically emphasizes the glory of Satan's position.

The language and syntax that Pope uses in invocation of Cibber (poetic name, Bays) is strikingly similar. His punctuation and periodic form even mirror that of Milton, as does the rhythm of the lines:

> High on a gorgeous seat, that far outshone
> Henley's gilt tub, or Flecknoe's Irish throne,
> Or that where on her Curlls the public pours,
> All-bounteous, fragrant grains and golden showers,
> Great Cibber sate: the proud Parnassian sneer,
> The conscious simper, and the jealous leer,
> Mix on his look. (ll. 1–7)

Cibber's attitude is similar to that of Satan, as both of them sit exalted on their elaborate thrones. Words such as "outshone" and "gorgeous" connect these two passages, as well as the "showering" of "gold" upon each. As with Satan, Cibber sits "high," intimating his innate superiority in addition to his political power. Their subjects bestow the same type of praise and obedience on them both. While perhaps we see Pope presenting himself here as an eiron—a classical figure in ancient Greek theater whose apparent simplicity ultimately undermines a cocky opponent—even more ironic than Satan, the similarities between Milton's Satan and Pope's Cibber suggest that the actions of the two characters will have similar effects on mankind. Satan caused man to fall from grace and into a life of toil; Cibber will cause the human mind and soul to lose its heavenly talents under the lethargic influence of dullness.

Yet it is the difference that Pope injects into his own description of Cibber's throne that proves of interest here, and the manner in which this difference upsets a purely imitative or celebratory reading of Milton's passage. Whereas the description of Satan's throne demands an epic comparison to "the wealth of Ormus and of Ind," Pope constructs the backdrop for Cibber as "Henley's gilt tub, or Flecknoe's Irish throne," a reference to pompous preaching and *MacFlecknoe*. More than indicating anxiety over the state of contemporary literary worth, this instance of bathos, the "plunging" quality of Cibber's existence, points to a diminution of an English sphere of influence. In Milton, the ironic glory of the throne can only be described by invoking the exotic riches of lands outside of England, suggesting that England's imperial prowess is capable of gathering these riches while constructing a government that is far superior in glory. Pope, however, empties this reading of the English national narrative, rooted as it is in "merit" and "hope," of credibility: that which Cibber's throne outshines reflects no greatness upon the nation. Rather than referencing generic cultural stereotypes of "Ormus" and "Ind," Pope, in an understanding of historical subjectivity, invokes two specific figures, both of whom represent gilded self-conceit and showy worth. The throne, for Pope, is not built on imperial wealth, but on gaudy self-representation and obscure literary value. The "sneer," the "simper," and the "leer" are the benchmarks of the satiric throne, not terms indicating hard work, resourcefulness, or aspiration. Notice the connection between the "Parnassian sneer" of Cibber and of the "Peer" whom Pope berates in *Epistle to Dr. Arbuthnot*, quoted above. Pope's lines perform a reduction of English concerns while Milton's stanza ennobles English governance ironically; Milton looks beyond England's boundaries to find his epic comparison, but Pope shrinks England inward, and ultimately finds a history conveyed through diminutive cultural figures.

The Dunciad does not dignify genealogical legitimacy through correlations with biblical stories, as does *Absalom and Achitophel* or *Paradise Lost*. In contrast, the kingdom of Dulness embraces the political history of the barbarians, a lesson that Cibber learns during his trip to the underworld. The Vandals, Ostrogoths, and Visigoths are reverently mentioned: "See the bold Ostrogoths on Latium fall; / See the fierce Visigoths on Spain and Gaul!" (book 3, ll. 93–94). These destroyers of the ancient civilizations of Rome, Spain, and Gaul are described as "stern," "bold," and "fierce" (ll. 91–94). Dulness's affinity for barbarian acts destabilizes a chronological sense of history as progressing forward away from a "darker," less sophisticated era, emptying cultural development of significant meaning. Pope relies on the narrative formula of historical degradation, of the fall from a civilized to a barbarian state, specifically predicated on the famous model of the fall of Rome into an effeminate, degenerate taste in arts and into political corruption. Pope's scatological inversions reinforce this regression, represented through the figures of bathos that plunge from the mind and sense to mere sounds of the body. Before Cibber is anointed king, he soliloquizes about the type of government that he will implement:

> Shall I . . . desperate in my zeal,
> O'er head and ears plunge for the commonweal?
> Or rob Rome's ancient geese of all their glories,
> And cackling save the monarchy of Tories? (book 1, ll. 209–12)

The progression of his thoughts from Commonwealth to Rome to monarchy and the party politics of Pope's contemporary milieu touch on multiple versions of possible historical alternatives—indeed, these lines depict Cibber as certainly fantasizing about which option he will embrace. Cibber's self-conceit is evident here, as he imagines having the power to "rob" Rome of their "ancient geese," a reference to the story that the Romans had been "warned by geese of the approach of the enemy when the Gauls attacked the Capitol in 390 BC, [geese that allowed] Manlius Capitolinus to resist the assault."[78]

In so fantasizing, Cibber longs to upset the standard historical record, to rupture the story of the geese by "robbing" them of "their glories." Silencing the geese, stripping them of their voice and their subsequent glory, would rescript not only the English national narrative but the collective narrative of western civilization as well. Pope's characterization of Cibber inclines us to read his words as proof of his desire to insert himself into the great historical myths of the past, to position himself as one of the great men of exemplar history, but in so doing Cibber stands as a threat to historical integrity as a whole. If, as Cibber claims, the various political options available to him merely form "the same rope" that the political parties "twist" from "different ends" (book 1, l. 207), then the choice itself is merely a formality, empty of meaning, as dullness defines all. The implications on historical inquiry are, then, dour.

Dryden utilizes biblical and classical typologies in order to trace a thread between the historical stories of the past and contemporary events, following Black's rendering of the utility of the past: "It was not simply a matter of a society that looked to the past for its codes of legitimate practice[;] . . . the belief that history possessed a cyclical quality, exemplified in the rise and fall of states, was strong, while the argument that major events had small causes, that were essentially due to the personal traits of the great historical actors, helped to undercut any sense of specificity through time or distinctiveness for particular historical periods."[79] Typological continuity recognizes history through "the great historical actors," the models of exemplar history, the invocation of whom supports a straightforward reading of chronological history in which the past can be mapped onto the present in order to produce futurity; *Absalom and Achitophel* functions in this way.

In contrast, *The Dunciad* upsets the veracity of genealogical legitimacy itself, suggesting that, through the poet's satiric vision, the collapse of historical myths taken as truth stands imminent. Pope positions Cibber as similar to Christ, Adam, and Aeneas, as a witness to the interweaving of temporalities during his trip to the underworld in book 3. Yet his guide and poetic father, Elkannah Settle, declares,

> All nonsense thus, of old or modern date,
> Shall in thee centre, from thee circulate.
> For this our Queen unfolds to vision true
> Thy mental eye, for thou hast much to view:
> Old scenes of glory, times long cast behind
> Shall, first recall'd, rush forward to thy mind:
> Then stretch thy sight o'er all her rising reign,
> And let the past and future fire thy brain. (ll. 59–66)

Cibber, as heir to Dulness, is privy to historical information of both "old" and "modern" periods, and, like his typological counterparts, receives this information in order to prepare him for his position as successor to the kingdom. However, Settle's emphasis on the extreme distance between the "old scenes of glory" and Cibber himself separates the past from the present instead of fusing them together. Settle tells Cibber that he has "much to view" *because* the "times [are] long cast behind," not readily accessible or intelligible. Cibber will need to "stretch" his mental capabilities in order to "let the past and future" direct his reign jointly. Temporal discontinuity threatens Cibber's reign from the outset.

The kingdom of Dulness may attempt connections with the past, drawing on the past to articulate itself, but, without the use of reason or judgment, it cannot truly understand that past. The poet's affirmation of Dulness as poetic inspiration suggests that the poem will end as it begins, with dullness, an assumption that anticipates an ending embedded within the beginning—a perspective that inherently denies difference and eradicates the possibility for productive cultural growth or the changing needs of a national Englishness: "Dulness! whose good old cause I yet defend, / With whom my Muse began, with whom shall end" (book 1, ll. 165–166). While trumpeting the glories of the past by invoking the techniques of writers such as Dryden and Milton, Pope also demonstrates their inability to speak to his contemporary concerns, thus indicating the great historical distance separating him from the very language he relies upon—that of the exemplar. Therefore, Cibber stands not as a typological counterpart to Christ, Adam, and Aeneas, but as the degraded figure of bathos, unable to discern the difference between himself and Christ, Adam, and Aeneas. Through its satiric form, *The Dunciad* commemorates that which it aspires to embrace (the texts and styles that precede it) and that which it actually represents (the fractured collective narrative). Seen in this way, *The Dunciad* cannot imagine recompense for the great acts of depravity its nation commits.

The Archive: A New Model of History

If past models of knowing history prove insufficient for elucidating eighteenth-century concerns, then what new models can replace them? The archival strategy of *The Dunciad* indicates a new way of formulating the national narrative and of articulating the individual's relationship to that collective. The memory system inherent to the archive relies not upon narrating the deeds of specific people, but upon the vast array of new *things* crowding eighteenth-century England, demonstrating the general shift away from narrative history toward Enlightenment interests in objects as purveyors of the past. Archival impulses "are marked by the insistence that only as archives can they bring order to and make sense of the contemporary world of letters and print."[80] This archival system was a new vehicle for preserving information. As Elizabeth Eisenstein points out, "There is simply no counterpart in medieval houses of studies or monastic libraries ... for the reference apparatus which accompanied them."[81] The attempts at creating an indexing and cross-referencing system did not develop until the seventeenth and eighteenth centuries with the rise of Enlightenment emphases on observation, categorization, and sorting—the key elements to archiving as understood by this book.

Pope's obsession with documenting every allusion to contemporary people and events reveals not only his fear that succeeding critics would preserve his work together with Grub Street writers and thus eliminate the distinction he wished to maintain from their work, but, more importantly, the period's changing relationship to accessing history. Historical knowledge would no longer simply reference great figures of ages past, as in narrative history; historical knowledge now included the immense quantity of *stuff* existing within collections. *The Dunciad*'s insistent satiric practice of naming replicates this archival zeal, straining the contours of the poem with its obsessive inclusion of names that frequently require footnotes for critical explanation of their significance.

Rumbold draws attention to one particular archival strategy Pope adopted when organizing the works of individuals later to emerge in *The Dunciad* as dunces: "Pope deliberately orchestrated the response to his *Dunciads*, as if to obtain indisputable testimony to the antagonism that he wanted to pillory.... He collected pamphlet attacks and had them bound into volumes, writing at the front of the first the biblical quotation, 'Behold it is my desire, that mine Adversary had written a Book. Surely I would take it on my Shoulder, and bind it as a crown unto me' [Job 31:35–6]."[82] Pope's "deliberate" collection suggests more than vengeance; the act of integrating into one text the disparate written attacks against him demonstrates an archival impulse, the same used by the poem. *The Dunciad*, because of its inherent acts of attribution, stands aside other archival endeavors of the period, such as Edward Cave's *The Gentleman's Magazine* (first published in 1731) and Ephraim Chambers's two-volume *Cyclopaedia* in 1728. Indeed, *The Dunciad* functions as an excellent source of general eighteenth-century knowledge, much like a reference manual.

However, *The Dunciad* demonstrates profound anxiety regarding the archival approach as a method of knowing history because the archive alters what constitutes historical value and how historical knowledge is disseminated. The indiscriminate amassing of items performed by the eighteenth century's enthusiasm for consumption disregards differing levels of originality or taste, thereby preserving in collective memory random, often useless, objects that have no cultural significance. The satiric archive emphasizes quantity rather than specificity, preserving items that have no intrinsic worth outside of being collectible. Harold Weber describes the archival impulse in England and Pope's reaction to it:

> The essentials of modern book collecting were established in England during the years 1660 and 1753, between the foundation of the Royal Society and the passage of the British Museum Act. . . . The poem represents an anguished protest against the breakdown in traditional structures of memory, and a sustained critique of the new (or newly redesigned) institutions—library, museum, and academy—that print culture helped to erect in their place. At the same time, Pope's successive revisions of the poem transform it into the very type of textual archive that he despises, for it memorializes and preserves the print industry that Pope both vilifies and exploits.[83]

The archival method, Weber suggests, institutionalizes national memory, placing it within the domain of the library, the museum, and the academy. These formal structures, I posit, become the discriminators of public knowledge about the historical past, acting as the liaisons between the individual and the collective. Access to the historical narratives increases, but *The Dunciad* implies that the items preserved do not adequately interpret and explain the past. The knowledge disseminated by a third-party mediator (such as the library) may prove faulty, incomplete, or worthless, thus hindering the ability of the individual and the nation to correctly extract moral-didactic lessons from the materials studied.

Despite our entanglement with it, *The Dunciad* suggests that the past can never be fully known because of the contentious versions arising, despite archival efforts at order. Paddy Bullard's thoughts on period miscellany might prove useful here: the "ordering of works within miscellaneous volumes was considered meaningful, even when authors or editors had no direct hand in their sequencing. Whatever the contingencies that cause a text to appear in a certain position among other works, that position becomes a fact in the work's history, often an unimportant fact, but sometimes a crucial one for its reception, or for its textual evolution."[84]

Bullard focuses on the arrangement of literature in miscellaneous collections, texts that bind together disparate literary genres, authors, and works into a single bound edition. He notes that the decision to include a specific piece in a miscellany influenced the audience's reception of that work, as the text "takes on an intertextual relationship with the poems printed immediately before and after it."[85] We can apply Bullard's logic to archival methods in general to help us understand the unease *The Dunciad* expresses. Pope's catalogs of individuals, events, and data related to both the historical present and the past attempts to bring order to historical knowledge, celebrating the copious amounts that we know, while simultaneously indicating the *lack* of what we know through the suggestion that there is always something absent that has not yet been found—or the concern that we have misfiled, misarranged, or miscatalogued items in the archive. The misuse of historical knowledge that Bolingbroke laments emerges from Pope's obsessive archiving. After all, items preserved are *curated*—that is, selected for inclusion based on a third party's assessment of their merit as part of a larger collection whose placement in that collection necessarily inscribes that third party's assessment onto the reading public.

In the archival formula as represented by *The Dunciad*, the past exists to be plundered for the benefit of collections; the past may be made visible through the displaying of collectible items, but those items represent the plenitude of the third party rather than the active investigation of knowledge by historically conscious individuals. The accumulation of objects in *The Dunciad* tends to the eradication of difference, posing a threat to individual identity. Seidel articulates this point clearly when he states that "the body of witlessness celebrated in the poem is capable of all sorts of births, and the participants in the recorded actions are usually incapable of distinguishing among them."[86] Throughout *The Dunciad* a multitude of "births" occur from the acts of "witlessness" committed by the various dunces yet they are indeterminate from each other. Certainly, within the world of Dulness abundance does not equate specificity, as Weber explicates: "A crowd of books, like a crowd of people, inevitably produces a leveling effect, reducing its individual members to a common and melancholy anonymity. A library may save the past and present for the future, but those preserved in the archive remain powerless to assert their unique status."[87] As Cibber aptly philosophizes in book 1, "What then remains? Ourself. Still, still remain / Cibberian forehead, and Cibberian brain" (ll. 217–18). Out of the entire four-book poem, what remains is that which is embodied by Cibber: simply dullness. The repetition of "still, still" emphasizes the satire's point that, despite the endless archiving and obsessive collecting depicted by the poem, what outlasts this type of history is Dulness herself—and recalls the opening lines describing Dulness "still" reigning ("Still Dunce the second reigns like Dunce the first").

In *The Dunciad*, Dulness oversees the curated archives that define the kingdom, making the choices about inclusion and exclusion that will mark the kingdom's values, an identity that the dunces will themselves assume. We see this in book 4 when Dulness authorizes the elimination of classic texts, an act that reduces exemplary narratives to mere objects and reinforces Pope's unease with archival methods:

> Let standard-authors, thus, like trophies born,
> Appear more glorious as more hacked and torn,
> ... Leave not a foot of verse, a foot of stone,
> A page, a grave, that they can call their own;
> But spread, my sons, your glory thin or thick,
> On passive paper, or on solid brick. (ll. 123–30)

Dulness identifies exemplary writing, the "standard-authors," as "trophies" adorning the kingdom. Yet these works are not "glorious" because of their moral-didactic quality but because they provide ample material for a bonfire. As kindling, Dulness references them as physical things her dunces can collect and ultimately harvest for parts rather than as the epitome of narrative history. Their erasure—ironically through their false appropriation by modern scholars, editors, and publishers—stands in honor of the "glory" of Dulness's "sons" and the lethargy that they are able to "spread" over the nation. In this apocalyptic vision, national stability arises from mishandling exemplary texts, texts narrating typical Homeric, Spenserian, Miltonic, or Dryden-like exemplars. The kingdom gains strength with each text "hacked and torn."

Of particular interest here is the recognition shared among Pope, Gray, and Richardson of the importance of burial procedures in securing historical visibility and, hence, value. In their respective texts, each of these writers includes interment rituals, positioning these practices as integral to determining individual worth to a larger national audience. Gray contrasts the showy, expensive forms of memorial by the elite with the unmarked graves of the rustics to secure their presence in national memory. Richardson uses Clarissa's obsession with crafting her coffin, will, and funerary dress as a method of asserting her self-identity after her rape. In

Pope, Dulness refuses to grant exemplary works a decent mode of burial in either literature ("a page") or in ceremony ("a grave"). In all three texts, burial is a form of archive, a practice dependent on acts of inclusion and exclusion, and raising questions about who controls the historical narrative attached to the individual.

In *The Dunciad*, the burial of the exemplary narratives forms a satiric archive, a collection of items that expresses for the kingdom of Dulness *what we are not*: the dunces are not readers of the classics, they have no meaningful connections to the past, and they prefer indulging physical appetites to contemplative activities. As readers, we are supposed to be properly aghast at what Dulness is doing to the exemplary texts—*because* they are canonical and hold historical value—and that reaction should motivate in us satire's instructional impulse. But connecting Pope to Gray and Richardson here pushes us to ask additional questions: Just because Dulness burns these texts, thereby renouncing ownership of them, does that mean that no one else can claim them as their own? If the kingdom refuses to incorporate them into its national archive, is it possible for them to still exist in personal collections that assert individual identity? To whom does the buried or burned object belong? *The Dunciad*, the "Elegy," and *Clarissa* deliberate these concerns, albeit using different forms of genre.

Exemplary narratives would imply that those items held in the archive possess especial quality, since they are being preserved intentionally by third-party mediators who are assumed to be well educated in their values, and thus more capable of arranging and categorizing their significance than others. However, the satiric depiction of the virtuosos in book 4 of *The Dunciad* demonstrates the lack of difference caused by the indiscriminate nature of the archive and its impact on historical knowledge. Most basically, the virtuosos are the enthusiasts for natural history, "amateur scientists and collectors," whose methods of scientific inquiry developed from Enlightenment emphases on rational inquiry and observation:[88]

> Then thick as Locusts black'ning all the ground,
> A tribe, with weeds and shells fantastic crown'd,
> Each with some wond'rous gift approach'd the Pow'r [Dulness],
> A Nest, a Toad, a Fungus, or a Flow'r. (ll. 397–400)

As Pope's collaborator, William Warburton, comments in his 1751 note to these lines, "the similitude of *Locusts* does not refer more to the numbers than to the qualities of the Virtuosi: who do not only devour and lay waste every tree, shrub, and green leaf in their *Course,* i.e. of experiments; but suffer neither a moss nor fungus to escape untouched."[89] Certainly, the satiric force of Pope's lines aims at dismantling experimentalist science as a valid form of information, but I argue that Pope also invokes the virtuosos here in order to vilify the eighteenth century's vogue for articulating history through indiscriminate collecting.

Virtuosos also embraced antiquarianism, the desire to collect "antique coins, medals, and statues; sixteenth-century Italian paintings and architecture; and cabinets of 'curiosities' or rarities."[90] In their assortments of oddities and bobbles, from both the natural world and the historic past, virtuosos seemed to embrace Enlightenment tenets of inquiry and observation while, as a verse satire like *The Dunciad* suggests, subverting "the developing empiricism of Sir Francis Bacon, William Harvey, and John Locke."[91] The danger thus posed by the virtuosos emerges from the manner in which they blur the divisions between historiographic strategies, drawing equally on the undiscerning hoarding of the archival method and the rationality of the Enlightenment. Russell West-Pavlov describes the method by which virtuosos would categorize the items studied: "Seventeenth- and eighteenth-century antiquarianism collected and arranged in spatial configurations a plethora of artefacts from the past, preserving them in elaborate engraved plates, as in Edward Gibson's revised 1695 edition of Camden's *Britannia*."[92] West-Pavlov stresses that the ordering system used by virtuosos was a visual representation of temporality wherein items were placed merely on the basis of visual identity.

Both Warburton's comments on the virtuosos and West-Pavlov's description indicate the indiscriminate nature of this ordering system. The charge leveled at the virtuosi by Warburton primarily foregrounds their interest in plenitude without regard for difference, while West-Pavlov indicates that a visual ordering system could be deceptive, especially since many natural items experience change during their own lifespans. The basic premise behind this form of archival collecting emphasizes continuity, the repetition within nature of similar types. This formula suggests stability between the past and present while providing a model of similitude for the future. Subjectivity across time remains unchanged and predictable, with no expectation of originality. Bolingbroke, like Pope, attacks antiquarianism as a form of illusion that misconstrues and misrepresents historical data: "All these systems are so many enchanted castles; they appear to be something, they are nothing but appearances: like them too, dissolve the charm, and they vanish from the sight. To dissolve the charm, we must begin at the beginning of them: the expression may be odd, but it is significant. We must examine scrupulously and indifferently the foundation on which they lean."⁹³ Bolingbroke writes of the necessity for Enlightenment-based history writing, one that investigates, discerns, and deliberates before narrating historical data.

Virtuosic endeavors and antiquarianism interested those imbued with historical visibility in the seventeenth and eighteenth centuries.⁹⁴ As public individuals connected to the nexus of authority and power in England, these high-ranking virtuosos used their collections as the means of accessing a historic past that would validate their own superiority in the face of a growing middle class and the new consumerism of the period, as Thomas A. King notes:

> If the initial impetus for virtuosic pursuits was the desire to contain social mobility by researching heraldry, and, in the cases of the Earl and Countess of Arundel, Buckingham, and other ambitious courtiers, to demonstrate the magnificence of great families and estates at home while promoting important, and often secret, lines of communication and patronage with powerful Catholics abroad, the ranks of the virtuosos leveled, following the Restoration, to include both gentlemanly collectors and scientists associated with the Royal Society. Both sign of and nostalgic response to the crisis of aristocratic legitimacy ... the virtuosos would themselves come to be marked as outside the public representation of private interests. Virtuosic pursuits, assimilating the elite men to an international aesthetic and political economy, failed to constitute a specifically national utility.⁹⁵

The virtuosos used the past to script a narrative of continuity for the elite class in which the past provided the rationale for continued presence in contemporary and future periods, particularly important during the historical upheavals of the seventeenth century.

The initial elite desire to maintain aristocratic presence in the face of the emerging middle class, to utilize a genealogical linearity as the historical model proving elite superiority, in fact relied on methods that technically undermined the official tenets informing historical subjectivity at the time—that is, the privileging of Protestantism over Catholicism and its attendant gestures of political exclusion. In so doing, elite virtuosos favored their own private desires over the demands of the public, English identity; within the "secret" negotiations between these elite individuals and Catholic countries exists a repudiation of the public self. Considering these years after the Restoration, when the Royal Society became marked by such virtuosic enthusiasm, King gestures toward the confusion arising from issues of linearity (and legitimacy). The "international" quality of virtuosic collecting, combined with its social "leveling" effect, shatters national certainty, and distinctions between private and public, as it likewise upsets what it means to be English at this time.[96]

King's thoughts move to the forefront those questions posed earlier regarding burial procedures in Pope, Gray, and Richardson, the shared anxiety emergent in these writers about whether a personal collection should still exist even if it stands at odds with perceptions about national identity. Such a concern seems especially pressing when we consider the danger archives pose to the items in their possession. Historical artifacts lose their educational and cultural legacies, transformed into items in a random collection aimed at diverting the attention of its owner until something of greater amusement arises, or, as in the case of Mummius, providing entertainment and sources of jealous competition among spectators eager to secure tangible benefits from them. During the court festivities, "in Book IV ... an antiquarian Dunce named Mummius ... fights for the possession of rare coins swallowed by another crafty collector."[97] In this scene, the coins function as the historical object worth preserving, the "nasty, trivial, and meaningless oddities," that the actions of Mummius satirically commemorate:[98]

> Down his own throat he risked the Grecian gold;
> Received each demigod, with pious care,
> Deep in his entrails—I revered them there,
> I bought them, shrouded in that living shrine,
> And, at their second birth, they issue mine. (ll. 382–86)

The "Grecian gold" is valuable because it alludes to an earlier historical period—but what is interesting is that because it is "historical" Mummius is willing to risk his own health in order to obtain it. Mummius is the ultimate historical collector, zealous in the pursuit of artifacts without explicating their significance beyond the fact that they are ancient. Recognized as "demigod[s]," each coin is treated as a sacred object, memorialized as the body of Mummius transforms into a "living shrine." The object itself ultimately loses distinction, becoming only one among many other instances of excretion.

The "birth" that Mummius explicates is not an ideological awareness built on historical knowledge but an excremental physical release that grossly eradicates the didactic purpose behind historical artifacts. Philosopher Eelco Runia argues that commemorative artifacts (such as Gettysburg or the Tomb of the Unknown Solider), rather than serve solely as sites of encomium for past events or figures, implicitly subsume the individual within a collective history, forcing the individual to appropriate the collective history as their own. The commemorative artifact forces the spectator, who most likely was not a participant in or witness to the actual historical event commemorated, into "a confrontation with what we don't like to be confronted with: with the fact that occasionally we behave in utter contradiction to what we regard as our identity."[99] Runia's thoughts helps readers to see the importance of Pope's construction of the Mummius scene: Mummius *enacts* the appropriation of the collective narrative by physically ingesting the historical artifact. Rather than philosophically "confronting" the artifact, the gold coin, Mummius consumes it. Pope satirizes what King explicates as a common critique of the virtuosos: "Criticism of the virtuosos thus remarked their failure to separate themselves, as (self-)conscious subjects, from the spectacles they amassed."[100] Mummius does not "separate" himself from the historical object or from the "spectacle" of entertainment his actions engender.

For Runia, commemorative acts involve a process of "externalization" in which the artifact stands as the physical embodiment of the collective memory and assuages the ontological contradictions arising from viewing the artifact.[101] For Mummius, though, there is no externalization (beyond excrement) as he literally internalizes the artifact in a maneuver that indicates his total possession. Externalization positions the memory of the historical event as a national artifact, but Mummius prioritizes only the individual self, without regard for how the collective will be damaged by his greed. Collectors like Mummius, Pope suggests, endanger collective narratives because of their emphasis on individual gain, much like the aristocratic attempts at legitimizing elite genealogies as described by King. In Mummius, temporality satirically collapses as the boundaries between past and present collide and yet produce no futurity beyond excrement. In *The Dunciad*, once the focus shifts away from exemplary narratives and turns toward objects, history devolves into a competition for *stuff* rather than for moral-didactic instruction. The archive and virtuosic collecting replace individuals as the motivators of historical change, displacing historical agency onto random items whose value is tenuously verified through the curated maneuvers of inept mediators.

Introspection and History

Noticing Pope's devaluing of the archive as a model of historical inquiry invites us to consider *The Dunciad* as both epitomizing Augustan verse satire and contributing to the introspection more obviously constitutive of melancholic, sentimental, and Romantic works. Although Pope does not directly question verse satire's effectiveness, as do Cowper and Shelley, there is an emotive trace that haunts the poem, anxieties that I believe place *The Dunciad* in conversation with the Augustan poems preceding it and the self-consciously reflective texts coming after, such as in Gray's "Elegy" and Richardson's *Clarissa*. The overwhelming despair that consumes the kingdom of Dulness, the dunces, and the reader at the end of *The Dunciad* arises from the knowledge that current historiographical and literary practices can no longer function. *The Dunciad* produces a historical record in which the act of knowing history potentially loses meaning. Each attempt at adequate representation—through the invocation of literary precedents, typological continuity, or virtuosic archiving—leads to the negation of a unique self. Both individually and collectively, the self cannot appropriate a relationship to the past that can sufficiently elucidate the present and thus generate a futurity. As a result of the inefficacy of the exemplar model of history and its attendant loss of subjective and temporal stability, Pope reconfigures history as succumbing to dullness.

Such an approach gestures toward Caruth's twentieth-century thoughts on trauma as outlined in *Unclaimed Experience*. Caruth locates trauma as "a break in the mind's experience of time" where the survivors of catastrophic events experience "the impossibility of living" with the knowledge that death has escaped them.[102] If Caruth imagines "the formation of history as the endless repetition of previous violence," then chronology cannot move forward.[103] A linear progression in temporality is prevented by the traumatic memories that are "experienced too soon, too unexpectedly, to be fully known and is therefore not available to consciousness until it imposes itself again, repeatedly, in the nightmares and repetitive actions of the survivor."[104] The cyclical violence of memory and pain trap the survivor, wherein the past event tortuously imposes itself on the present, disavowing the possibility that a futurity, free from the traumatic wound, could exist.

Caruth links the traumatic event with historical time in a way that allows us to read Pope's kingdom of dullness in surprising ways. Pope does not offer us trauma in the direct way that Caruth describes: an actual event, immanent to history, with verifiable individuals who daily experience the trauma of escaping death from the event. The spirit of Caruth's description of trauma resonates with *The Dunciad*, though, the hopelessness of moving forward in chronological time replicated by the stagnation consuming the kingdom. Each heroic game or event that occurs in the poem represents the ongoing torture of Pope's apocalyptic vision. Rumbold rightly describes the heroic games as Pope's "imagined nightmares," and I offer that the poem *is* his traumatic nightmare, the ongoing assault of devolution and the horror of modernity that Pope daily experienced and lived in fear of.[105] The unrelenting power of dullness in the poem echoes the "endless repetition" of violence described by Caruth: the dunces are imprisoned in the unchanging dullness, much like survivors who cannot progress forward, who cannot achieve recompense for a wound inflicted.

The inability to narrate difference—between the dunces, the past and present, the objects collected—speaks to a traumatic experience where the individual (and history) cannot progress forward, inundated with random memories and vestiges of the past that weigh them down, like the lethargy choking the kingdom of Dulness. The introspective quality of *The Dunciad* takes on new meaning when we pair Caruth and Runia in conversation. Runia imagines that history occurs when thinking and reflecting individuals encounter a commemorative object, an artifact that represents the past, thus placing individuals into a relationship with the past, ultimately shaping their appreciation of the past and their future identity. But Caruth suggests that when such fusion between individual and memorial cannot occur, trauma exists: "The shock of the mind's relation to the threat of death is thus not the direct experience of the threat, but precisely the *missing* of this experience, the fact that, not being experienced *in time*, it has not yet been fully known."[106] For Runia, viewing commemorative objects provides invaluable knowledge about the past to the individual, yet Caruth maintains that not all historical knowledge is intelligible or can be gained without direct experience of the event. In *The Dunciad*, the past cannot be reconciled to the present, cannot be assimilated or fully known; instead, a deep-rooted despair permeates the text. The kingdom not only perpetuates dullness but also a traumatic rendering, a severing, from the past. The dunces cannot establish a relationship to the past because they misread and mishandle the past, much like a traumatic psyche grappling to heal the "break in the mind's experience of time." *The Dunciad* does not narrate the infliction of an extant traumatic event but the experience of an unnamed trauma, articulated over and over again in various ways throughout the text, without the possibility of compensatory repair.

The complexity of *The Dunciad* rests on the reader's ability to accept that "the poet, for Pope, is not a hero of univocal stamp who slays the dragon of chaos once and finally," as in exemplar narratives, but one who instead propels dullness forward.[107] During Cibber's trip to the underworld in book 3, Settle prophecies Dulness's triumph through a series of visions. The early eighteenth-century vogue for pantomime, with its elaborate stage effects, dancing, and miming, creates a parodic apocalypse in which the basic distinction between heaven and hell crumbles:

> Hell rises, Heav'n descends, and dance on Earth:
> Gods, imps, and monsters, music, rage, and mirth,
> A fire, a jig, a battle, and a ball,
> 'Till one wide conflagration swallows all. (ll. 237–40)

Pope showcases that entertainment previously confined to fairground booths have infiltrated theatrical programs (creating new areas of financial speculation that Pope detested, such as fire insurance), thus bringing City elements into the Town. More than this, though, the danger for Pope arises from the implications on historical consciousness and agency. In this vision, "gods" mix with "monsters" in movements that confuse natural boundaries between such emotions as "rage" and "mirth" and such movements as "battle" and "ball." Pantomime may develop from a desire to provide amusement, but its effect is nothing less than fiendish, not because it brings hell to earth but because it collapses hell into heaven, making intelligibility between the two impossible. This loss of articulation, this inability to narrate difference, between virtue and vice, divine and profane, exemplary and common, informs pantomime's threat and propels the final line of the stanza—"'Till one wide conflagration swallows all"—that eerily anticipates the last line of the poem itself: "And Universal Darkness buries All" (book 4, l. 656). The inferno culminating the prophetic vision in book 3 stands as the forerunner of the much more lethal lethargy that ultimately consumes the universe in book 4.

Other Augustan verse satires contain undercurrents of anxiety and frustration when confronted with the disparity between past and present, such as *Absalom and Achitophel* and "The Vanity of Human Wishes." Pope's commitment to the breakage of historical time, though, stands in marked contrast to both Dryden and Johnson, as potentially best seen by the defeat of History herself in *The Dunciad*. Traditionally, history and satire represent two different models; history, as linked to tragedy, valorizes the actions of the great, those who conventionally inform the historical subject of exemplar narratives; satire, through its connection to comedy, focuses on the actions of the common, those customarily excluded from historical visibility. Significantly, Pope positions satire—not history—as remaining immune from Dulness's call to silence in book 4. Beneath Dulness's throne, science, wit, logic, morality, and mathematics lay chained, unable to precipitate action. Like Sir Thomas Hanmer, personified History fumes silently, incapable of initiating change in the kingdom:

> But sober History restrain'd her rage,
> And promis'd Vengeance on a barb'rous age.
> There sunk Thalia, nerveless, cold, and dead,
> Had not her Sister Satyr held her head. (ll. 39–42)

Both History and Hanmer retreat offstage, so to speak, allowing their offended honor to simmer, unable to access heroic action of past models, the "promise" of their future retribution holding no meaning for the present.

Moreover, *The Dunciad* consistently casts history as a satiric object in itself, such as in book 3 when History is given "her Pot" (l. 196)—that is, her pot of ale. In this depiction, history is personified as a woman gossiping while drinking her liquor, an image that empties history of wisdom, replacing edification with idle conversation. Rather than stressing ancient beliefs that attributed the creation of beer to various goddesses, this image reinforces the trivialities that degrade history writing. History's interest in trifles, not in the exemplary, emerges even earlier in the poem. In book 1, when discussing Cibber's library, Pope suggests that history manifests from those books managing to be "redeem'd from tapers and defrauded pies" (l. 156)—in other words, from the books not used to light candles or line baking tins. Both of these moments in *The Dunciad* remove history from its insulated space as privileged caretaker of memory, marking it as the property of those rhetorical showmen Bolingbroke laments.

The heroic games of book 2, Pope's "imagined nightmares," are certainly designed to appropriate history within the realm of dullness, especially the final competition to resist the urge of slumber when read a book, in parody of Odysseus's ability to withstand the song of the Sirens.[108] The winner,

> To him we grant our amplest pow'rs to sit
> Judge of all present, past, and future wit;
> To cavil, censure, dictate, right or wrong,
> Full and eternal privilege of tongue. (ll. 375–78)

The reward for staying awake is not escape from death, as in *The Odyssey*, but the power to become "an arbitrary and prescriptive critic."[109] However, I argue that there seems to be more at stake within the import of this game than the satirizing of critics. Like the historiographer, the judge represents a collapse of temporality in which linearity does not exist. The configuration of time in line 376 specifically rejects linearity as present precedes "past." The satiric construction of the passage, though, upsets any assignation of integrity to the judge's position, suggesting that the judge's danger lies not so much in the judgments he will make on literary works, but on the effect of his presence on historical temporality. Indeed, by line 420, when all of the dunces fall asleep, different aspects of constituting history have particularly been invoked as victims of the game's slumber: law (line 397's attack on the lawyer and translator Eustace Budgell); religiosity (line 399's attack on the deist Matthew Tindal); the arts (line 411's attack on the playwright Susanna Centlivre); and compilations of current events and recent history (line 413's attack on Abel Boyer, who produced through installments bulky works Pope denigrated, such as *The History of the Reign of Queen Anne, Digested into Annals*, published between 1703 and 1713). The triumph of the "judge"—and hence Dulness—is a triumph rooted in the widespread evacuation of sense from all means of representing, with integrity, history, and disseminating knowledge about the past's meaning for the present. Here, Pope elucidates a traumatic emptiness of experience, the present unable to lock into the significance of the past, knowing that the past exists but attaining only, at best, a foggy connection to it.

Even the muses, the revered forces bringing the articulation of arts to the world, are

> Closed one by one to everlasting rest;
> Thus at her felt approach, and secret might,
> Art after Art goes out, and all is Night
> ... Physic of Metaphysic begs defence,
> And Metaphysic calls for aid on Sense!
> See Mystery to Mathematics fly!
> In vain! They gaze, turn giddy, rave, and die. (book 4, ll. 638–48)

The commemorative suggestion within "everlasting rest" successfully buries, as does the final line of the poem, the muses as dullness indiscriminately obliterates the multiple modes of constituting history—"metaphysics," "mystery," and "mathematics." These methods of formulating the past turn "giddy" and "raving" as they too become victims of dullness's invasive presence, upsetting historical agency and the ability to establish a relationship with historical temporality.

The Dunciad dislocates history from its traditional position as caretaker of the exemplary. In book 4, Satire succeeds where History proves immovable by rebelling against Dulness. The 1751 note from Warburton on book 4 indicates that only Satire retains intelligibility beneath the weight of Dulness: "She alone of all the sisters is unconquerable, never to be silenced, when truly inspired and animated (as should seem) from above, for this very purpose, to oppose the kingdom of Dulness to her last breath."[110] In so doing, Pope seems to be validating his own satiric project and the pretensions of formal verse satire generally. His consistent ridicule of history, while supplying the figure of Satire with the rebellious action in book 4, indicates an investment in a historical model that extends historical visibility to those typically disassociated from historiographic authority, subjectivity, and agency, thus rethinking class assumptions of exemplary writing. Yet I wonder if we should read Pope's tribute to satire as circling back on itself, ending not with the reification of verse satire but in the crippling of history. Satire remains, but at the loss of historical integrity, a loss that ultimately crushes the foundation of the kingdom of Dulness and initiates the "Universal Darkness." Again, the past for Pope is not "dark" in the sense of information not gleaned, but in its distance from us.

The devastating effect of the poem's dullness manifests in its invasive nature, the manner in which it batters historical inquiry, targeting everyone in it, not just any of the specific exemplary Hanoverian figures with which the poem began. At the outset of the poem, the transmission of dullness through historical succession occurs in a linear, unbroken fashion, giving Dulness much pleasure:

> Much to the mindful Queen the feast recalls
> What City Swans once sung within the walls;
> Much she revolves their arts, their ancient praise,
> And sure succession down from Heywood's days.
> She saw, with joy, the line immortal run,
> Each sire imprest and glaring in his son. (book 1, ll. 95–100)

The coronation of Cibber reminds Dulness of past laureates and her firm grip on the world. The promulgation of dullness promises "sure" linearity, the stability and security of succession, "the line immortal," that reproduces the replications of fathers by sons. The affinity between predecessor and successor is "glaring," to the point that the father is indelibly stamped, "imprest," upon the son, just as Pope describes in his 1717 defense of the ancients: in the preface, as discussed earlier in this chapter, Pope ridicules those who claim that our "faces are not our own, because they are like our Fathers." Curiously, we see Pope deriding this same logic when placing it in the mouth of Dulness here in *The Dunciad*.

Succession suggests a linear model of history based on the exemplary accomplishments of great men, epitomizing history as constituted through verifiable individuals and events. Indeed, succession stands as a public event, of the kind often narrated in exemplary history. Late seventeenth-century occasional poems, for example, often commemorated royal successions. Poets depicted these public events, such as the Restoration of Charles II to the throne in 1660, as opportunities for national healing, inaugurating a new period of civic stability and peace. Consider, for example, Dryden's commemoration of Charles II in *Astraea Redux* (1660). Dryden praises the restoration of Charles's rule as a return to peace after the turmoil of the Cromwell years and specifically identifies Charles as the "blest example" capable of bringing stability back to England.[111] Dryden crafts Charles as the explicit figure responsible for ushering in a new, healthy political era, seamlessly fusing Charles the individual, Charles the monarch, and England:

> Oh, happy age! oh times like those alone,
> By fate reserved for great Augustus' throne!
> When the joint growth of arms and arts foreshow
> The world a monarch, and that monarch you.[112]

Concluding his panegyric with an emphasis on "you," Dryden clearly reinforces the unity between Charles and England's present and future power. Charles's reign will unite, Dryden imagines, both military and artistic expressions of English fortitude, creativity, and strength. In keeping with exemplary narratives, Dryden assigns to Charles responsibility for historical change and grants him the agency needed to bring harmony to the chaos caused by Cromwell's rule.

In *The Dunciad*, Pope does not attribute such unification to Cibber's monarchy. The coronation does not emerge as a triumphant victory over an opposing force; after all, Cibber replicates the dullness that has always characterized the kingdom. Seidel argues that "the main action of the Poem [is] by no means the Coronation of the Laureate, which is performed in the very first book, but the Restoration of the Empire of Dulness in Britain, which is not accomplished 'till the last."[113] The placement of the coronation first decentralizes the specific, public, royal function as *The Dunciad*'s subject—that is, what would be considered the exemplary event of traditional ceremonial history writing. The coronation of Cibber does not cleanse the kingdom of chaos, as Dryden believes Charles will do, aptly demonstrated by the poem's concern over bloodlines that continues well after Cibber is crowned in book 1.

Book 4 returns to succession as a point of unease, particularly since monarchical succession provided a model for other familiar and titular successions: "So may the sons of sons of sons of whores, / Prop thine, O Empress! like each neighbor Throne" (ll. 332–33). As with every other weighty topic, Pope, too, reduces succession, removing it as a hallmark of high political events and instead positioning it in the realm of bodily appetite and amusement, shifting it away from the elite to all classes. Rumbold notes "contemporary fears about sexual indulgence on the Grand Tour" that led to "a demographic crisis in which many distinguished families were failing to reproduce themselves," as well as the continuation of noble families reliant on "the ennoblement of illegitimate children of royal mistresses."[114] Rumbold specifically points to the Duke of Grafton, the grandson of a mistress of Charles II, who had appointed Cibber as poet laureate. The fears arising from the reliance on illegitimate children to sustain royal and noble families raise concerns of the purity of bloodlines (as well as the activities of young men embarking on the Grand Tour), yet these concerns point to the complexities of historical visibility as well. Succession embodies chronology, but the sexual and reproductive energies of individuals destabilize simple categorizations of legitimacy that break down linearity.

Again, if we connect *The Dunciad* to Gray and Richardson, then we can position succession as not ennobled by associations with the exemplary; instead, issues of succession emerge from interpersonal sexual relationships driven by private desires that are typically ignored by exemplary narratives—and that involve humanity in general. These relationships upset linear recompense by their refusal to follow direct causal interactions founded on genealogy and matrimony. Gray deliberates the sexual genealogy of the poor in the rustic graves, while Richardson forefronts it as a motivating factor in Clarissa's story. Likewise, Pope acknowledges sexual acts as inherent to discussions of historical recording and visibility, upsetting history's reputation as the voice box of public, exemplary individuals and events, free from the bathos and appetites of the vulgar.

The result, as imagined by *The Dunciad*, is, as the Italian opera singer–harlot flaunts, "another Phoebus, thy own Phoebus" (book 4, l. 61), thus stripping history writing of its exemplarity. "Thy own Phoebus" turns its back on the past as a source of legitimate authority and emotive stability, dispelling the greatness of exemplar figures, such as Apollo, often rendered as Phoebus, the god of poetry, in order to create a poetics that preserves, poignantly, the stagnation and similitude that dullness promises.

Recompense in *The Dunciad*

"Thy own Phoebus," though, is not necessarily a negative literary-historical development for Pope. Although it recognizes a break from the historical past, and although it is founded on a self-consciousness regarding its ability to enact meaningful change, as a force it is powerful enough to engulf Pope's kingdom of Dulness. Devoting over two decades of his life to writing *The Dunciad* I think proves Pope's respect for the Phoebus his poem describes and his obsession with articulating it correctly. History seems to be a victim of *The Dunciad*'s all-consuming lethargy, but perhaps the interpretative frame of recompense can offer a more nuanced assessment of the poem's legacy and its connection to historical inquiry.

The publication history of *The Dunciad* is in many respects the history of the early eighteenth century. Pope enriched and altered his satiric objects as his preoccupations changed over the decades. As Maynard Mack elucidates, "The poem thus encompasses a nearly complete record (a few of its lines date back in their first versions as far as 1708 or earlier) of Pope's experience as a writer, crippled, quick-tempered, highly sensitive to slights, at times vengeful, carving out a career by sheer genius and relentless application in the face of envy, religious bigotry, and almost continuous slander."[115] Yet we cannot read *The Dunciad* as solely "Pope's experience" enshrined in verse; Pope witnessed the changes that occurred in England spanning half a century, and he commemorates them in *The Dunciad*, his "publick Epitaph."

What is crucial about *The Dunciad*, and what separates it from other verse satires of its period, is the breadth of revision involved in its production. As Abrams aptly elucidates, "There is one consolation: out of non-art itself, out of matter without spirit and substance without essence, the poet creates his own final artistic triumph, and makes a poem."[116] The "consolation" that interests Abrams is precisely what I will call the "recompense" of the poem. Pope's revisionary process reveals his changing attitudes—and those of the eighteenth century—to the figures and events he makes visible in his poem at various times, depending on the edition of the poem considered. Like Hume's *History of England*, *The Dunciad* underwent many revisions, resulting in four volumes. As Graeme Slater points out in his discussion of Hume, "The 'definitive' edition of the *History of England* of 1778, posthumously incorporating Hume's final revisions, was a rather different work from the first version of the *History of Great Britain under the House of Stuart*."[117] The same could be said for *The Dunciad*. Rumbold labels it "the culminating achievement of Pope's career," and certainly "culminating" is an apt term, pointing to the revisionary history of *The Dunciad* itself.[118] Nokes likewise stresses that "Pope, as we know, was an indefatigable reviser who continued to make alterations, both major and minor, to such poems as *The Rape of the Lock* and *The Dunciad* throughout his life."[119]

The Dunciad, over its history, transforms from an attack that is primarily personal to one deeply attached to issues of English national identity. Thus Colley Cibber replaces Lewis Theobald as king of the dunces, as "Cibber had been for years a favorite butt of Pope's earlier work. The antipathy of the two reached as far back, in fact, as 1717 or earlier."[120] Initially begun as a rebuttal against Theobald's criticism of Pope's translation of Shakespeare, the satire evolved—as did its king—into a dense allegory sharply questioning the changes England faced. Theobald specifically represented a type of scholarship Pope devalued, what Pope understood as a modern relationship to literature, one in which a text's complexities could be dissected with methods similar to those espoused by Enlightenment science. Rumbald clarifies that "Theobald's *Shakespeare Restored* extended to an English author the principles of historicist analysis establishing the books Shakespeare would have known, and comparing his grammar and idioms with those of his contemporaries, produced answers to textual problems very different from those which had resulted from Pope's reliance on taste rooted in assumed universal standards."[121] Theobald's methodology offended Pope's literary taste and evaluation of aesthetic value along humanistic lines.

Cibber's so-called crimes were much more expansive, making him a figure of more generalized animosity than Theobald. Occupying such roles as poet laureate, playwright, and actor as well as supporter of the Whig government, Cibber "presented a potent focus for the alleged vicious circle of Whig corruption, cultural commercialism and the decline of taste."[122] Others, such as Defoe, Swift, and Fielding, also produced critiques of Cibber's involvement in culture and politics. The critical language used by Mack to explicate the change in *The Dunciad*'s key figure is telling:

> There had been, in short, sporadic feuding between the two men [Pope and Cibber] for years.... Such change of heroes would have much to recommend it. Theobald was ancient history by now, and his actual edition of Shakespeare, when at last published in 1734, had won acclaim. Cibber, on the other hand, was considerably an ass and perpetually in the public eye. As laureate, he thrust in the face of heaven the taste of the minister and king who had appointed him. As court sycophant, he demeaned what Pope believed was the proper dignity of a subject and the proper role of a poet.[123]

Mack specifically states that "Theobald was ancient history"; his perhaps flippant use of the phrase is nonetheless extremely pertinent here, considering *The Dunciad*'s interest in history. Pope's poetic and historical interests moved beyond the vengeful, rooted instead in large-scale scrutiny of the eighteenth century, indeed becoming a "public Epitaph," a poetic lamentation of national importance. These interests corroborate his own engagement with the exemplar mode, as he turned away from the specific instance of Theobald's *Shakespeare Restored* to consider the more nuanced, and hence more dangerous, threat represented by Cibber.

The shift from Theobald to Cibber also returns us to the apparently straightforward trajectory offered by recompense. Lurking behind Pope's decision to switch his hero is the problem of origins. By replacing Theobald with Cibber, traditional tort law would assume that the injuries inflicted by Theobald have either been assuaged or are no longer relevant, yet *The Dunciad* remains with a new originating event substantiating the inclusion of Cibber: the punishment (the verse satire) remains although the aggressor has changed. The poem's revisionary history considers the way that personal affronts assume public meaning in an increasingly commercial and literate society, and the complications that arise when attempting to ameliorate them. In addition, *The Dunciad* opens up discussions about the nature of national restitution for injuries inflicted on private citizens, particularly whether wholesale compensatory gestures are adequate testimonials of public apology. As Runia intimates, can modern readers be held accountable for the dullness engulfing the kingdom at the end of the poem, charged with the crimes Pope enumerates, despite the temporal divide between the eighteenth and twenty-first centuries? Does the emotive pain and violent immersion into dullness in book 4 become *our* trauma, as Caruth imagines, constitutive of our own national and personal consciousnesses?

The Dunciad is remarkable because it involves voices beyond that of Pope, making it a capacious representation of eighteenth-century England. It was well known in the period that many of the notes and commentaries affixed to the text, starting with the 1728 version, came from the members of Pope's select coterie, who read and reflected on the poem; in this way, The Dunciad reflects the opinions of others historically present in Pope's milieu. Yet, "by the time he was revising for *The Dunciad in Four Books* of 1743, many of his early friends were dead or, in the case of Jonathan Swift . . . isolated by distance and failing health" in Ireland.[124] The copious and meticulous revisions to *The Dunciad*, as with his earlier works, indicate Pope's obsession with perfecting his text, at enabling its intelligibility for an unknown audience beyond that of the intimate coterie who would be privy to his poetic meanings. The Dunciad stands as an object of commemoration for the friends Pope relied on, as well as for the passage of time ushering Pope away from his early mentors and into his later relationship with Warburton, one that upsets *The Dunciad*'s own history.[125] In their detailed study of the publication practices utilized by Pope throughout his career, David Foxon and McLaverty point out that the collaboration between Pope and Warburton complicates critical knowledge of the ownership of the notes: "The problem is made much more difficult by the fact that the death-bed editions, out of all Pope's works, are the very ones where it is almost certain that accidentals have been changed by Warburton and perhaps by their printer Bowyer."[126] Rumbold likewise describes Warburton's particular desire to "emphasize his importance to the project."[127] More positively, though, *The Dunciad*'s debt to many voices generates its recompense: it extends beyond Pope, assimilating into itself the thoughts, reactions, and ideas of a larger range of individuals.

Fundamentally, *The Dunciad* reflects the period: the people, the events, the debates, the issues that constituted it. The various additives to the poem become the poem just as surely as its lines of verse. One of the great paradoxes of the poem is that, as it criticizes the hazy labyrinth of nonsense that Dulness weaves, the meaning of the poem is itself concealed beneath layers of allusion and mockery that make it partly farcical, "a garbage heap" of people and events.[128] Alvin Kernan elaborates on this potential convolution by stating that "advertisements, . . . remarks by various critics, letters to the publisher, testimonies by other authors, arguments for each book, extensive learned notes, and four different editions, including a variorum, accumulate grotesquely to bury the poem itself under the weight of the bibliographical apparatus made both possible and inevitable by print."[129] Weber claims that "Pope's *Dunciad* cannot simply be considered a poem. . . . The poetic text cannot be understood apart from its relationship to the extensive and varied critical apparatus that came to surround it. . . . The poetic text loses its primacy, and attempts to understand its significance must take into account its status as part of a much larger work."[130] Similarly, Rumbold states, "after 1728 the *Dunciad* ceased to be simply a poem: succeeding versions were composite texts of verse and prose. Lavish care and ingenuity went into the elaboration of annotations, prefaces and appendices, and much of the fun of the *Dunciads* is lost if they are overlooked; moreover, once they began to appear, the reader's experience of the work became vastly more complicated, as eye and judgement were diverted into negotiation between poem and surrounding prose."[131] Kernan, Weber, and Rumbold point to the historicalness of *The Dunciad*, its immersion in extant eighteenth-century England, through its accumulation of literary attachments and appendages.

Yet if we peel back the layers of dullness from the kingdom Pope depicts, looking beyond history as attribution, then we also find England as Pope imagined it *could* be, its potentials and possibilities that the literary imagination could assist him to script. To again invoke Hammond, "Pope does not quite mean what he is ostensibly saying," thus requiring us to see him as more than "the oppressor of other writers, the Canute trying to send back the waves of professional progress, the satirist who attempted to preserve the property of literary appreciation in the hands of his own and his adopted class-fraction."[132] Importantly, Hammond writes that *The Dunciad*'s "vision is not an objective, value-free description of social reality."[133] Doing so acknowledges the fantastic and fantasized that often informs extant historical events. Like Gray, who uses his historical imagination to endow the rustics with exemplary status in the "Elegy," Pope confers visibility onto his dunces, enfranchising those qualities not typically enshrined by historical writing. Moreover, like Richardson, Pope elevates private intentions as central to the decisions and actions of individuals imminent to historical data. In *The Dunciad*, personal deliberations and goals are usually equated with base physical desires, but nonetheless their inclusion, as in *Clarissa*, implies that history is more than the sum of recorded, verifiable action. Pope's kingdom represents an elaborate and fanciful vision of England at its worst, but he does so by pushing the limits of historical inquiry, daring to expose that which exemplary history conceals.

If we alter our approach, looking not at Pope's apocalyptic England, that which *The Dunciad* overtly expresses, then perhaps we can find its foil—the ideal England abundant in the values and beliefs that enamored Pope. Pope's imagined England is in many ways more inclusive than the one he experienced daily as a cripple and as a Catholic. By challenging the elite class in his poem, Pope opens up the possibility that the nonelite could enter a historical narrative. In his depiction of the negation of difference in *The Dunciad*, perhaps there is a desire, born out of decades of harassment and abuse, for an England that in reality was not marked by difference but by similitude. Hammond suggests such a reading in his own biographical sketch of Pope: "In politics he supported a government of national unity, subscribing to a 'patriot' programme capable of uniting all those elements not already recruited to the banners of Whig plutocracy or Tory legitimism. In matters religious he played down his Catholicism in order to foreground those aspects of a reasonable Christianity calculated to appeal to all but extremists and fanatics."[134] Most important, similitude, for Pope, would be embodied by literary and artistic ideals acknowledged by all, and, more basically, free of stigmas attached to bodily health.

Pope, in his preface to his translation of *The Iliad*, describes the creative genius of Homer as "boundless" and as expansive "vast Invention."[135] The heroic journeys of *The Iliad* and *The Odyssey* present exemplary feats of courage and intelligence, motivated by the oratory skills of Achilles and Odysseus, who are able to exhort their comrades into action, truly the examples that Bolingbroke advocates for in his *Letters*. Dennis Todd suggests that *The Dunciad* explores Pope's "most cherished notions of the power of art, what its possibilities are and how it can be misused," particularly his belief "that trivial art is not a technical failure, but a sin, and that bad art, because it has no power to move the audience or because it has no audience at all, has the power to destroy civilization."[136] In *The Dunciad*, no exemplary voice rises to the forefront to assuage the cacophony and discord promulgated by Dulness's games, or to rally the participants into heroic feats. There is no Achilles or Odysseus. Rather than a definitive sign that England has already succumbed to dullness, the lack of a hero at the end of *The Dunciad* frees England from the strictures of historical exemplarity, suggesting that new forms of behavior and inquiry are required.

The Dunciad is a showcase of degraded England, a lamentation for past exemplary formulas, *and* an exemplary representation of verse satire and nascent introspective writing, made possible by the very denigration it bemoans and "buries" by the last line ("And Universal Darkness buries All"). According to Runia, history "is a kind of burial: we take leave of ourselves as we have come to know ourselves and become what we as yet do not know. In the process we come to see what is lost forever: what we are no longer."[137] Applying this logic to *The Dunciad* allows us to read its final lines as potential rather than as conclusive, as challenging us to confront the instability arising when current historical and literary modes of self-representation prove inadequate. The burial at the end of *The Dunciad* buries everything and everyone; there is no one left in the poem to erect an epitaph or other commemorative artifact. Yet, in so doing, Pope invites the reader of *The Dunciad* to engage in the processes of self-reflection that Runia describes as at the heart of viewing public memorials, transforming readerly assumptions about English national identity and our own relationship to it. Much like the memoirs written by survivors of extant traumatic events, *The Dunciad*, with all its revisionary baggage, represents catharsis, that which remains to edify other readers, despite the trauma narrated in its lines.

Although Mack's seminal biography of Pope, *Alexander Pope: A Life*, has come under scrutiny for its humanizing approach, I support such a reading, as it forces us to consider Pope as nuanced individual rather than as elite exemplar.[138] To return to Pope's question in the *Epistle to Dr. Arbuthnot*, "You think this cruel?" (l. 83): Do we consider *The Dunciad* and its strategy of verse satire to be cruel? We celebrate Pope canonically, meaning we celebrate him as a victor, triumphing over his misfortunes, enduring despite his manifold disabilities; that, after all, is what an exemplar does. But *The Dunciad* forces us to rethink Pope, to think of him not as a victor but, like the history he examines, as a resilient yet perhaps fractured caretaker of national discourse.

Further Introspection, Another Burial

Before moving into the chapter on Gray's "Elegy," I think it worthwhile to consider Pope's earlier "Eloisa to Abelard" (1717). In both *The Dunciad* and "Eloisa," Pope imagines the poem as recompense for the pain endured within the poetic lines, as offering readers the imaginative space to reanimate historical circumstances and to forge an emotive connection to those individuals and events described. This recompense breaks from the traditional recompense as embodied by tort law, one that rejects binary appellations of victim and aggressor, that reconstitutes the intimacy associated between two opposing parties and refutes the assumption that a specific punishment can obviate a crime. *The Dunciad* and "Eloisa" use burial as the foundation of this recompense, which relies on an anonymous reading audience made possible by the new commercial and printing developments. The existence of—or hope for—this new audience replaces the older tort law system and paves the way for a discussion on the "Elegy."

As in *The Dunciad*, Pope based "Eloisa to Abelard" on the romance between actual historical individuals: Peter Abelard, a medieval scholar, and his pupil, Heloise. Eloisa's grief at her separation from Abelard motivates the myriad of emotions she articulates. The subject of the poem demanded that Pope use his historical imagination in order to convey adequately the Gothic setting of Eloisa's convent and the integrity of the male-authored female voice he adopts: "In *Eloisa*, for the only time in his career, Pope tells a story wholly through another's voice."[139] Eloisa's varying emotions represent a type of historiographical scripting in which the search for the proper mode of expression emerges, as Eloisa's struggle to succumb to earthly or divine desires engage with two different temporalities, that of the human and the heavenly. The result, as Abrams explicates, is Eloisa's "fantasy" of God and Abelard competing "for her soul."[140]

Most important for our discussion here, Eloisa specifically invokes the grave at the close of her lament as the physical artifact capable of transcending the limitations of earthly temporality. The "one kind grave" will "unite" her name with that of Abelard, connecting them in ways denied by their families and religion.[141] The imagined comfort of the grave brings peace to Eloisa's turmoil because of its ability to place her in close proximity to her beloved—and, indeed, historically, Abelard and Heloise are buried beneath the same monument in the monastery of the Paraclete in France. Yet the visibility Eloisa seeks is twofold: not only does she desire to be interred near Abelard but she also desires a place in a historical record. She envisions the grave as offering her the means of accessing "ages hence" (l. 345), of thrusting her voice into a futurity wherein her "tender story" (l. 364) finds intelligibility. Eloisa engages with more than just earthly or divine temporality; indeed, neither of these opposing options proves capable of assuaging her pain. She seeks historical subjectivity and imagines the grave as the means of providing her with the agency of attaining it.

In fixing the grave as the means of conveying her historical worth, Eloisa gestures toward an audience upon whom rests the reanimation of her history. She harbors the hope that "two wandering lovers" (l. 347) shall come across the grave and be moved to "falling tears" (l. 350) in mourning for the sad story enshrined. This emotive connection between the imagined spectator and Eloisa supplies the memorial with its potency, collapses temporal and historical differences, and ultimately allows the manifestation of recompense—what Eloisa terms as "forgiveness" (l. 358) attained by the reconciling of "heaven" (l. 357) and "one human tear" (l. 358). Only through the exposure of her inward, private story (typically consigned to invisibility in exemplary narratives) by an act of commemoration can her suffering find meaning. Particularly, Eloisa goes on to iterate, her story—and, consequently, herself—gains visibility; she imagines "some future bard" (l. 359) poeticizing the details of her story, which allows her "pensive ghost" (l. 365) to find succor from the knowledge that another individual empathizes with her suffering. That empathy, the ability of an imagined stranger to engage and enliven her history, enables the "bard" to be "well-sung" (l. 365), to be productive of an aesthetic creation of beauty—and creates an interweaving of individuals across time.

Eloisa ultimately finds comfort in the imagined subjectivity offered by the grave, the commemorative artifact, which, she envisions, provides her with a historical consciousness regardless of physical death. The poetics scripted by future spectators of the grave, as well as by future readers of the poem, offers recompense for her estrangement from Abelard. Eloisa hopes that future travelers will enact Runia's process of commemoration, being transformed by the story they read on the grave. In so doing, "Eloisa to Abelard" demonstrates affinities with not only *The Dunciad* but also Gray's "Elegy" written over three decades later. These poems envision what Eloisa terms "death all-eloquent" (l. 335), the self-articulation made possible only through burial, rituals that, as Runia describes, allow us to "become what we as yet do not know."[142] Rather than indicative of loss, death—physical, literary, historical—reaffirms identity in *The Dunciad*, "Eloisa," the "Elegy," and *Clarissa*, encouraging the anonymous reading audience to reanimate and empathize with the scenarios depicted, thus expanding historical inquiry beyond exemplarity.

2
"Their Artless Tale Relate"
Pastoral Elegy and Geography in "Elegy Written in a Country Churchyard"

Pope's legacy as the exemplar of Augustan verse satire suggests that, often for canonical writers, literary genre reflects historical biography. Pope's poetic subjects—the City, the elite, the controversial—are mapped onto his biography, creating the phenomenon that Suvir Kaul describes as the "(re)creation of the biographical subject through an unproblematic culling of selected quotations from his poetic subjects."[1] Whether consciously or not, we often read Pope *as* Augustan verse satire, unproblematically committed to attacking the vices of "the Great" through unabashed and relentless practices of naming, exposure, and denigration. Pope seems to recognize the power of his own name when he writes in his *Epistle to Dr. Arbuthnot*, "What tho' my Name stood rubric on the walls? / Or plaister'd posts, with Claps in capitals?"[2] Pope references the practice of eighteenth-century booksellers affixing signs to boards in front of their shops, advertising the title-pieces of their books. By 1735, when these lines were published, Pope would certainly have been rather blasé about the predicament he describes, accustomed to the commercial and celebrity status of his own name. The use of verse satire to present these lines, though, reinforces the association between the genre and his name, "plaister'd" together in a financially fruitful but perhaps cramping way.

The same can be said for Gray. The fame of Gray's mid-century masterpiece, "Elegy Written in a Country Churchyard" (1751), fixed Gray as the icon of both elegiac and melancholic verse, a description codified by such works as Thomas Warton's "Sonnet: Addressed to Gray."[3] As Michele Turner Sharp aptly notes, "Though Gray seemed largely indifferent to its progress in the world, his 'Elegy' created an enduring persona for Gray as the pensive poet," much like *The Dunciad* did for Pope's own exemplary status.[4] Gray's legacy is reflected by his choice of genre in the "Elegy," reifying him as the exemplar of the so-called graveyard or churchyard school, wherein rural spaces become the focus of the poet's introspective musings.[5] Such an assessment seems in line with Gray's biography, sheltered as he was at Cambridge, where he donned the Regius Professorship of Modern History.

Generally disliking publication and the public presentation of his work, Gray eschewed his celebrity status. Yet Gray's stylistic mastery of form evident in the "Elegy" established him as one of England's premier poets, despite his reclusive reputation. Somewhat paradoxically, considering Gray's active disassociation from what he deemed nongentlemanly persons and occupations, traditional readings of the "Elegy" since Matthew Arnold emphasize the poem's allure, particularly its cultivation of a "generic feeling-state" of commonplace emotions recognizable to and shared by all readers.[6] Amy Louise Reed, writing at the beginning of the twentieth century, reiterates the comfort offered by the "Elegy" to eighteenth-century readers, delivered through allusions to the great retirement poems preceding it: "For the reader of 1751, [the 'Elegy'] was a marvelous synthesis of the thoughts and feelings of the melancholy poetry produced in the past fifty years, which had been so widely read and admired."[7] Eric Parisot, writing in 2011, continues the practice of fixing the "Elegy" as representative of mid-century graveyard verse, especially noting that the joint publication of Gray's "Elegy" with Robert Blair's "The Grave" proved popular from the first appearance of "The Grave," in 1761, "culminating in twenty-eight editions by the century's end."[8]

The trouble with Gray's lasting fame as the exemplar of elegiac and graveyard verse, as well as Pope's legacy in terms of Augustan verse satire, is that such biographical renderings of genre fix these two writers as exemplars of particular types of writing, at the exclusion of others, interested in a narrow range of issues. Marking Pope as *The Dunciad* or Gray as the "Elegy" or, indeed, Richardson as *Clarissa*, produces a "sterilized account" of the imaginative prowess of each writer and their text.[9] John Sitter's remarks on the difference between Augustan and mid-century poets perform this collapse of biographical subject and genre choice: "When we look directly at the poetic procedures in the middle of the century, those which are often most interesting are procedures of avoidance, and they show that the poets are seeking to avoid history."[10] When Sitter states that there is an "avoidance" of history, he identifies a marked separation in how history itself is viewed between poets like Pope and Gray. At stake in Sitter's idea of avoidance is the assumption that the graveyard poets, in their emphasis on individual sensation and emotive agency, remove themselves from worldly and historical concerns, while poets like Pope see themselves "as historian of his own times."[11]

Certainly, Gray, like the other graveyard poets, sought a new poetic style, one that M. H. Abrams has termed "at once intimate and prophetic" and "more lyrical and fanciful than that of Alexander Pope's generation."[12] As such, Gray's poetry reflects many of the same eight common elements that Peter Thorpe recognizes as shared by mid-eighteenth-century poets, including death, the transitory nature of life, places of burial, a funereal tone, reconciliation (usually Christian) toward death, and a solitary speaker.[13] The introspective musings and contemplation of nature's symbiosis with the individual find resonance in Gray's "Elegy" as well as with the other graveyard poets. William Collins, with whom Gray is so often linked, shares Gray's interest in the interweaving of mood and landscape common to graveyard poets, as seen in his "Ode to Evening." The poet positions the poetic voice outside of history, as disassociated from the strategies of articulating history (naming specific figures and dealing with public issues) that typically inform Augustan—and ceremonial—texts.

When we think about Gray as interested in history, we think of the Pindaric odes, such as his 1757 "The Bard," which retells Edward I's conquest of Wales. As mentioned in the introduction, these odes follow exemplary narratives by taking as their subject verifiable events and extraordinary individuals. Gray's meditative poems, in contrast, are typically viewed by scholars as enacting that "avoidance" of which Sitter writes, withdrawn from worldly concerns of wealth, society, and the large institutional structures of politics, economics, and religion. Yet, as I've already shown in chapter 1, there are surprising moments of connectivity between Pope, Gray, and Richardson that trouble the rendering of Gray as an exemplar of melancholic verse disassociated with historical concerns. Pope's satiric inversion of exemplarity marks the introspection and potential self-doubts that we would not consider as constitutive of Augustan verse satire but more easily recognizable in melancholic or later satires. Gray, similar to Pope, assesses the available modes of (melancholic) representation, dismisses them as inadequate, and creates a new poetics.

To do this, Gray, like Pope and Richardson, considers burial practices as both the literal and figurative way of creating a new mode, one that is more capacious than the exemplar model, and turns them into acts of commemoration.

The enduring legacy of the "Elegy" as the pinnacle of graveyard and elegiac verse seriously limits critical understanding of eighteenth-century historical inquiry, ignoring Gray's investment in the dissemination and constitution of historical knowledge. Thorpe points to the fallacy embedded in such logic, particularly noting "that the major and famous graveyard poems of Parnell, Young, Blair, and Gray appear in the first half of the century," yet "one would at first tend to think that it should be the other way around, for it is the second half of the century that readers have come to associate with the kind of sensibility displayed by the graveyardist."[14] Indeed, the publication dates of *The Dunciad*, the "Elegy," and *Clarissa* undermines—or, at the very least, challenges—such an easy segregation. The close temporal proximity in the publication dates of these texts supports the premise sketched in the introduction to this book: that eighteenth-century England meditated traditional forms of knowing history, taking shape across a myriad of genres, deliberating various models as effective means of conceiving period history.[15]

Raymond Williams, in his work on poetic representations of the country and the city, shows that all poems are embedded in historical processes and indeed reflect those processes even when history is not invoked as the explicit subject of the text. As a Marxist critic, he reads eighteenth-century poetry as made possible by the historical upheavals defining the previous century. To do so, Williams does not position the country-house poems that are the subject of his study as overtly exploring political and economic exploitation (such as through labor and enclosure), but instead reads the invocation of the nostalgic, through the pastoral, as performing this political and economic work. Williams, conceiving of history as the *longue durée*—history as a set of beliefs and emotions held in stasis despite the actions of specific conscious actors and the superstructure of institutional and social life—could never imagine the poet as outside of history; indeed, history shapes both the poet and the poetry. Derived from the French Annales school of historical writing, the longue durée prioritizes the longevity of embedded historical structures (cultural and social traditions) over the extant events and individuals prioritized by a method of attribution. The cyclical patterns informing the frameworks of community life rather than the investigation of a specific, named, traceable figure informs historical knowledge and temporality in this theory.[16]

Reading Gray's "Elegy" as engaged with history as the longue durée positions Gray as embedded in, not alienated from, issues related to the historical subject and historical time, and allows us to see how Gray reimagines the meaning the past holds for the present. Such a reading builds off the scholarship already begun by Kaul and Henry Weinfield, who locate eighteenth-century sociopolitical and economic concerns in Gray. Doing so frees critical scholarship from the premise—perpetrated by the Victorians and advanced by Gray's life as a scholarly recluse at Cambridge—that Gray is otherworldly and unconcerned with English national events. Similar to Pope's *The Dunciad* and Richardson's *Clarissa*, Gray's "Elegy" gives rise to significant historical concerns: If "great men" no longer form the basis for writing and understanding history, then who becomes the subject of historical inquiry, who possesses historical agency, and how is historical consciousness written? Using the theory of the longue durée expands eighteenth-century historical inquiry beyond the referential specificity found in the exemplar model, offering anonymity and rural geographic locations as legitimate sources for constituting historical knowledge and temporality. Gray challenges the assumption that history emerges solely from the actions and decisions connected to a nexus of power and attempts to reimagine the geography usually associated with exemplars. To do so, he meditates on the efficacy of the idyllic pastoral as an adequate mode of expression; finding that the pastoral cannot ease the self-alienation felt by the poem's speaker or offer recompense, Gray considers the grave and burial rituals as the means of constituting history.

Moreover, reading the "Elegy" alongside the longue durée troubles recompense as a purely straightforward transaction. Prioritizing the longevity of custom over the desires of a named individual indicates that wounds and gestures of repair may have longer timespans than the *OED*'s definitions of recompense might suggest. Rather than a quick requital, the adjudication process for crimes committed could spill over generations, potentially outlasting the actual participants involved, as becomes the case with the quarrels articulated in *The Dunciad*. With the forward movement of time, the origins of the disputes might fade from memory or become altered as historical data becomes more difficult to ascertain—an issue that Clarissa seeks to avoid through the negotiation of her will as indisputable legality.

If *The Dunciad* is on the cusp between formal Augustan verse satire and the introspective writings epitomized by Gray, then I see the "Elegy" as likewise caught between earlier heroic texts and those explicitly sentimental writings to come. Clarissa, as a mid-century novel, is also positioned between older romances and the later didactic novels that emerged. As I will discuss in the following pages, the speaker of the "Elegy" wants to assume the role of exemplar, the champion of the rustics, but he also wants to assimilate into their hamlet. The "Elegy," as mentioned in chapter 1, uses an archival approach to understanding the genealogy of the hamlet on par with Pope's satiric maneuvers, deliberating the archive as a method of articulating Englishness and England's relationship to the past. If we see these connections, we can acknowledge another instance of a major 1740s-era text that expands historical inquiry and in so doing engages in nascent English nation building.

Perceiving the shared emphasis on alienation in Pope, Gray, and Richardson in the opening lines of their respective texts allows us to reevaluate Gray's canonical legacy as melancholic poet. In the "Elegy," stanza 1 constitutes history as the changes brought by the passage of time *and* as the inevitable shaping of consciousness by the historical structures in which it is embedded. By inserting the "me" into line 4, the speaker establishes himself, without apology, as a historical subject attempting to enter into discourse with historical time, "the world" outside of himself. From the outset, then, Gray both invokes and remakes the exemplar model, relying on a singular individual to motivate the poem, but refusing to grant that individual named specificity. Furthermore, the poem immediately establishes the speaker as exemplary not because of heroic action, but because of the meditative prowess demonstrated. In both name and character, Gray disturbs assumptions regarding ceremonial verse and the dissemination of historical knowledge; the "Elegy," then, seems to be hearkening back to exemplary models while looking forward to the introspective verse dominating the later eighteenth century, on the cusp of two different models similar to that of *The Dunciad* and *Clarissa*.

It may seem surprising that I would devote almost seventy pages to Gray's "Elegy," but I continue the work begun by Weinfield's book-length study of the poem. Rather than regard the poem retrospectively, I take it line by line as it evolves. Doing so allows us to recognize the tonal changes of the poem, as well as the gradual construction of the speaker's own historical consciousness.

Articulating History through the Pastoral

The tolling of the church bell signaling the end of day for both animals and workmen opens Gray's "Elegy":

> The curfew tolls the knell of parting day
> The lowing herd wind slowly o'er the lea,
> The plowman homeward plods his weary way,
> And leaves the world to darkness and to me.[17]

Interestingly, the "Elegy's" first line contains a double emphasis on the closing of day, first with "curfew" and then with "parting day," fixing this as a poem that begins with a focus on an ending. Curiously, this recalls *The Dunciad*'s affirmation of Dulness in the first lines of Pope's poem as the "good old cause I yet defend, / With whom my Muse began, with whom shall end" (book 1, ll. 165–66). As discussed in the previous chapter, this gesture to Dulness collapses temporal distinctions, reaffirming that the poem will both begin and end with dullness. Similarly, in chapter 3, we see the same anticipation of the ending early in Richardson's *Clarissa*. Anna Howe's emphasis on the "story" of Clarissa, rather than the woman herself, references the status Clarissa embodies at the end of the novel although Anna's letter occurs at the beginning. All three texts invalidate historical linearity as an authentic means of narrating and of constituting the historicalness of self-consciousness. This, in turn, challenges our readerly assumptions about the differences in genre and subject existent in Pope, Gray, and Richardson.

The opening of the "Elegy" follows Howard Weinbrot's description of the poem as the overthrow of earthly self-interest in favor of a divinely inspired life of "sincerity of soul," one where a religious presence manages the structure of daily time.[18] Curiously, though, this presence remains an unfocused object to the speaker of the poem, the "me" who translates the evening scene into a profound reverie of self-reflection. With the insertion of the "me" into the natural and architectural descriptions, the speaker immediately positions his relationship to the tolling bell as central to the poem's meaning. The "ivy-mantled tower" (l. 9) of the church, although entrusted with the task of marking the passage of time, remains at a hazy distance from the speaker, eerily present in the gloom but incapable of dispelling the speaker's growing sense of self-alienation from the comfort assumed by its punctual tolling. After all, the church as a physical architectural space emerges as both a regulator of time and its subject, vulnerable to the changes passing time brings. The speaker's ambiguous relationship to this religious presence in the opening stanza firmly establishes that a form of alienation is taking place, either his own self-alienation from a belief in a godly being or from a historical landmark that locates its power in a time past, thus indicating the links between physical space, human time, decay, and spirituality.

Locating self-alienation in the opening lines of the "Elegy" can potentially help us read Pope and Richardson in new ways. Rather than as climactically building over the course of their respective texts, this sense of estrangement from temporal, historical, and literary linearity seems, as in Gray, to be constitutive of the infrastructure itself. Certainly, the differences in genre manifest significantly: in Pope, the "I" is not the singular meditative "I" of Gray's elegiac contemplations, and, in Richardson, the "I" that is Clarissa is endowed with much more psychological and realistic prose details than Gray's speaker. However, the shared "I" figure in all three texts indicates an alienation from genre and its ability to express adequately historicalness, impacting each text's compensatory gestures of repair. In the "Elegy," the speaker's awareness of historical time surrounding him and his desire to insert himself into a relationship with it destabilizes a traditional, comforting, reading of the poem as representative of stock emotional responses, particularly undermining Weinbrot's reading of the reconciliation of the individual and the social to Anglican notions of God's orderly universe, an interpretation that offers an easy recompense for a human life of toil. Instead, the opening line's collapse of beginnings into endings introduces the interest of the "Elegy" in the interweaving and overlapping of multiple times and histories (past/present/future), as well as its complication of linear recompense.

The speaker who opens his thoughts in the first three stanzas describes the surroundings of the hamlet in typical pastoral reverie, the pastoral here most basically defined by Williams as "significant writing about country life."[19] It also follows Pope's description of the pastoral in his *A Discourse on Pastoral Poetry* (1709) as "that solitary and sedentary life," full of opportunities for shepherds "to celebrate their own felicity" and "tranquility" through singing.[20] The homeward tread of the "lowing herd" (l. 2) and "the plowman" (l. 3) interests the speaker in the "Elegy," as well as the "fading" (l. 5) of "the glimmering landscape" (l. 5) into the "solemn stillness" (l. 6) of evening, the repetition of the "s" emphasizing the mythic recurrence of the night's events. The sounds of a "moping owl" (l. 10) and the "droning flight" (l. 7) of a beetle dominate the speaker's poetic vision, providing a nonthreatening view of the obscure hamlet. Soon after, the speaker invokes the domestic activities of the village, the pervasive presence of religion in the "incense-breathing Morn" (l. 17), and "the blazing hearth" (l. 21) around which the happy children "kiss" (l. 24) and play. The speaker positions himself amid what Sharp terms "the resounding echoes of the pastoral tradition," and allows this tradition to craft his poetic storytelling.[21] The speaker chooses to envision a happy pastoral rather than meditate on the potential dangers of practical rural life, embracing a version of rural England that is mythic in its harmony, plenitude, and filial affection. An idyllic pastoral setting, the hamlet abounds with "jocund" (l. 27) activities and rich harvests.

Yet the speaker's self-alienation from stanza one casts a shadow over these subsequent images of pastoral wealth, with the speaker's interest in knowing history maintained. If history could include those processes and structures not acknowledged by exemplar history, such as the emotive and natural agencies informing the longue durée, then the speaker's use of the pastoral becomes the means of covertly exploring his own relationship to historical subjectivity and temporality. Williams's thoughts in *Marxism and Literature* on the "structures of feeling" present within communities, the "lived" experience existing in contradistinction to institutional and formalized organization, coincides with the conception of historical knowledge in the "Elegy" as constituting the personal and nonspecific longevity of alternative space—here, the rural inhabitants of a quiet hamlet and the daily tolling of a church bell.[22] Like Pope with verse satire and Richardson with the epistolary novel, Gray meditates on the way the conventions of the specific genre, pastoral elegy, impact the delivery of historical knowledge.

The alienation immediately indicated by the speaker filters down into this depiction of rural life and upsets an easy reading of the pastoral tradition in the "Elegy." Paul Alpers claims that "conventional pastoral genres seem to lose their vitality . . . roughly, around the turn of the seventeenth century," in this case meaning that Gray invokes poetic deference to the tradition rather than a straightforward mapping of it onto his poem.[23] The pastoral landscape provides a form of rhetorical antecedent under whose influence the speaker labors. Such deference, however, acts as an inherent recognition of distance, as if in the process of aesthetically creating the rustic village the speaker nonetheless figures himself as inhabiting a different time than that represented by the village—much like

Pope, who both uses and critiques the conventions of formal verse satire, and like Richardson, whose hyperawareness about the epistle grants his novel its self-conscious reflections on genre. As the speaker of the "Elegy" recognizes his own separateness from the pastoral scene, the thread of alienation continues in which there can be no rhetorical, temporal, or phenomenological reconciliation between the former tradition of the pastoral and the present elegiac setting the speaker creates—indeed, in stanza 1, the speaker clearly describes the plowman and his herd as "leav[ing]" him, isolated and alone, to his meditations.

The essential concern of Gray's "Elegy" rests on how poetically to deliberate and resolve the problem of constituting history when confronted with a geographically and ideologically different space than that of the City. As a satirist, the focus of Pope's aesthetics are the elite as legitimate poetic subjects; Gray, in contrast, considers individuals outside of court and the ministry, and their valuation in poetics and history. The nature of elegy as "abundant in detached images of seclusion and protection," as "a world which is often visually indistinct or darkened," and as a genre "where consolation is prized over confrontation, stasis over strife" (key features of the mid-century graveyard school) deepens in historical, if not specifically political, intensity in Gray's hands.[24] Seen in this way, Gray's relationship to history is not avoidance in the sense of ignorance but manifests in spaces typically disassociated from public view. As the speaker ponders the rural hamlet, he attempts to grant the inhabitants historical subjectivity equal to that found in exemplar narratives, even though the poem certainly lacks the heroic action and extraordinary feats found in ceremonial verse. Finding the pastoral inadequate for this task forces the speaker to look elsewhere for a poetic form capable of elucidating their—and, by extension, his—historical value.

The Grave and the Longue Durée

Buried within the lulling comfort of the natural and familial picture offered by the pastoral are the elegiac images of "moldering" graves tucked soundly

> Beneath those rugged elms, that yew tree's shade,
> Where heaves the turf in many a moldering heap,
> Each in his narrow cell forever laid,
> The rude forefathers of the hamlet sleep. (ll. 13–16)

Such description substantiates the fame of the "Elegy" as one of the period's premier graveyard and melancholic poems, but it also propels the movement of the poem away from the predicable pastoral formula and toward a constitution of history as the longue durée. The line "the rude forefathers of the hamlet sleep" provides the transition from the poem's pastoral emphasis on the lowing herd and plowman in stanza 1 to the poem's interest in death and the commemorative practices involved in burial rituals—forms of articulating history that can reimagine the exemplar model.

While the description of the forefathers as "rude," emphasizing the untaught and lowly condition of those who are buried in the churchyard, and by extension suggesting the intellectual superiority of the speaker who views them, is clearly iconic and thus potentially nonthreatening in its commonplace usage, the term "forefathers" itself bears significance. "Forefathers" continues the poem's opening suggestion of the interplay of past, present, and future. Weinfield positions the forefathers as representative of a lost world whose function in the poem is to undercut any trite sentimentality associated with the speaker's pastoral vision of their graves: "The Forefathers, after all, now belong to the past—not only as individuals but in a generic sense. In other words, what is now *past* is not only the lives of the Forefathers individually, but—given the social transformations of the eighteenth century—the life of the peasantry as a whole, and hence the idealizing mode."[25] Weinfield emphasizes that the forefathers "now belong *to* the past, not *in* the past," a distinction that positions the forefathers as *possessed* by an outdated historical consciousness.

The forefathers as indicators of something lost pairs well with the pastoral as a form of history that suggests an English "type" belonging to a golden age, a lost world. Pope in his *A Discourse on Pastoral Poetry* likewise draws on the examples of Theocritus and Virgil to situate the pastoral as "an image of what they call the Golden age. So that we are not to describe our shepherds as shepherds at this day really are, but as they may be conceiv'd then to have been," in "exposing the best side only of a shepherd's life, and in concealing its miseries."[26] This "Golden age," though, indelibly connects poetics and history, according to Alpers, as "the shepherds of pastoral are figures devised to engage certain issues of poetry and poetics, to express certain ethical attitudes, and to locate poets and readers in cultural and political history."[27] Sitter elucidates that "one secular version of history which had been available to poets who wanted to retain the idea of a Golden Age was a correspondingly secular version of the Fortunate Fall: being expelled from a cultural Eden . . . leads man to exert his energies, learn, build, make laws, and so on . . . But increasingly toward the mid-century the Fall into society and history is seen not as a fortunate fall but as a catastrophe."[28] Parisot attributes the rise of graveyard poetry to "the ubiquitous presence of death and disease during the early half of the eighteenth century, which resulted in periods of severe decline in population and life expectancy."[29] Along with Sitter's description of the mid-eighteenth-century view of "the Fall," Eric Parisot's account of mortality rates helps make clear how pastoral reverie became attractive for writers. Gray's depiction of a jocund pastoral landscape stands juxtaposed to and alienated from the postlapsarian world where society and history act as catalysts for catastrophe, death, and disease, those "miseries" of which Pope hints.

Yet we cannot read the pastoral in Gray as fundamentally in opposition to a current historical frame but rather as engaged in the aesthetic processes of retrieval and innovation that Alpers explicates. Indeed, Alpers makes clear that the "pastoral historically transforms and diversifies itself."[30] In this context, Gray's use of elegy and the pastoral tradition are mutually invested in one another, allowing Gray to constitute historical knowledge in new ways, particularly by using genre to shape the speaker's relationship to his surroundings and to provide historical meaning. The speaker's depiction of the forefathers does not only point to the insufficiency of the pastoral as an idyllic mode but it also performs the historiographic work of invoking the longue durée. In direct opposition to Weinfield, who argues that the forefathers are representative of a past historical situation that cannot be recovered, I argue that Gray identifies continuity in pastoral relationships that furthers the poem's efforts of undermining categorization based on temporal and literary boundaries. Alpers writes that the pastoral "takes human life to be inherently a matter of common plights and common pleasures. Pastoral poetry represents these plights and these pleasures as shared and accepted, but it avoids naiveté and sentimentality because its usages retain an awareness of their conditions—the limitations are seen to define, in the literal sense, any life, and their intensification in situations of separation and loss that can and must be dealt with, but are not to be denied or overcome."[31] Alpers's emphasis on the commonality of the shared experience of "separation and loss" captures well the emotive agency in Gray's "Elegy," suggesting a repetition that stands regardless of a forward movement of chronological time.

"Forefathers" means ancestors, those who came before, those who engaged in the same acts of continuity that the present plowman does in stanza 1—or, to use Alpers's own language, both the forefather and the plowman perform acts common to "any life," the nondifferentiation in "any" pointing to the shared experience and repetitive nature of the village's genealogy. The forefathers and the plowman act together, engaging in the same repetitive acts of "plights and pleasures" that ensure the continuation of the hamlet and inform the structures of the longue durée. When paired with the adjective "rude," this invocation of history undermines the very rudeness of the sentiment. Rather than being rude, these forefathers were learned in the things that would keep the community fostering into the future, indeed ensuring that the present moment described by the speaker could occur. The plowman, then, is seen not only as the present inhabitant of the hamlet but also as a future forefather to a future plowman through the repetitive pastoral awareness of both the "plights and the pleasures."

Notice that Gray describes the graves as actively imposing their will on the landscape: "Where heaves the turf in many a moldering heap" (l. 14). The dirt "heaves" in the present tense; Gray imagines the grave as continually impacting the natural landscape. Gray does not write in the past tense, where the grave was *once* dug and now serves no other generative purpose. Instead, the grave engages in action, perpetually cast in movement: laboring, exerting, rousing the earth from tranquility. Like the hamlet's fields, which seasonally transform and produce, the grave also exudes vitality. Such energy elevates the grave, raising its stature and importance to the hamlet; Gray demands respect for it, its ceaseless toil altering our reading of the otherwise sedentary "shade" and "sleep" of the graveyard's description. The grave of the forefathers represents a tribute to the pervasive nature of historical consciousness, of the way that the knowledge of the past builds into the present and futurity of a community.

As in chapters 1 and 3, I am here reminded of Eelco Runia's notion that through burial we learn about ourselves. For Runia, history "is a kind of burial: we take leave of ourselves as we have come to know ourselves."[32] As in Pope and Richardson, Gray depicts burial and the attendant death of the corporeal body not as an ending but as the link forging connections between the past and present, recasting death's purpose beyond narratives of Christian redemption. In stressing the importance of the forefathers and the graves, Gray radically reimagines sources of historical inquiry.

Not only does Gray locate the graveyard as a site of ample historical knowledge, but he also celebrates the forefathers using a form typically reserved for the elite exemplar: the elegy. Enticing to readers since the publication of the "Elegy" has been the mysterious nature of the "Elegy" as an *elegy*. Critical appraisals, while celebrating its elegiac qualities, also recognize crucial distinctions between Gray's elegy and the elegiac tradition as represented by Milton's *Lycidas*, typically positioned as more definitive of the form. When considering the genre, Sharp elucidates, "poets use the death of a fellow poet as a means to secure their own poetic stature," with the poetic act allowing the private grief of the mourner to insert the poet into the public gaze, offering "compensatory closure" to the bereaved.[33] Sharp's words echo the trajectory of recompense, where the poem stands as a gesture of repair for a wound (the death of a poet) inflicted. Although Gray's first biographer, William Mason, argued that the poem, in standard elegiac fashion, grew from the unexpected death of Gray's close friend Richard West in 1742, thereby following linear recompense, the "Elegy," unlike *Lycidas*, is not clearly addressed in commemoration of the specific death of an individual, as one would find in late seventeenth-century occasional poetry or exemplar narratives. Even Gray's close friend fellow writer Horace Walpole refuted Mason's claim based on the date it was written.

Instead, Gray's subject is not a single named individual, but the mass of forefathers collectively occupying the graveyard. Rather than simply decaying in a "cell" (l. 15), discursively silent, these forefathers continue to influence—to heave—the present inhabitants through a practical, physical, and genealogical contribution to historical consciousness that is embedded in the acts of memory and memorial performed by both the living inhabitants of the village and by the speaker. Thus, the speaker invests the dead with historical subjectivity, a capacity to participate in a functioning community consciousness, historical valuation usually reserved for the educated elite.

Pointing to the forefathers draws our attention to the reproductive continuity of the village. Not just historical or cultural repetition is at stake in the speaker's vision of the pastoral landscape. Like Pope and Richardson, who both identify sexual genealogy as a valid component of historical inquiry, the "Elegy" considers reproductive and intimate history as worthy of preservation. The use of fore*fathers* raises issues of the fundamental generative functions of the individuals that secure the collective survival of the village. Coupled with the idyllic domestic images of affectionate home life, the speaker crafts a pastoral vision in which physical intimacy is, significantly, not marred by the demands of physical labor. John Goodridge, in his study of rural life in the period, emphasizes the importance of the cottage door image as an ideal trope, stating that "in eighteenth-century portrayals of labour, home is the ultimate compensation, the symbol of warmth, food, safety, comfort, nurture and the 'miniature kingdom' of family."[34] Tracing the tradition back to *The Odyssey* and to Sappho, Goodridge juxtaposes its conventional use—the transformation of a physical space into an ideal literary space—with the way rural poets of the early decades of the period such as Stephen Duck, Mary Collier, and James Thomson portray it. Unlike these other poets from the 1730s, Gray refuses to spoil "the reassuring motif of the cottage-door scene."[35]

Indeed, in the "Elegy," the homeward-bound plowman receives the affection of his family eagerly, without complaint of his own weariness caused by a day of work, as found in Duck's "The Thresher's Labour" (1730):

> The sweat, and dust, and suffocating smoke,
> Make us so much like Ethiopians look,
> We scare our wives, when evening brings us home;
> And frighted infants think the bugbear come.[36]

For Duck, working-class labor transforms the identity of the worker, altering him physically so that he becomes unrecognizable, donning the disguise of a foreigner to his family. Such a transfiguration damages the domestic, fraught by the effects of labor and fatigue, and critiques, through its invocation of "Ethiopians," what it means to be English. For Gray, though, such distress does not exist in his rural hamlet, where the physical demands of labor do not impede the jocund family hearth or raise issues of nation building.

Similarly, Gray does not threaten the feminine with realistic hardships. In the "Elegy," the wife is not overcome by the demands of domesticity or motherhood, as in Collier's "The Woman's Labour: An Epistle to Mr. Stephen Duck" (1739):

> We must make haste, for when we home are come,
> Alas! we find our work but just begun;
> So many things for our attendance call,
> Had we ten hands, we could employ them all.

> Our children put to bed, with greatest care
> We all things for your coming home prepare:
> You sup, and go to bed without delay,
> And rest yourselves till the ensuing day;
> While we, alas! but little sleep can have,
> Because our forward children cry and rave;
> Yet, without fail, soon as day-light doth spring,
> We in the field again our work begin.[37]

For Collier, women bear double duty in laboring-class scenarios, since they must not only perform the hard toil required by fieldwork during the day but they must also fulfill all familial tasks at night. Although the male laborer may retire to the domestic setting—essentially waited on by the female—secure of a good night's rest, Collier argues that childcare and housekeeping duties prevent women from achieving any such solace. "Without fail," each day brings an unceasing pattern of toil. Read side by side, as they often are, Duck and Collier depict animosity across gender, an unrelenting battle to decide which endures more hardship. For Gray's speaker, however, no distinction exists between men and women: both happily perform their chores, contributing equally to their separate spheres. Children, in Gray's depiction, likewise suffer little by the hard work demanded by rural life; they are not burdened by malnutrition or fatigue from premature enforced labor.

Thomson's "Winter" (1726–30) critiques the cottage-door motif in a slightly different manner than either Duck or Collier, by removing the emphasis on family and children. Thomson, in contrast to Gray, imagines the cottage as the retreat of a bachelor-shepherd, one who survives the harsh winter months in "high converse with the mighty dead, / Sages of ancient time."[38] For Thomson, the philosophers and heroes of Greece and Rome sustain the individual, despite "the ceaseless winds" (l. 255) that batter the cottage. In settling his bachelor in "a rural, sheltered, solitary scene" (l. 256), Thomson reimagines the traditional compensatory purpose of the cottage door. Rather than the warm embrace of family, the bachelor finds solace in "silence! thou lonely power! the door be thine" (l. 296). Wrapped in the weighty tomes of history, the bachelor receives "humour ever gay" (l. 300). Happiness, for the bachelor, arises not from relationships with others, but from his own scholastic pursuits.

Affection and love exist between parent and child in Gray's rural imaginings, as opposed to the absence of children in Thomson's bachelor-shepherd, the clear burden children represent for working women in

Collier's domestic scene, and the horrific reaction of the children to their sweaty and dusty father in Duck's rendering. For Gray, the sexual life of the village, like all the other jocund activities depicted, is healthy and fertile. The importance of the forefathers, then, is not just to direct the speaker's aesthetic vision toward a historical continuity built on community rather than exemplars. More than this, the forefathers indicate that historical continuity is dependent upon a healthy physical vitality. By scripting the forefathers and domesticity as organically fused with the necessary labor required to maintain rural life, Gray turns away from the poetic interests of Duck, Collier, and Thomson in order to depict his village scene using a pastoral, idealizing frame.

In so doing, the speaker turns away from the historical veracity indelibly grounding the works of Duck, Collier, and Thomson, that of the real hardships of the laboring class. For these poets, articulating history manifests from rendering the past and past literary forms as unintelligible for the present, requiring completely new modes and apparatuses capable of appropriating and representing the historically real—that is, changes in the landscape and economy, and transformed attitudes toward labor and service. In this poetic moment of the "Elegy," the speaker chooses to retreat into a more familiar pastoral convention, not performing an obvious reversal of the cottage-door scene as in Duck, Collier, and Thomson, but following Pope's adage that pastoral poetry "expos[es] the best side only of a shepherd's life" and "conceal[s] its miseries" (120).

This decision could be indicative of the latter 1740s as an especial ideological decade, one welcoming a more inclusive and positive rendering of history that imagines the laborer as sufficiently recompensed for their physical toil by the comforts of home. However, I argue that Gray's use of the cottage-door convention too performs a critique because it occurs as evidence of the speaker's sense of alienation, or what might be termed his awareness of the compensatory failings of the ideal. The sense of alienation that pervades the description of the forefathers stems from the speaker's own inability to embrace fully that which he envisions because he cannot assimilate himself into the imaginings. Although he may narrate the cottage-door scene, he cannot incorporate himself into it. As Weinfield recognizes, "Paradoxically, however, the meaningfulness of this perspective to the present is rendered possible only by the fact that its representation as nostalgia is simultaneously the representation of its annulment."[39] Pastoral reverie, or "nostalgia," inherently involves "annulment," the distance that is at once predicated upon the use of the tradition and separation from it.

Weinfield's use of "annulment" proves an interesting term when we remind ourselves that we are considering the burial of the forefathers. Reading the first stanzas of the poem, the reader is potentially lulled by words such as "sleep" (l. 16) and "bed" (l. 20) to overlook the speaker's actual focus on death, thereby successfully burying the dead beneath his poetic rhetoric. He himself has not buried the physical body, the individual, but what he has succeeded in doing is burying the individuality of the death and extracted from it its collective significance. Through the poetic act the speaker transforms the annulment of the healthy sexual vitality of the men that ensures the genealogical continuity of the village and instead emphasizes the nostalgic role that their unified presence gives to the village. Thus, the speaker alters the annulment fundamental to death itself by shifting the forefathers' historical contribution. The nostalgia that is created is not intended as grief over the personal loss of a specific person, as found in standard ceremonial verse—and, indeed, the forefathers are not differentiated by individual name or family—but an act of commemoration in recognition of the service that these individuals collectively offered to the community during life, and the service they offer in death: namely, the intertwining of the past with the present for the survival of the village into perpetuity. The forefathers form an archive, not satirical as in *The Dunciad*, but one that collects the individual people, highlights their similarities, and assembles them into a larger metanarrative about the hamlet. Such a move fundamentally alters the standard conception of historical knowledge found in exemplar narratives, as it shifts history away from named "great men" with personalized stories to the enduring legacies celebrated by history as the longue durée. Recompense emerges, then, as the ongoing process of archiving the deceased.

Line 29: Hostility in Genre and History

The speaker, however, does not end his poetic act here with the rhetorical burial of the forefathers and the tribute that his poetic musings grant them. Beginning at line 29, the speaker disrupts the tone of relative pastoral and graveyard comfort he has presented thus far, replacing it with spite toward the privileged classes, whom the speaker anticipates as scorning the lives of the rural inhabitants. Here, Gray follows more closely the work of Duck, Collier, and Thomson by introducing into his poem instability, not through a reversal of the cottage-door scene, but by acknowledging a world beyond the isolated community of the hamlet and finding insufficient recompense. Crucially, the speaker's attack against such elite figures is not directed at a specific individual, an exemplary representative of those outside of the village such as a parliamentary figure, titled aristocrat, or country squire. Instead, the speaker's aggression arises suddenly, unexpectedly shattering the lulling melancholic and pastoral landscape. The jocundity of the first part of the poem vanishes, replaced by an abruptly prescriptive tone:

> *Let* not Ambition mock their useful toil,
> Their homely joys, and destiny obscure;
> Nor Grandeur hear with a disdainful smile
> The short and simple annals of the poor. (ll. 29–32; emphasis added)

The speaker's remarkably sharp intonation marks a distinct separation from the preceding stanzas, showing the discontinuity of the speaker's voice itself over the unfolding of the poem.

Only upon the intrusion of an elite set of expectations into the speaker's mind does the description of the graves suddenly need defending from the "disdainful smile" of those outside of the hamlet. Whereas, previously, the speaker had reveled in the lulling images he described, *now* there is a defensive tone in the face of this unseen, unheard, unrepresented elite force. Significantly, the speaker dresses such elite in the fashion of exemplars, complete with "heraldry" (l. 33), "pomp of power" (l. 33), "beauty" (l. 34), and "wealth" (l. 34)—words that call to mind Pope's description of Sir Thomas Hanmer in *The Dunciad* discussed in the previous chapter. Beginning at line 29, then, Gray directly sets his speaker in opposition to—and, perhaps we could even say, an enemy of—the exemplary. The speaker's tone clearly aligns his poetic empathy and his historical interest in those disenfranchised from elite systems of historical valuation, as it alters from pastoral reverie to embody, surprisingly, the hostility typical of Pope's verse satires.

Traditionally, this section of the "Elegy" is read for its claims of the leveling force of death that eliminates social distinctions or for its demonstration of a Hegelian dialectic of class struggle. Weinfield's 1991 book *The Poet without a Name* performs such a reading, expanding history beyond the recovery of facts. Gray's "Elegy," as understood by Weinfield, "has little do with history in the ordinary sense, either with past events or their interpretation" but focuses on "the thematic constellation of poverty, anonymity, alienation, and unfulfilled potential."[40] The "problem of history" that the "Elegy" articulates "is not the loss of the particular individual through death," as is found in traditional elegy, "but, in an ironic reversal, the loss, for the majority of humanity, of the potential for individuation in life. This theme is obviously of major significance, yet it does not emerge prior to the *Elegy*."[41] Weinfield's book-length study of Gray's "Elegy" offers superior insight into the nuances of the poem's engagement with class, capitalism, and "the logic of commodities" in the wake of the Industrial Revolution.[42]

However, rather than rigidly defining historical knowledge in the "Elegy" as the death-in-life problematic, or as a Hegelian dialectic of opposing classes, I suggest reading Gray as sharing earlier satiric anxieties concerning historical subjectivity and temporality. Indeed, beginning at line 29, Gray positions himself much like Pope in *The Dunciad*, in an attitude of active aggression, seeking out the exemplary in order to destroy its integrity through ridicule. The plenitude of description used to characterize the burial practices of the elite reveals scorn, as well as distaste for misplaced and misguided use of human privilege. The overabundance of detail provided in lines 41–44 not only charges the elite with vanity, but also shapes that vanity into folly:

> Can storied urn or animated bust
> Back to its mansion call the fleeting breath?
> Can Honor's voice provoke the silent dust,
> Or Flattery soothe the dull cold ear of Death?

The unceasing attempts of the elite to exercise control over death and mortality through embellished tombs and fancy decorative urns indicates, for the speaker, idiocy on par with Pope's derision of the Hanoverians.

Gray's tone also reflects the same contempt as exhibited by Johnson in his satire "The Vanity of Human Wishes," published shortly before the "Elegy," in 1749. Johnson, like Pope and Gray, dismantles the glitzy reputation of the heroic exemplar:

> The festal blazes, the triumphal show,
> The ravished standard, and the captive foe,
> The senate's thanks, the gazette's pompous tale,
> With force resistless o'er the brave prevail.[43]

Johnson enumerates all the trappings of exemplary status, the myriad ways that fame emerges for the exemplar: the banners, the displays and parades, the trophies of war, the praise from those in power, and the enshrinement in ceremonial verse. Yet, cast as they are in a verse satire dedicated to eschewing the "pompous" nature of such elitism, these vestiges of honor indicate naught but foolish, empty vanity. Johnson meditates on military prowess as the traditional home of exemplary individuals and events; Gray, though, applies Johnson's disdain for the exemplar to burial practices, a move that challenges not only assumptions about exemplary heroism but also sources of exemplary pride—as well as the elegy's capacity as a genre to attack with satiric relish. The rhetorical questions flung at the elite in lines 41–44 of the "Elegy" mark the first questions posited by the poem, and certainly Gray's speaker anticipates no response, since reason seems absent from exemplary assumptions regarding death and burial.

The discontinuity in the speaker's poetic contemplation, arising at line 29, traumatically ruptures the "Elegy," clearly separating the comforting pastoral and graveyard meditations of the first 28 lines from the speaker's subsequent thoughts. Alpers states that "some kind of violence" is necessary for poetic originality, and, indeed, the aggressive tone of Gray's speaker commits violence against the "Elegy."[44] This violence, though, shatters both poetic and historical knowledge in the poem. In "On the Concept of History," Walter Benjamin also emphasizes the importance of ideological violence, arguing that history, and historical consciousness, emerges at "moments of danger."[45] He rejects the idea of a "universal history" in which all moments in the history of humanity follow a single chain of causality, like a thread that is pulled tightly and neatly forward and thus reduces all events to stale categories, such as childhood or maturity. Instead, rather than scripting history as unfolding due to neatly packaged causes and effects, Benjamin fosters a notion of historical awareness as ever-changing, as remaining obscure in its details except for moments when "the genuine historical image ... briefly flashes up."[46] The appropriation of history, for the historical subject, occurs through the "movement and arrest of thoughts."[47] The shift in tone evident in Gray's speaker certainly performs this type of work as described by Benjamin, as it inhibits pastoral or meditative comfort from dominating the "Elegy." The speaker rouses himself from the nostalgic assumptions of the pastoral, committing violence to the genre and to history as he angrily expostulates against the elite.

Richardson handles burial a bit differently in *Clarissa*. Unlike in Pope and Gray, Richardson does not adopt an aggressively hostile tone when describing Clarissa's obsessive arrangement of her own funeral and burial.

Clarissa's fixation on the objects memorializing her life provide her with peace and give the remaining days of her life meaning. However, Clarissa is driven to orchestrate the commemoration of her death because of the need to reassert control over her identity. Her burial rituals are predicated upon an act of violence that, as discussed in chapter 3, destroys historical linearity in keeping with Benjamin's constitution of temporality. When read alongside *The Dunciad* and the "Elegy," we can appreciate the latent hostility undermining Richardson's description of Clarissa's actions, manifested by the violence that precipitated her efforts. All three texts accuse elite burial practices of concealing the folly and human vanity that led to an injury, what Benjamin terms "rupture." The brief sketch of a funeral procession that Pope provides in his own elegy, *Elegy to the Memory of an Unfortunate Lady* (1717), reflects the tonal hostility that permeates Richardson and Gray:

> On all the line a sudden vengeance waits,
> And frequent herses shall besiege your gates.
> There passengers shall stand, and pointing say,
> (While the long fun'rals blacken all the way)
> Lo these were they, whose souls the Furies steel'd,
> And curs'd with hearts unknowing how to yield.[48]

Pope imagines a moral-didactic retribution manifesting in the rapid succession of deaths afflicting the household of those whose coldness toward their "charge too good" (l. 29) precipitated a woman's suicide. Significantly, Pope locates the procession of the hearses as the opportune time for this moral critique to emerge, a detail that curiously aligns with Clarissa's fantasies of her own death as recompense for the personal and public degradation explicated by her narrative. As in Richardson and Gray, Pope refuses to let the burial trappings of elitism (here intimated through the family's access to multiple hearses and funerary displays) obscure the folly of those commemorated.

The problem that Pope, Gray, and Richardson seem to be fighting against relates to historical origins. The origins of injuries are hard to locate when there is no single person responsible for the crime and when the impact of that crime is more apparent than its infliction. Even in Pope's "Elegy," based loosely on verifiable circumstances, the crimes committed are moral in nature, not quite punishable by law and only made visible by the lady's death. Likewise, in Gray's "Elegy," the disparities in burial practices are symptomatic of a larger injury sustained by the rural poor—but that larger injury cannot be pinpointed because it involves a web of injustices stitched into the fabric of the nation. The speaker feels the frustration of the inhabitants, incorporates it into his own emotive register, and attempts to repair it through verse. While noble, this attempt cannot assuage the very real poverty of the village or limit the excessiveness of the elite.

The intrusion of an educated, elite, urban world external to the rude hamlet points to the speaker's awareness of a conflict over what counts as authoritative, accurate, and authentic history, and how genre is impacted when we look beyond the traditional sources of historical knowledge. This conflict proves dangerous to the speaker because it reveals the differing social standards by which the communities of the rural hamlet and the outside world are separated. Elite, exemplary strategies of power, beauty, and wealth form a distinct community of identification in the mind of the speaker that is at odds with the "homely joys" (l. 30), "destiny obscure" (l. 30), and "simple annals of the poor" (l. 32). Lucinda Cole explains that "community" was a fraught term in the eighteenth century, containing "strategies of exclusion, displacement, normalization, or containment" that are "based upon disidentifications" involving categorizations of sameness and difference.[49] Gray's speaker demonstrates an interest in such strategies as he contemplates the differing burial practices of the rural and elite, and the shared inevitability of death.

Like Benjamin, Cole hints at rupture as "a constitutive feature in the formation of community."[50] This rupture traditionally arises from the threat of death, capable of leveling the infrastructures of class and society erected by the elite and reinforced through exemplary models of history. For instance, Nicolas Poussin's early seventeenth-century pastoral painting of shepherds gathered around a tomb, with its title of *Et in Arcadia ego* (Even in Arcadia, there am I), emphasizes the permeating force of death even in a utopia. Weinfield contributes to this discussion by arguing that what intrudes into the "Elegy" is the concept of death in life, or the reality of poverty within the rural situation, that undercuts the vision of pastoral plenty opening the poem and creates a class-based community. "Such polarities as poverty and wealth, obscurity and fame, absence and presence," Weinfield states, are "polarities that now begin to take a firm grip on the poem," only being "meaningful from a historical perspective that conceives of the division of men into classes."[51] Indeed, the shift in tone and topic that occurs in line 29 of the "Elegy" ("Let not Ambition mock their useful toil") acts as an aesthetic rupture that disturbs the speaker's initial pleasure (despite his sense of alienation) in the pastoral community, precisely, as Weinfield notes, because of the speaker's awareness of the man-made constructs—what Weinfield labels "a historical perspective"—of class. This perspective is in opposition to the idyllic state of nature.

Yet if we read the speaker's experience as performative of the violence suggested by both Alpers and Benjamin, and integral to the interpretative frame of recompense, then it is possible to consider the knowledge of history in the "Elegy" for *itself* rather than as the means to a Hegelian discussion of class or economics. The speaker brackets and externalizes the discontinuity of external determinants of historical events, such as economics, labor, and death, those overarching political and historical structures providing a linear, progressive frame. Instead, the site of significant rupture in the poem is the speaker's emergence of historical consciousness marked by loss, by reflections on complex temporalities, and by poetic alienation from the present aesthetic moment. His prescriptive "Let not Ambition mock their useful toil" marks a change in the speaker's complacent acceptance of the pastoral and the meditative as adequate forms of poetic expression. Instead, he realizes that he must navigate a history of poetic conventions, verse satire included, as well as a history of socially constructed conventions involving issues of class, geography, education, and, significantly, modes of commemoration, in order to mitigate the circumstances of external history. These circumstances, enshrined as they are by the exemplar model he deliberates, typically prevent rural, unnamed inhabitants from occupying a place of value in historical inquiry and experiencing adequate gestures of recompense. The speaker therefore performs his own form of violence, both in the poem and against the genre.

With his prescriptive tone, the speaker suggests his break from the historical time offered by the pastoral, his inability to access fully the comfort embedded in the genre, and the resulting emotional turmoil he feels. Here, on par with Pope's *Dunciad* and Richardson's *Clarissa*, Cathy Caruth's work on trauma as outlined in her book *Unclaimed Experience* proves useful in understanding the emotional state of the speaker at this moment in Gray's "Elegy." Caruth writes, "The shock of the mind's relation to the threat of death is thus not the direct experience of the threat, but precisely the *missing* of this experience, the fact that, not being experienced *in time*, it has not yet been fully known."[52] By describing the impact of witnessing yet escaping death on survivors of traumatic events, Caruth fuses historical knowledge with chronology. Linear progression through historical time becomes impossible if the past cannot be fully known or understood. Such is the turmoil experienced by the speaker of the "Elegy" as he attempts to use the pastoral to elucidate his own present moment. He finds himself unable to access the historical-literary heritage offered by the pastoral genre, although all the trappings of pastoral seem easily in reach around him: the quiet hamlet, the "rude forefathers," the fertile hearth. Because he cannot completely decode the past, he cannot use it to articulate a generative present moment. More broadly, the speaker is surrounded by the vestiges of nationhood: the documents, the monuments, the objects that evidently preserve national identity. The speaker, though, cannot map those public expressions of selfhood onto an awareness of his private values because he cannot appropriate the past in an adequate manner.

Similar to *The Dunciad*'s typological discontinuity and Clarissa's mad papers, the "Elegy" articulates the breakage in historical time, genre, and self-consciousness. The speaker's acknowledgment of an elite, exemplary other, abruptly arresting (to use Benjamin's term) him in line 29, functions as the profound means by which he can begin to analyze his historian's gaze, forcing him to reflect back on his own use of history and genre in the opening stanzas. What intrudes, then, upon his meditations is not the pomp and privilege of exemplary expectations, however defined as either "death as leveler" or "death in life." Rather, the full awareness of the inauthenticity of the pastoral vision he seeks to erect—to which a painting like *Et in Arcadia ego* gestures—assaults his consciousness: he becomes aware of the inadequacy of the genre for legitimately disseminating his historical experience and offering recompense.

Weinbrot writes that "Gray's poet learns to tell the tale of the dead around him and to preserve their memory."[53] Indeed, it should be emphasized that the speaker of the "Elegy" needs to *learn* how to tell his tale because the genre is ruptured. Weinbrot reads the learning process of the poem as one involving a move from secular to divine knowledge in order to attain "sincerity of soul," but to do so is to limit the poem, to confine it within one particular mode of knowing history, one that follows the linearity of traditional recompense.[54] The speaker grapples with his own self-imposed role as poet-historian as he struggles with feelings of alienation even as he scripts a pastoral ideal. In learning to tell his tale, then, the speaker must learn the process of scripting a narrative of nation building under the force of the "crushing presence" of history.[55] The speaker experiences a transformation of historical consciousness and the necessity of adapting poetic form. The speaker's encounter with the rural populace, which he had initially expected to represent through the conventions of an enameled pastoral, shatters his own elite/urban ideologies of status and ambition and thereby ruptures his relationship to that enameled pastoral and to genre in general, generating his experience of traumatic alienation from temporality. The intrusion of external historical agents, such as economics, impinges on the poet's consciousness not for itself but by the way it proves the inadequacy of the pastoral genre for rendering moments of arrest and for assuaging the hardships of the poor.

Questions of community, nationalism, and especially history push to the forefront, demanding voice, under the weight of the tale the speaker attempts. Thus, although it is not an exemplary representative, external to the rural setting of the poem, who specifically sparks the affective rupture of the speaker, such an elite force nonetheless prompts the *historicalness* of the poetic consciousness, reminding the speaker of the external, public determinants of history (economics, politics, religion), producing changes in interiority and self-consciousness regarding genre.

Line 37: Articulation and Community Exclusion

The outside elite defines both proper burial procedures and refined society in terms of the lack that the rural hamlet supposedly possesses—specifically, memorial "trophies" and attendant remembrance. Lucinda Cole points out that "discourses of community usually involve one or another lack," meaning that groups unify around a shared set of cultural characteristics, the "lack" of which indicates an individual's exclusion from the unified group.[56] Weinfield and others are correct when they identify a lack of money or status as key characteristics that separate the rural inhabitants from elite formulations of history, but these two characteristics assume importance in the poem through depictions of physical burial procedures. Lines 37–44 address the interlocking role of memory, burial rituals, and history:

> Nor you, ye proud, impute to these the fault,
> If Memory o'er their tomb no trophies raise,
> Where through the long-drawn aisle and fretted vault,
> The pealing anthem swells the note of praise.

Deepening his attack against the elite he opposes to that of the rural hamlet, the speaker specifically changes the pronoun he invokes. Rather than the personified abstraction of "Ambition" of line 29, in line 37 the speaker pointedly remarks, "Nor *you*, ye proud" (emphasis added). The "you" of this line subtly indicates a discontinuity in the speaker's relationship with the rural hamlet. No longer the wistful, comforting tone of the opening stanzas, line 37 continues the scorn introduced in line 29. This time, though, when he forcefully maligns the "you" of the "ye proud," he situates himself within the very pastoral his own historian's gaze has challenged as inauthentic.

In giving voice to the elite, to whom memory arises from elaborate burial rituals, the speaker does not simply rehearse the attitudes and values of their community but once again reveals his own uneasy position. Excluded from both communities, the elite and the rude, the speaker unknowingly reveals himself as the "lack," to use Cole's term, the exclusion through which each community acquires identity. His consistent sense of alienation throughout the poem has distanced him, both spatially and temporally, from that which he imagines, preventing him from fully envisioning himself as one of the pastoral ideal, such as during the cottage-door scene.

However, his ability to recognize and voice the characteristics and "disidentifications" (to invoke Cole) of the elite indicates his own fluency with their idiom, a fluency that implicates him as having profited by an elite education not available to the rural inhabitants he champions. Such a reading of the speaker's predicament breaks with traditional understandings of "post-Augustan retreat" typically applied to graveyard poems. In these poems, as Sitter elucidates, "'nature' typically means a place without people (or without any people but me) and where 'society' is seen as radically 'unnatural.' This is the complex of assumptions which started becoming conventionally 'poetic' during the middle and later years of the eighteenth century."[57] In extracting the discourse of the elite from the elite body while simultaneously rejecting that elite body, the speaker complicates a depiction of a "natural" setting since that "natural" setting can only be imagined by a speaker versed in an elite, or "unnatural," language. By opposing the hamlet against the elite, the speaker ignores the nuances of the distinction between them, potentially overlooking the subtleties of their interlocking nature, and the complexity of his own position.

The troubling relationship of Gray's speaker to both the rural and the exemplary, his exclusion from both communities, arises from a fundamental tension in the act of discerning history: in order to envision the past one must rely on the tools of the present. Here, the speaker's tribute to the rural depends on elite rhetorical skills, which destroy the illusion of an insulated and isolated rural past, kept inviolate from the contamination of the elite present. Williams locates temporality based on continuity and discontinuity present in constituting history, specifically the way that older forms persist despite innovation. Various versions of the past collide, drawn from differing perspectives of historical fact.[58] The pressures of tradition in a mythic understanding of the past apparently seem at odds with an Enlightenment conception of progress and change, and yet such nostalgic renderings nevertheless persist and influence present developments. The speaker of the "Elegy" attempts to depict a rural hamlet isolated from the folly and avarice of a contemporary elite, but his strategies for articulating history, his utter dependence on elite discourse, demonstrate that such an endeavor must fail.

The speaker contrasts two different physical specimens of commemoration, one the classical, Roman-inspired "storied urn" (l. 41) and "animated bust" (l. 40) of the elite, whose traditions hearken back to a mythical historicity of its own, and the "lowly bed" (l. 20) of the "rude forefathers" (l. 16). Indeed, this binary opposition reflects the dichotomy in *The Dunciad* between those writers espousing the ancients and those whose impulse to write comes from the material circumstances of survival. To the elite community in the "Elegy," described as "Honor's voice" (l. 43) and "Flattery" (l. 44), physical memorials attest to more than just the wealth and status of the deceased, indicating historical subjectivity. As Weinfield describes, "In order for an individual to be remembered by History, that person would have to have been *present* to his society in a manner that would have marked him out beforehand as an individual *to be* remembered."[59] In other words, the memorial process is both the cause and the effect of its concrete manifestations. Those carried down "the long-drawn aisle" (l. 39) of the privileged occupy the historical memory of the community in a way that is fundamentally opposed to that embodied by the "neglected spot[s]" (l. 45) of the rural poor. Those memorialized by the elite represent an exemplary mode of history (one hailing conspicuous figures, events, and the superstructure of society) that is inherently at odds with the history represented by the hamlet (the nonspecific, emotive, and natural determinants). The rural dead can never be visible to the elite collective—a viewpoint the speaker challenges by the end of the poem—because the rural inhabitants are emblematic of a history in which individual greatness is "neglected," effaced, or made anonymous in order to allow for a larger, composite meaning. Commemorative practices achieve the position of primary importance in this poem, beyond that of death as leveler or death in life, because of the way they challenge the speaker's assumed knowledge of historical valuation.

That is not to say that death does not function in crucial ways in the poem. Indeed, what the speaker is able to recognize, despite the opposition of elite and rural, is the element common to all memorial gestures, that of "the silent dust" (l. 43) and "the dull cold ear of Death" (l. 44). Death is not an end itself here; instead, the abstraction of death connects with the poem's historical inquiry. Interestingly, the speaker describes the leveling act of dying by emphasizing the negation of voice and sound present in death. The "dust" is "silent," as if it could ever speak to begin with, and the "ear" of "Death," while predictably "cold," is "dull." "Dull" connects with "silent" in its connotations of mute speech. The speaker's earlier interest in the voices and sounds of the evening falling upon the hamlet has been transferred to his description of the absence of these within death. To invoke Cole's logic, the speaker identifies a community built upon a lack—the lack of speech and hearing, the fundamental elements of storytelling itself. In the "Elegy," death negates the potential for aesthetic creation and historical speech (narrating and accessing history). Linked together—by their annulment threatened by death—is the poetic act of imagining and the retelling of the past. By contemplating the commemoration that memorials offer, the speaker threatens the very nature of the storytelling that is at the heart of history.

Historical Fantasy and Named Specificity: Memorials as Recompense

Because of his knowledge of elite education and values, the speaker can imagine both literary and historical potentials buried in the obscure hamlet, "some mute inglorious Milton" (l. 59) or "some Cromwell guiltless of his country's blood" (l. 60). No longer confined to images of domesticity and the hearth, the speaker imbues the rustics with historical subjectivity by poetically endowing them with "celestial fire" (l. 46) and "ecstasy" (l. 48). In so doing, he reimagines, as does Pope and Richardson, historical processes as involving fantasies—that is, alternative versions to externalized, codified historical events and figures, typically unmarked by historians. He imagines the rustics as possessing the potential to become full, elite, historical subjects, if they had proper "Knowledge" (l. 49). Indeed, as Sharp points out, the speaker thrusts these potentials, these figures traditionally endowed with historical visibility, upon the rustics, "inscrib[ing] these terms in the rural churchyard and in the lives and deaths of the hapless poor."[60] The rustics are confined to their "neglected spot" (l. 45) because they could not learn how to attain the greatness of the alternative community space, the exemplary strategies of valuation, but the comparison to the elite should offer recompense for this lack of education. The story that the speaker imagines, and the subsequent manner in which he envisions the history of this solitary village, is likened to "a flower [that] is born to blush unseen" (l. 55), again invoking sight as the metaphor here. In these lines, the speaker focuses on individual figures in English history whom poetics has traditionally memorialized.

In contradistinction to the theory of history he has been thus far exploring, here Gray's speaker invokes explicit personages. Weinfield points out that these are the only direct names in the poem, "figures who embody different types of greatness and who are symbolically linked with the Revolution of 1642"; their appearance "poses the issue of heroic presence in immediate historical terms, and in the process it complicates the political (and ethical) associations that are linked to this theme."[61] In other words, Gray's speaker apparently relies on the exemplar strategy of valuation in order to celebrate the unnamed rural inhabitants, hoping to bestow on them a compensatory gesture sufficient to ease their obscurity. Milton and Cromwell embody greatness (either literary or historic) against which the lack felt by the speaker is measured—but these figures, too, are absent from the text and are indeed dead. To make his point, the speaker must rely on exceptional individuals as indicative of the nation, yet these figures are not present within the poem despite the heroic stature granted them ideologically. Gray uses the invocation of "great men," as do Pope and Richardson, not to affirm a history of attribution and referential specificity, not primarily to celebrate those exemplary individuals, but to undermine acts of tribute traditionally belonging to the genre.

The references to Milton and Cromwell evoke a specific revolution, a particular breaking point in the continuity of English history, a rupture that demanded the rescripting of Englishness itself. It is curious that Gray chooses to use a revolutionary advocate (Milton) and a regicide (Cromwell) as the people indicative of the historical subjectivity against which the rural inhabitants are measured. These two individuals represent a specific English mode of representation, that of anti-monarchicalism, that shattered a linear model of progressive history. Through the speaker's commemoration of them, the speaker appears to celebrate Milton and Cromwell for their ability to question whether the assumed mode of representation (that of linear monarchical succession) adequately narrates period history. However, the speaker's own uneasy relationship with both the rural and the elite suggest, instead, that the rescripting espoused by Milton and Cromwell is too dangerous, too threatening to English identity, to be the object of commemoration. The speaker's sense of self-alienation when confronted with the knowledge that the traditional elite model proves problematic clouds his depiction of Milton and Cromwell as the great men to whom the rustics should aspire. The speaker attempts to rewrite *their* presence within the historical register, as well as that of the rural dead, by imagining an alternative history in which their heroic stature is not predicated upon rupture.

The speaker's words imply that the glory of Milton and Cromwell, and the exemplary model of history they helped to perpetuate, is, if not criminal, then at least invested with guilt—much like the underlying guilt the speaker feels at realizing his own inability to accept the conventions that the traditional pastoral model offers. In daring to rescript the imagined nation, Milton and Cromwell offered an alternative mode of literary and historical representation, making them exemplary, yet in so doing they subsequently damaged the nation through the ideological ruptures they espoused, raising concerns over the integrity of their actions. In the "Elegy," the speaker attempts to retain their presence while simultaneously purifying their guilt, thus infusing his imagined rural hamlet with a fantasized version of England's past. The speaker does not condemn Milton and Cromwell overtly for any crime, nor does he celebrate them for the particular politics they supported; instead, the speaker uses them to register the poem's larger interest in the way that genre manipulates and reimagines versions of history that appear inviolate. As in Gray's clearly historical poems "The Bard" and "The Progress of Poesy," the "Elegy" performs Odney's assessment of Gray as a "self-reflective" writer who manipulates "versions of the past" when writing history.[62] The nod to Milton and Cromwell here certainly positions Gray's meditative verse alongside his Pindaric odes as crucially invested in articulating history and historical origins.

Milton and Cromwell demonstrate that once again the speaker finds himself in the troubling position of having to rely on knowledge reified by the outside elite in order to celebrate the rural obscure. Weinfield casts this problem as evidence of the link between poverty and commemoration that he argues is the grounding for the poem:

It does happen to be true, of course, that Memory and Knowledge are associated with the rich and powerful, but that is another matter entirely. For if Memory raises no trophies over the graves of the poor, and if Knowledge fails to unroll her ample page for them, it is not the fault of Memory and Knowledge but rather of "Chill Penury." We are not asked to take a dim view of Memory and Knowledge per se, but we are led to the awareness that these abstract functions are controlled by the upper echelons of society and consequently are not available to the poor.[63]

The knowledge of Milton and Cromwell, then, on which the speaker draws represents his essential historical alienation from the rural populace—the rural villagers would never have access to such historical knowledge, according to Weinfield—while simultaneously providing him with the aesthetic means of paying tribute.

The pastoral, made inauthentic by the speaker's realization of its inability to stand alone without the rhetorical tools of the elite to assist him, falters as the speaker reimagines English history. The pastoral, with its reliance on generalized shepherd figures cast as ideal *because* of their lack of individuality, can only be heralded by this speaker through the use of particularity. Only by gesturing toward specific individuals, the Miltons and the Cromwells, in a way that rethinks exemplar narratives, can this speaker adequately convey his own aesthetic imagining of the hamlet and its inhabitants. The speaker finds himself, then, in an uneasy and perhaps unsatisfying position of attempting poetically to script a pastoral ideal but recognizing that ideal cannot be scripted without the use of "living" (to invoke Williams)—although they are technically dead—or historical referents.

In celebrating the unfulfilled potentials of the rustics, they also acquire both faults and virtues, thus rupturing the placid image the speaker held of them at the beginning. It is "Chill Penury" (l. 51) *and* rural isolation that

> their growing virtues, but their crimes confined;
> Forbade to wade through slaughter to a throne,
> And shut the gates of mercy on mankind. (ll. 66–68)

Their isolated life, not just their penury, prevents both their "virtues" and their "crimes" from being known to history. Rather than the pastoral image of the plowman and the domestic felicity in the early stanzas, here, following the abrupt intrusion of the elite, the speaker recognizes the complexity of human nature and sees that "slaughter" and "mercy" combine in every human heart, regardless of the socioeconomics of the community, an idea that further undermines his desire for a pastoral ideal. Indeed, eighteenth-century viewers often interpreted Poussin's painting *Et in Arcadia ego* as suggesting that even in Arcadia, in a utopian land, all manner of human—not simply idyllic—pleasures existed. This same reading emerges from Gray's "Elegy" and most fully points to the inauthenticity of the pastoral genre, since, with altered circumstances, he can now envision a history in which these rustics emerge from their idyllic world in order to embrace all aspects of the living. We should recall the poem's emphasis on forefathers, on the passionate and earthy rather than on the chaste and pristine. Just as the showy vestiges of wealth might hide the crimes and vices of the elite (remember Pope's scatological purpose in his poem, as well as Lovelace's rank and connections in Richardson's novel), so might the pastoral obscure the avarice and immorality of the poor. Gray's speaker severs the distinction that Williams points to as a post-Renaissance conception of the pastoral, since the speaker collapses the boundaries between rusticity and elitism by linking them together in common "crimes" and "mercy."

Forming a link between the rural inhabitants and the elite causes the speaker to question the veracity and integrity of his own historian's gaze. If the pastoral becomes inauthentic and if the pastoral figures become implicated in interests usually associated with the elite (honor, ambition), then the speaker's sense of a forward-moving history, chronologically progressing from an era of a golden age, a happier rural past, shatters. In order to establish a relationship with historical knowledge and historical time, the speaker must be able to navigate often contentious historiographies, such as that of the rural and the elite. Writing history becomes a stitching together of disparate visions, and the danger lies in it subsequently becoming incomprehensible. The pastoral, for the speaker, is an ideal, and if he cannot overcome his commemoration of that ideal, then Benjamin's conception of the "genuine historical truth" escapes him: that of realizing pastoral figures cannot ever quite *be* his ideal pastoral because they, too, operate on elite values.[64]

The speaker's musings over the course of the poem indicate his resistance to the idea that these emotions do exist in the rural hamlet. After suggesting in lines 65–66 that their penury prevented their crimes from finding expression, the speaker removes the possibility that these crimes could have existed at all:

> Far from the madding crowd's ignoble strife,
> Their sober wishes never learned to stray;
> Along the cool sequestered vale of life
> They kept the noiseless tenor of their way. (ll. 73–76)

Cloistered within their "vale," separated both geographically and ideologically from "the madding crowd," the speaker maps onto the rural inhabitants "sober wishes" in a move that makes crimes unintelligible to them. By rejecting the myth of the pastoral and by rejecting the pastoral's affinity with elite values, the speaker may be capable of envisioning these pastoral figures *outside of* the moral frame of the pastoral—or beyond elite fantasies concerning rustic life. This move, while reassuring to him, nonetheless contains the threat that he may not be able to script the narrative correctly to ensure that others will be compelled to read these figures sympathetically as existing both within and outside of the pastoral myth (much like the readers of *The Dunciad*'s vitriolic attacks who Pope, we could assume, wanted to read the dunces as deserving of his contempt). Knowing history eludes him if he cannot adapt to new, and perhaps horrifying, rereadings of historical data. In the "Elegy," the speaker, rather than being a sublime figure of "Memory and Knowledge" in the poem, the protector and discriminator of cultural thought processes, becomes unable to narrate the past if he cannot reconcile himself to the disparate versions he encounters.

Indeed, the position of the speaker while pondering the life of the rustics embodies the role of the traditional historian as described by Benjamin as one in which "transplanting himself into a remote past, [he] prophesies what was regarded as the future at that time but meanwhile has become the past."[65] Benjamin's use of "transplanting" is apt here, as it suggests geography, the movement and immersion that the historian dons in order to examine the past. In voluntary exile from the myths through which the past is ordinarily seen and made valuable, the historian, in seeking "the genuine historical truth," explores the ways that the past becomes meaningful in the present as the origin of the present. The danger exists, therefore, of recognizing no past as the stable origin of the present if knowing history is predicated upon genre. How, then, can an adequate recompense be offered? The speaker of the "Elegy" attempts to decode history by using specific methods of writing that history: the pastoral, the exemplary, the elegiac. However, as in *The Dunciad* and in *Clarissa*, Gray's speaker finds that each model offers a different version of the past, creating a cacophony of voices and a series of competing narratives.

Is the English past to be found in shepherds and hamlets? In the actions of elite figures? In commemorative practices?

Transplanting, moreover, suggests a geographic movement of importance and connects with Gray's interest in reimagining the geography associated with constituting history. The speaker of the "Elegy" gives no explanation for his sudden poetic exclamations over the hamlet that he views, nor does he provide insight into what circumstances brought him to this particular place. Rather, the speaker emerges as fully exiled, as transported to the scene that will destabilize his understanding of pastoral origins. Benjamin's words indicate the overlap of temporalities assaulting the historian, and the negation of a direct chain of causal history: the past cannot remain isolated from the present or the future because the future has become the present that at its moment of creation becomes another past. The historian's gaze sees not compartmentalized time but overlapping and intertwining time, which complicates a poetic vision that attempts to confer a stable history on a cohesive nation and offer recompense for injuries inflicted. Indeed, the historian's gaze, rather than simply being a tool for the speaker, becomes integral to the poem's development and the poem's deliberation of history.

Despite the fact that the rustics will never "read their history in a nation's eyes" (l. 64), separated from elite narratives of historical memory, the speaker insists, through the use of "Yet" in line 77, that there is something precious preserved by the memorials of the rural dead:

> Yet even *these* bones from insult to protect
> Some frail memorial still erected nigh,
> With uncouth rhymes and shapeless sculpture decked,
> Implores the passing tribute of a sigh. (ll. 77–80; my emphasis)

Rather than protecting the "bones" of the deceased, the physical decay of the body, from the landscape's continual progress (another type of temporality), or indeed even the pastoral ideal that has become inauthentic, the speaker focuses on the "insult" of an outside community whose scorn the speaker has already imagined. Most basically, the speaker recognizes the similar memorializing acts subsisting between the rural community and that of the elite. This shared commemorative gesture truly levels the exemplary and the rural, not the duality of the diabolical and angelic within both the rustics and the elite, nor the leveling force of death or the reminder of poverty and class structure.

The speaker's concern that the rural memorials be protected questions what these rural burial practices offer that elite acts of commemoration do not. Rather than extracting certain individuals out of specific, named subjectivity, individuals that embody progression and change, the rural formulation celebrates the eradication of self-interest and promotion in order to continue the traditions and life of the past, elements constituted by history as the longue durée. Upon death the individual ceases to be of primary importance and instead becomes a testimony to the longevity and continuity of the rural community itself. The specific individuality of the dead—their characteristics, preferences, abilities, desires—remains private, closeted within the domestic mourning of the wife and children depicted earlier in the cottage-door scene. Parisot claims that "the symbolic reproduction" of such elements as night, solitude, and refuge formed the "cloistered conditions in graveyard poetry," proving attractive to the eighteenth century, which increasingly valued private modes of grieving (as opposed to publicly delivered funeral sermons).[66] Certainly, the relegating of bereavement to the domestic space in the "Elegy" points to this shift in the methodology of mourning.

In addition, Gray offers a radical transformation in period understanding of historical knowledge and temporality, providing an alternative location for valuable historical individuals and events. Critical desire to pinpoint the exact individual whom Gray commemorates with his elegy (such as West) runs contrary to the impulse of the poem. As mentioned in the introduction to this book, Gray rejects the elegiac utterance of *Lycidas*, with its lament for the specific, nameable individual and instead manipulates the tradition of the pastoral in which shepherds are given conventional names in order to typify their universality; Gray suggests that there is no room for individuality in Arcadia. The rustics may never be able to "read their history in a nation's eyes" because of their illiteracy and because their specific stories will not enter the historical consciousness of the nation, remaining behind the cottage door. But even if the rustics do not have this form of recognition, they still possess historical value. As members of an isolated hamlet, the villagers may not be concerned with the elite world outside of the rural space, but they are kept in memory by those who are educated outside of the hamlet. Indeed, it is the "trembling hope" (l. 127) of the speaker that their collective story will indeed be read not only by himself but also by those passing by their graves; this provides him recompense.

The voice that emerges from the memorials to the dead, no matter how "frail" (l. 78), offer a voice that counters the negation of speech and sound attributed to Death earlier: "Even from the tomb the *voice* of Nature cries" (l. 91; my emphasis). "The unlettered Muse" (l. 81) proves the most eloquent for the speaker, as he sees in these "simple annals" (l. 32) an abundance of knowledge about alternative formulas for constituting and disseminating historical knowledge. The local customs and traditions informing village life prove significant for Gray's speaker, because they generate the connections between past, present, and future that perpetuate continuity and stability. Sharp argues that the generalized nature of the individual dead in fact prevent them from entering into historical subjectivity, that "the 'Elegy' does teach its learned poet that neither his knowledge nor the memory stored up in all the books he has read can be sufficient to bring forth the rural scene. Poet and poem, richly formed by the spoils of time and nurtured at the hearth of knowledge, cannot remember *these* dead, beneath *these* trees, in *this* neglected spot. The poem cannot remember them because its poet does not know them. The rural dead recede ever further from the poet."[67] Sharp looks for the exemplary in the "Elegy" and returns empty-handed, as Gray intends. Although there is an absence of formalized historical awareness and speech, of the sort embraced by elite strategies of burial, in the rural community, historical knowledge emerges in other forms.

The speaker critiques the belief that elite fanfare better preserves the wealthy elite in historical memory. Instead, Gray argues that even the rural graveyard, with its unimpressive headstones, contain individuals worth preserving in historical memory, individuals whose lives narrated moral-didactic lessons and whose actions continue to serve as models of imitation for both the rural and the elite—even though he does not know their names. Such anonymity emphasizes the private and the familial, rather than the public and the civic, as cornerstones of English national identity. Rural practices of commemoration and manifestations of the longue durée mark historical time and continuity, defying not simply death but a chronological understanding of history itself, with the poetic act of aesthetic creation reevaluating the value of memorial acts and possibilities of genre. Origins, then, as envisioned by the speaker, begin with burying the dead.

The Epitaph, the Speaker, and Elegiac Mourning

Although the "Elegy" ends with a memorial, it is not a memorial to the rustic forefathers. In fact, the epitaph in the "Elegy" serves a different commemorative purpose than traditionally found in elegiac verse; it is entirely in tribute to the speaker himself, his final means of assuaging the alienation that has consistently grounded the poem:

> *Here rests his head upon the lap of Earth,*
> *A youth to Fortune and to Fame unknown.*
> *Fair Science frowned not on his humble birth,*
> *And Melancholy marked him for her own.*
>
> *Large was his bounty, and his soul sincere,*
> *Heaven did a recompense as largely send;*
> *He gave to Misery all he had, a tear,*
> *He gained from Heaven ('twas all he wished) a friend.*
>
> *No farther seek his merits to disclose,*
> *Or draw his frailties from their dread abode*
> *(There they alike in trembling hope repose),*
> *The bosom of his Father and his God.* (ll. 117–28, italics in original)

As in Pope's "Eloisa to Abelard" and in Richardson's *Clarissa*, the speaker constructs a way to maintain his subjectivity even after death. This stands in marked distinction from the earlier elegiac conclusion of *Lycidas*, Gray's foremost literary exemplar, where the speaker ultimately leaves Lycidas to his watery grave with tranquility and inspiration for future poetic creation.

Typical elegiac verse, as in Milton's elegy, celebrates the poet even as it memorializes an exemplary figure. The point of the elegy is to provide the poet with the means of self-transformation, where, in discussing the virtues of the deceased, the poet may critique and ultimately ennoble his own abilities.[68] Milton's speaker extracts from Lycidas's death a lesson regarding his poetic desires. The speaker of *Lycidas* likens his lost friend to the sun that sets but always returns more brilliantly the next morning, which then allows him to figure his death in religious terms among "all the Saints above" (l. 176).[69] The resolution of the poem exists in the speaker's elevation of Lycidas's place of death into a site of commemoration. The "large recompense" is the body of poetic work Lycidas leaves behind as anchors aiding the unknown "all" that may happen to "wander" among the "shore" of poetry.[70]

Like Milton, Gray positions his speaker as invested in the commemorative properties of spaces indicating death. The commemorative artifact for Milton, though, the "wat'ry bier," is ever changing and ever moving, like the disparate strains of history itself, "large" in its geographic space, but incapable of fixing the dead.[71] Indeed, the speaker imagines the corpse of Lycidas treated indiscriminately by the ocean:

> Whilst thee the shores and sounding seas
> Wash far away, where'er thy bones are hurl'd;
> Whether beyond the stormy Hebrides,
> Where thou perhaps under the whelming tide
> Visit'st the bottom of the monstrous world.[72]

The language of "where'er," "whether," and "perhaps" underscores the speaker's inability to establish the outcome—the physical end—of his friend's life, although "hurl'd" suggests the speaker's fear of the mistreatment of the body, of the lack of proper burial procedure. With the line "Look homeward Angel now" (l. 161), the speaker ultimately moves past these ruminations to regard Lycidas not as a corpse tossed within the ocean but as the guardian of the shore. Milton's poetics indicate the transformation of the individual loss into collective gain, the movement from private to public property, where the body becomes the acquisition of oceanic, poetic, and national identity.

In contrast, Gray's epitaph reinforces interiority as the instigator of the historical consciousness of the speaker of the "Elegy." The epitaph, unlike the ocean, marks a solid, physical burial space capable of securely *placing* the speaker's own death alongside the deaths of the rustics to whom he offers such encomium, thereby elevating his own passing into a realm of "enameled" pastoral reverie.[73] The speaker of *Lycidas* may be able to turn away from his commemorative scene "to fresh woods, and pastures new," but Gray's speaker can imagine no such escape—and, certainly, he desires no such escape.[74] The epitaph becomes indelibly linked to the speaker's identity, his relationship to his aesthetic creation, and to historical inquiry itself.

Gray's speaker attempts to find resolution for his traumatic poetic experience by crafting his imagined epitaph and thus creating a cohesive, lasting identity of himself, one that fuses the disparate attempts he has made in articulating the significance of the hamlet. Runia argues that commemoration involves both "closure and perpetuation," two elements that seem at odds with one another but that are vitally linked by the mourner's desire to transcend the physical impediment of death and to keep the dead alive.[75] With this epitaph, the speaker performs an act of transplantation where he may finally imagine himself as fully integrated into the rural hamlet, an act of closure that will exist into perpetuity. The epitaph invites not only the passing imagined individual to stop and ponder the speaker's life but also the audience reading, reciting, or listening to the "Elegy" itself. The speaker displaces the imitation behind exemplar narratives onto an engagement with his epitaph and creates the sense of commonality that Alpers attributes to the pastoral, where an elite form of commemoration nonetheless embraces the rural poor. He tries to enact what Lycidas accomplishes, the linking of private and public self: he becomes the possession of a national reading audience (a didactic function) while also becoming the possession of the graveyard (literally thrusting his body into the geographic dirt of the hamlet).

Curiously, Pope imagines a similar fate for the lady of his own *Elegy*, especially since she, like the rustics, will not be commemorated by traditional elegiac rites:

> What tho' no weeping Loves thy ashes grace,
> Nor polish'd marble emulate thy face?
> What tho' no sacred earth allow thee room,
> Nor hallow'd dirge be mutter'd o'er thy tomb? (ll. 59–62)

Similar to the situation of the rural poor, the death of Pope's lady does not instigate the construction of the "polish'd marble" headstone or the singing of a "hallow'd dirge." To replace these traditional elite formulations of value, Pope's speaker, like Gray's, insists on the grave as generative, producing "rising flow'rs" (l. 63) and the "green turf" (l. 64) encouraging "the first roses of the year" (l. 66) to bloom. These natural signs of health and vitality mark the grave as "sacred" (l. 68), rather than the man-made institutions of tombs and religious services. For Pope, the strongest critique of the elite that he can offer exists in denying those who had scorned the lady their own graves:

> So peaceful rests, without a stone, a name,
> What once had beauty, titles, wealth, and fame.
> How lov'd, how honour'd once, avails thee not,
> To whom related, or by whom begot;
> A heap of dust alone remains of thee;
> 'Tis all thou art, and all the proud shall be! (ll. 69–74)

Pope's description emphasizes anonymity, stripping the elite of the named specificity that endows them with traditional power: family name, genealogical legitimacy, social and financial wealth. Like Gray, and like Richardson's Clarissa, Pope insists that the lady has *earned* the right to possess physical marks of commemoration through her morality; in contrast, the elite have no virtue and so deserve no such distinction in historical preservation.

Gray's speaker intends that his grave and its attendant epitaph will serve as restitution for elite denigration of the rural community, as well as the ruptures he himself has experienced as the poem unfolded. Again, as in Pope and Richardson, we find the desire for linear recompense, but it is unclear whether the speaker's imagined restitution can truly assuage the divisions, the historical realities, subsisting between the elite and poor (or between the empowered and disenfranchised in Pope, and between the domestic gentlewoman and landed gentleman in Richardson). After all, the speaker ultimately represents neither the traditions of the rural nor the values of the elite. Despite the speaker's desire to transplant himself into the world of the rustics and to represent his epitaph as the melding of rural and elite, his epitaph, because of its dependence on exemplifying his own achievements, prevents him from fully assimilating into the hamlet's graveyard. The speaker becomes the exemplar because of his own pretensions to particularity, rejecting the anonymity cultivated by the unnamed forefathers. The speaker concludes his poem by falling back into old forms: the swain, when lamenting his loss, describes the "dirges" that "in sad array" (l. 113) the mourning shepherds sing as they parade "through the churchyard path" (l. 114), details that curiously invoke the traditional elegiac rituals of the procession of grief that is absent from the speaker's own description of the rustics. Unsure of himself, unsure of the future, the speaker can only imagine an epitaph and a swain's description in unsatisfying references to a past tradition that he earlier found inadequate. The "counterfeit quality" of the swain's musings turn the speaker into a "caricature" of a poet, thus devaluing and casting as inauthentic the entire poetic endeavor of his poem.[76]

The closing verses of the "Elegy," with their tepid references to "dirges" and "the bosom of his Father and his God" (l. 128), prove unable to evoke empathy—that is, the reader's acceptance of the legitimacy of the speaker's endeavor and resolution. Parisot states that "graveyard poetry may well function as a private and occasional expression of grief for the author, but to remain an analogous experience, the graveyard poem must also remain generic enough to facilitate empathetic transfer between poet and reader."[77] Parisot's thoughts underscore the role of the audience in validating the elegiac lament as poetic creation, as does Sharp when she asks "how commemoration remains possible when poets 'speak' to unknown readers about decedents whom these readers cannot know" in an increasingly commodity-driven marketplace.[78] Sharp resolves this dilemma by arguing that "elegy becomes epitaph, an abbreviated, gnomic trace or shadow of the writer's heartfelt response in the face of loss."[79]

In the "Elegy," the speaker endeavors to tell the story of the rustics, but, curiously, the poem ends removed from his own voice in contradistinction to the general impulse of elegiac verse; the speaker alienates his voice first to the "hoary-headed swain" (l. 97) and then to the physical edifice of the epitaph. If the historian poignantly stands at the point of intersection between past, present, and future, what does it signify that the speaker of the "Elegy" is denied speech in a poem that, firstly, is interested in the pervasive eloquence of speech over death, and, secondly, is interested in the interweave of beginnings and endings? George Haggerty argues that "the elegy form, then, promises consolation, release, resolution, but it brings these only in the form of loss" in Gray's text.[80] Although Haggerty writes specifically with male-male desire in mind, his general reading of the way in which the poem offers and then subsequently denies fulfillment of the speaker's desires works well here to underscore what Haggerty terms the speaker's "isolation."[81]

Not only does the speaker's vision lack a traditional heroic presence but it also lacks the ideal pastoral shepherd, as Alpers describes: "In pastoral elegy, a dead and exceptional herdsman is commemorated by his fellows, so as to ensure the continuity of the diminished social group. The laments, recollections, and mimings which represent the dead herdsman are definitive, we have argued, of pastoral poetry, because they define what becomes of poetry and its power in the absence of a hero."[82] In Gray's "Elegy," there is no commemoration of a herdsman by his fellow rustics; there are no "laments, recollections, and mimings" outside of the meager imagining of the epitaph. As Sharp notes, "We find no procession of mourners, no catalogue of flowers, and no refrain of grief."[83] In attempting to figure himself as the "exceptional herdsman," the speaker reveals his disconnection, in no way functioning as one of the rude forefathers—in other words, as ensuring "the continuity of the diminished social group"; hence his concluding "hope" for aesthetic "repose" is "trembling" (l. 127), unlike the reassured speaker of *Lycidas*.

Weinbrot claims that the progress of the "Elegy" follows the speaker's movement from feelings of self-alienation to those of contentment as he makes the moral choice to live among the rustics and embrace a religious-inspired life of spiritual reward.[84] Weinbrot's close reading of the shift in pronouns used by the speaker in referring to his relationship to the rustics supports his argument and leads him to the conclusion that the speaker "emerges as more attractive" to readers "because he chooses to be their retired social and moral equal."[85] But, in this choice, I posit, lies the eternal difference between the rustics and the speaker: according to Weinbrot, he *chose* to become one of their lifestyle, but they, as far as the poem allows us to see, did not. In praising the alignment of the speaker with the lives of the rustics, Weinbrot reads a spiritual triumph in which "Heaven has recompensed him with its own and with human friendship not for his worldly achievements but for his sincerity of soul."[86] Similar to Weinbrot, Thomas Carper argues that the speaker's poetic journey leads him "to be cherished in heaven."[87] In reading this recompense, Weinbrot and Carper emphasize the distaste for secular knowledge that competes with his moral choice as well as the apparent ease with which Gray ameliorates the speaker's wounds. Yet the rustics possess no such learning, no such historical consciousness, and so are incapable of making the moral choice of the speaker: "Their sober wishes never learned to stray" (l. 74). The epitaph may champion the speaker's generosity to the poor and his "large ... bounty" (l. 121), but in fact it is only "a tear" (l. 123) that the speaker bequeaths to "Misery" (l. 123), upsetting an easy reading of the speaker's spiritual transformation and accompanying movement away from sin and guilt.

Indeed, the concern that the epitaph may not, after all, provide the connective link between the rustics and the elite and, moreover, may not adequately represent the speaker himself recalls to mind Pope's question as posed in his own *Elegy*. Pope asks, "What can atone" (l. 46) for the death of the lady? At first, he offers the grave as assuaging the loss of her virtue in the world, since the melding of her corpse with the earth proves generative of life: flowers, grass, rain. Readers might expect additional recompense as existent in the poem itself, the hope of the poet, as in *Lycidas* and "Eloisa," that future readers will reanimate the lady's story and continue to condemn the elite, just as the poet has done. However, the last stanza of the poem forcefully negates such optimism through its claim that "poets themselves must fall, like those they sung; / Deaf the prais'd ear, and mute the tuneful tongue" (ll. 74–75). Once the poet dies, as he inevitably will, the lady, too, comprehensively vanishes, preserved in memory only as long as the poet remains to speak her story. Pope emphasizes, like Gray, the negation of speech and sound, the "ear" and "tongue," essential to poetic and historical storytelling. Pope writes, "Then from his closing eyes thy form shall part, / And the last pang shall tear thee from his heart" (ll. 79–80). Notice the emphasis on the solitary poet as caretaker of the lady's legacy; there is no gesture to an outside reading audience. The emotive connection between the speaker and the lady's memory is so substantial that it cannot last beyond the poet's mortality, perhaps because no one else is capable of forging that emotive connection. Such a rendering fixes the speaker and the lady as especial individuals, locked in an exemplary, insulated relationship that resists intrusion from a public reading community.

In both elegies, Pope and Gray tackle the issue of elite privilege: in granting visibility to those traditionally outside of—or at best adjacent to—elegiac rituals, they claim that historical value exists in alternative classes and geographies than those typically enshrined by exemplary narratives. At their best, these poems offer visibility to the nonelite and to the nonmale. Yet Pope's question about atonement and Gray's odd return to those elite practices he had earlier derided cast these poems at their worst, as explicating the real threat that elite privilege represents—namely, its insidious and unyielding control over historical and literary forms that denies speech to voices outside of itself. Although Pope, Gray, and Richardson insist that these voices are fundamental to national identity, their texts nonetheless contain the fear that such hopes are, in fact, fantasies.

Keep in mind that the act of commemoration, for Runia, involves the memorialization of deeds seemingly in opposition to the accepted narrative of ourselves. Runia argues that "by doing things that are at odds with our identity, we place history outside ourselves. Committing history thus," by viewing history as the constant rescripting of our identity through moments that seem most at odds with our conception of ourselves, acknowledges our identities as unstable and changeable.[88] Historical preservation, in Runia's conception, is self-alienation instigated by the collision of private individual and national narrative. When the speaker crafts his epitaph in the "Elegy," he acknowledges his various struggles over genre and its implications on his self-consciousness, choosing the epitaph as the most inviolate means of representing his poetic journey (as Clarissa does with her will). At the heart of the speaker's epitaph is "the story of a wound that cries out, that addresses us in the attempt to tell us of a reality or truth that is not otherwise available. This truth, in its delayed appearance and its belated address, cannot be linked only to what is known, but also to what remains unknown in our very actions and our language."[89] Tacked on to the end of the poem, the epitaph emerges belatedly, and in its "belated" appearance marks the speaker's trauma and his desire for recompense. It is a poignant attempt, made desperate by his overwhelming sense of traumatic helplessness when confronted by the crushing inadequacy of historical and genre forms.

Writing the Nation in the "Elegy"

In chapter 1, I argued that *The Dunciad*'s iteration of "thy own Phoebus," the poetics capable of articulating Pope's apocalyptic vision, does not necessarily indicate a negative development for Pope. Instead, it allows Pope to deliberate and to express the traumatic recurrence of dullness in eighteenth-century England. Likewise, the inefficacy of Gray's epitaph as an authentic rendering of elegiac expression is celebrated by the poem as the most legitimate mode of representation. By recasting the speaker's individual voice as the point of translation between the exemplar and the anonymous, between the particular and the general, Gray's epitaph reconfigures history writing as an act of historical consciousness rather than about specific actions and events, an inward exploration into an affective relationship between the individual and the external. The "Elegy" does not support temporal divisions, along the lines of what Williams terms the "single escalator" carrying us toward progress and further away from a tranquil, happy pastoral past.[90] The speaker, through his epitaph, hopes to dissolve temporal distinctions by transcending the limitations of his own death and impacting futurity—as do Eloisa and Clarissa.

Common to readings of mid-eighteenth-century poetry is the strategy of retreat, as Sitter describes: "We have seen how the conflict and violence of public history as it is conceived metonymically by many of the poets leads to images of Retreat, images of shepherds fleeing as they sing, for example, hurrying toward the shelter of shady groves or the protection of caves, and we have seen that these images of seclusion are also metaphors for the solitary poetic imagination itself."[91] We might find this description slightly amusing if we consider that Pope, Gray, and Richardson, after establishing themselves in their professions, performed such a retreat (although it is hard to imagine Pope as a shepherd fleeing as he sings). As mentioned briefly in the introduction, Pope fashioned

Twickenham as his gentlemanly refuge from City degradation, although, as *Epistle to Dr. Arbuthnot* bemoans, the ridiculous and the vain certainly followed him to his grotto nonetheless. Likewise, Richardson distanced himself from his business and from London by residing at the North End estate, where he wrote his novels. Both Pope and Richardson donned the role of gentleman on these properties, although they were not landowners themselves. Similarly, Kaul writes, "As one of his [Gray's] biographers, William Jones, puts it, Gray's 'tastes fit the tradition of the more literary landed gentry of his time . . . But he had not estate . . . [and so] he played the gentleman by reading and studying at Cambridge in winter and visiting his friends at their homes and estates in summer.'"[92] In the actions of all three writers, we see a physical removal that points to the potency of geography in establishing one's identity, particularly by associating the country with contemplative possibility and the City with monetary concerns. This interest in location lends itself to reading their respective texts as cognizant of geography being steeped in national consciousness.

In the "Elegy," the "conflict and violence" done to the speaker's pastoral vision over the course of the poem (albeit through his own aesthetic logic) certainly forces him to "retreat"; in this case, though, it is not to "shady groves" or "caves" that the speaker escapes but to his own aesthetic vision—the epitaph. However, Gray's epitaph, *because* of its refusal to mimic the standard elegiac conventions described by Sharp, Parisot, and Alpers, invests in historical inquiry. Gray situates a pastoral landscape as the ideal resting place for his speaker because of the pastoral's capacity for engaging with historical concerns, specifically asking us to reimagine rural geographic spaces as more than reminders of a lost golden age. Instead, the rural hamlet expands English national identity beyond the court and urbanity, incorporating older strategies of life, thus placing the past in the present and as an active figure in the creation of futurity. "Retreat," in this sense, does not indicate active removal from worldly concerns but, as evident from the biographies of Pope, Gray, and Richardson, acknowledgment that Englishness resides beyond the limits of fashionable London.

In the "Elegy," historical consciousness manifests in the rupture from received modes, including referential history centered on named individuals, the enameled world of Renaissance pastoral, or the creation of external artifacts as national commemorative objects as in Milton. In a discussion of "the relation of literary works to their predecessors" and "the continuity of literary forms and expression," Alpers, taking issue with Fredric Jameson's genre theory, argues that "literary value consists precisely in breaking old molds, doing some kind of violence to received conventions and forms of expressions. I think we all assume that good poems either extend the possibilities of expression or in some way revitalize the capacities of literary form and language."[93] Although Alpers does not directly discuss Gray's work, his appreciation of the flexibility of the poetic process to "revitalize," "extend," invent, and, if I may add, *sever* assumed literary practices in order to produce new "forms of expressions," joined with Weinfield's characterization of Gray's "Elegy" as enacting a literary "dissolution," removes Gray's "Elegy" from the dusty gloom of nineteenth-century critical appraisals of its commonplaces. Indeed, we find that Gray's elegiac utterance "diverges significantly from elegiac conventions," performing aesthetic ruptures with the poetic past in order to move beyond exemplary constitutions of history and historical time.[94]

Fundamentally, the project of the "Elegy" changes from an exploration into an individual locale's relationship to an elite, exemplary other to, instead, an interest in the individual speaker's relationship to the past. Sitter claims that "the specter which seems to be lurking behind much of the poetry of the generation after Pope's and Swift's, however, is the fear not of the loss of history but of its crushing presence."[95] Sitter's use of "crushing" to describe the terror behind the speaker's engagements with history is apt—although I argue that historical inquiry is a shared connection between Pope, Gray, and Richardson. The poetic process ushers the speaker toward a realization of himself as historical—that is, he learns that to be constituted as different from the past is precisely to become historical. Or, as Haggerty so concisely puts it, "'I' is the source of grief, that is, rather than 'he' or 'you'" of elegiac tradition.[96] In the "Elegy," history is moved inward, becoming the provenance of a subjective, deeply personal understanding of the self's relationship to temporality, creating a more capacious historical consciousness that enfolds past, present, and future while rooted in the private, intimate self.

The final address of the speaker in the line beginning "For thee" (l. 93) shifts his contemplative process one last time, granting the poem its interest in nascent English nationalism:

> For thee, who mindful of the unhonored dead
> Dost in these lines their artless tale relate;
> If chance, by lonely contemplation led,
> Some kindred spirit shall inquire thy fate (ll. 93–96)

The speaker's various attempts at securing an adequate mode of disseminating historical knowledge leave him unsure of his own relationship to history, much like Benjamin's historian, who is precariously perched between visions of the past, present, and future. Presuming to be the interpreter of rustic ways to a larger community does not necessarily indicate his assimilation into that rustic group precisely because of his historian's gaze. The speaker is unsure if by "chance" (l. 95) his memory will be the subject of musings; here we have the manifestation of another outside element in the poem, but this time it is not the elite disdaining the rustics. Instead, the speaker deliberates the desire for "some kindred spirit" to happen upon knowledge of himself and to instigate the production of his own "artless tale."

With the epitaph, the speaker imagines life among the rustics, acting as his attempt to assuage the rupture from past historiographic modes that he has envisioned in his own poetic creation. Indeed, the imagined "hoary-headed swain" (l. 97) addresses an imagined audience when he says, "Approach and read (for thou canst read) thy lay, / Graved on the stone" (ll. 115–16), his words appropriately emphasizing the literacy of those who view the speaker's imagined grave as if it is a tourist attraction—or, to invoke Runia, a site of commemoration that forces a nation to readjust its master narrative of itself. As with *The Dunciad* and *Clarissa*, the boundaries of the poem break as the epitaph invites not only the passing imagined individual to stop and ponder the speaker's life but also the audience reading, reciting, or listening to the "Elegy" itself. In witnessing the imagined grave of the speaker, the speaker transforms from witness to speaker to poet, as he wishes his future audience to participate in a national act of rescripting the collective consciousness of what constitutes historical value.

Writing history proves to be the underlying traumatic element in Gray's poem; hence the pressure placed on the poetic depictions of voice and utterance. Runia's understanding of history as a national project of *narration* is clearly at work here in Gray's eighteenth-century frame, expressing the problem of how to speak a nation's collective story: Who will speak it, to whom shall it be addressed, and what shall it say? In the "Elegy," the speaker stands as the self-elected ambassador for both the rustic population and the elite, attempting, through the epitaph, to script a resolution allowing for the fusion of these two disparate groups into his imagined collective. Indeed, the tropes of death as leveler or death in life espoused critically underscore the melancholic ways in which scholars typically read the investment of the "Elegy" in this nation building. Gray's speaker contemplates an understanding of history in which all figures collapse in "the attempt to make poetry nonreferential, to free it from the realm of memory and mimesis, at least from the mimesis of verifiable events and things."[97] The democratic binding of all types of individuals—rustic and elite—into historical knowledge creates a national narrative that emerges through difference. Because of the emphasis on self-consciousness as constitutive of history, both nation and history become imagined objects, fantasies of the speaker's consciousness, rather than as an extant "history" as we might define it today. In this way, the "Elegy" connects to *The Dunciad* as imagining *what could be*, not just historical realities.

"Eton College" and Historical Consciousness

In order to understand the recompense available from the "Elegy," I think it useful to turn for a moment to Gray's "Ode on a Distant Prospect of Eton College" (1747), also contemporaneous with *The Dunciad* and *Clarissa*.[98] "Eton College" likewise showcases Gray's interest in constituting history outside of the exemplary, further proving Gray's myriad interest in history beyond the Pindaric odes. When the speaker of "Eton College" juxtaposes his own state of maturity and its attendant suffering with the lightheartedness of the college youths, the knowledge that "Ah, tell them they are men!" forms the heart of his lament.[99] "Eton College" unfolds around the speaker's personal grief as he deliberates whether to enlighten the youths to the futurity they will inevitably experience. As he watches the youths "play" (l. 52), figures of maturity layer his aesthetic vision. Into his awareness of the frolicking of the youths enters images of their future misery: "Yet see how all around 'em wait / The ministers of human fate, / And black Misfortune's baleful train!" (ll. 55–57). The speaker identifies these "ministers" and "train" as hovering around the oblivious youths in a manner that collapses distinct boundaries between past, present, and future. The ministers are not passive but actively "waiting" for the moment to pounce upon the youths. What follows is a catalog of "black Misfortune's" misery, such as "Passions" (l. 61), "Jealousy" (l. 66), and, as mentioned in the "Elegy," a key term associated with the historical rendering of the elite, "Ambition" (l. 71).

This catalog following his lament "Ah, tell them they are men!" performs a type of poetic violence, shattering the internal harmony of the poetics to create a bitter, furious introspection. All youthful promise of "invention ever new" (l. 46) as the defining characteristic of humankind is eradicated, replaced by thirty lines of undifferentiated misery in which all individual experience is effaced. Indeed, the speaker anticipates the whine of a youth demanding his individuality, which he sums up abruptly and unremorsefully: "To each his sufferings: all are men / Condemned alike to groan" (ll. 91–92). The only individualization that exists in this barrage of misery is that "each" individual has his own "sufferings" which he cannot share. This gesture toward the individual plea is syntactically short, followed by a colon that explains the uselessness of such a plea. The inevitability of "condemned" combines with "alike" to completely eradicate any hope, any exception, anything other than the march toward self-erasure. In both meditative poems, "Eton College" and the "Elegy," Gray positions a speaker bitterly antithetical to the exemplar formula where individuals emerge as heroes overcoming impossible odds.

In considering whether he should inform the youths of Eton College of the inevitable suffering of adulthood, the speaker debates the morality of his choice, boldly deliberating the catalog of misery that ruptures the scene of innocence and challenges the integrity of the college. More than simply critiquing the exemplar, though, "Eton College" envisions the danger posed to English national identity when history is moved inward, becoming an expression of subjective desire, a movement that *The Dunciad*, the "Elegy," and *Clarissa* all perform.

The victimization of the youths in childhood, albeit unbeknownst to them, inherently shatters the linearity of chronology, on which the notion of historical change as maturity depends. Line 95 of "Eton College" finds the speaker reapproaching his essential dilemma as iterated in line 60: "Yet ah! why should they know their fate?" Here, in the final stanza of the poem, the speaker turns away from the youths, arguing that "ignorance is bliss" (l. 99). Rejecting the option of intruding upon their "play" (l. 52)—note the similarity with Pope's depiction of "Eaton's sons for ever play" in book 3 of *The Dunciad*—the speaker allows ignorance to claim space in a poem that initially pledges its own adoration of the learning performed at Eton College. For the speaker, the most useful lesson to come out of Eton is ignorance, rather than lessons on the inevitability of "doom" (l. 51) awaiting the attendees.

The Dunciad considers a similar collapse in temporality, particularly through a reference to Eton College in book 4. When satirizing the proclivity of teachers to flog their students, Pope stresses its widespread contamination throughout England:

> O'er ev'ry vein a shudd'ring horror runs;
> Eton and Winton shake thro' all their Sons.

> All Flesh is humbled, Westminster's bold race
> Shrink, and confess the Genius of the place:
> The pale Boy-Senator yet tingling stands,
> And holds his breeches close with both his hands. (ll. 143–18)

The educational practice of flogging permeates "All Flesh," including Eton and Winchester schools, rupturing linear progression toward maturity. "Westminster's bold race," the former youths of Eton and Winchester who enter Parliament, continue to suffer physiological and psychological effects from the violence done to them during their school days. Rather than being "bold," then, the parliamentary member, the figure of maturity and accomplishment who is ready to foster English triumphs, figures as "the pale Boy-Senator." He is "pale," rendered useless with the manifestation of remembered "tingling" that transcribes itself onto his present self as a here-and-now tingling. This tingling forever unites the "Boy" with the "Senator," indelibly links the youth with the adult, in such a way that collapses temporal distinctions and eradicates linear chronology as in Gray's "Eton College." The futurity of the elite—the advocates for and protectors of Englishness—is bound to the past and an ever-ruptured present unable to move beyond the past in order to create a new future, thus reinforcing and reinvigorating the "Genius" that is Dulness.

"Eton College" echoes this same interweave of temporalities; the speaker's aesthetic decision to turn away from the youths suggests the inherent burden of moving forward in time, as considered by the last line of the poem, that it is "folly to be wise" (l. 100), as well as the burden that historical consciousness creates. Such thoughts echo Caruth's ideas on trauma when she describes trauma as "a break in the mind's experience of time," an experience rendered poignantly by the students depicted in both *The Dunciad* and "Eton College."[100] The inability of the students to move forward in temporality, and the remembered, repeated, memories of pain experienced at the college, haunt the poems and suggest a fractured relationship between past, present, and future. This trauma troubles the privilege the elite supposedly possess, as it empties the elite of volition, upsetting a binary rendering of history as victim and aggressor.

Indeed, as emblematic of the elite national self, the student of Eton College should be versed in the wisdom of "Henry's holy shade" (l. 4), which would allow him to lead his country to glory. The youths of Eton College represent the elite, educated, aristocratic set who have the privileged representativeness that the speaker of the "Elegy" contrasts to the anonymity of the rural poor. Yet the poetics of "Eton College" and the historical knowledge it presents elicit the concern that it is impossible to *ever* pinpoint a national self within a national narrative if one's past is always encountering one's present and thus creating the future self at the time of the present. If the "doom" (l. 51) of futurity cannot be avoided or eradicated by such promising youths as those at Eton, what hope can England have for its own development if development results only in "moody Madness laughing wild" (l. 79)? When the rhetoric of a nation is grotesquely altered into "Madness" and "wild," indecipherable utterances of laughter, how can a national narrative arise that is at once coherent and indicative of the efforts of individual triumphs? Is it indeed *useful* to consider the notion of scripting a definition of one's identity if that identity is constantly in flux, constantly being reevaluated by individual private events and reencounters with older selves and imagined future selves, as the speaker encounters in his return to Eton?

It is helpful to note here that Gray's conception of the students of Eton College "laughing wild" comes from the same poetic destabilization of institutional, typically historically present, spaces as legitimate markers of historical value and veracity as does Pope's in book 3 of *The Dunciad*. At the conclusion of Cibber's trip to the underworld, Settle prophecies the degeneration of the distinguished educational locations as evidence of Dulness's triumph:

> Proceed, great days! 'till Learning fly the shore,
> 'Till Birch shall blush with noble blood no more,
> 'Till Thames see Eaton's sons for ever play,
> 'Till Westminster's whole year be holiday,
> 'Till Isis' Elders reel, their pupils sport,
> And Alma mater lie dissolv'd in Port! (ll. 333–38)

The major educational institutions responsible for molding elite boys into "English" men—Eton, Westminster, Oxford, Cambridge—are cataloged here, by both professors and students, as sites of infantile "play," drunken revelry and "sport." Pope's imagining, like that of Gray, is a wild cacophony of dissolution in which there is no solid subjectivity, either of private self or public institution, to foster the scripting of a historically viable Englishness.

"Eton College" rejects the chronological progression of England toward improvement and innovation by undercutting the fundamental educational system responsible for that progression. Yet what remains at the conclusion of "Eton College" is not an imagined epitaph but Eton College itself, impervious to the lines of students weaving in and out of its registry, oblivious to the ministers of fate who hover around the youths. In remaining, the space of Eton College fixes the story that history narrates: it is the triumph of the academic institution that pervades historical memory, the hallowed walls of "Henry's holy shade," not the aesthetic terror envisioned by a lone speaker. Indeed, the speaker himself suspects the significance of the story Eton tells, evident by the fact that he returns to Eton in the first place, reifying it as home to privilege and historical visibility.

Ironically, by turning his back on the youths and refusing to pass on the historical knowledge he possesses, the speaker guarantees that Eton's narrative—an elite narrative—will prevail in English history. Both Eton College and the epitaph of the "Elegy" offer stories that are fraudulent; the imagined *un*reality embodied by the epitaph's optimistic scripting of national unity, and the college's insistence on excluding the nonelite and the traumatic from its legacy. For Runia, commemoration and history are acts of narration; "Eton College" and the "Elegy" meditate on the dangers posed to national identity when individuals refuse to narrate their experiences for the benefit of the public, thus repudiating the moral-didactic function provided by exemplars.

Recompense in Gray's Poems

Yet a national project of commemoration, as pondered by the speakers of these poems, as in Pope and Richardson, does not depend on founding a universal subjectivity but enfolds in itself multiple voices, precisely those of the various readers constituting—although loosely, comprised of disparate parts—a "readership," albeit one that does not indicate a collective, stable Englishness. The ultimately bitter commemoration of Gray's two poems can be read as an authentic rescripting of identity rather than alienation, since the function of the poem is to reinvoke the experience of mourning for others through the act of reading or reciting the poem. In the final resolution of the speaker of the "Elegy" to turn away from his present and imagine his epitaph, and in the final resolution of the speaker of "Eton College" to turn away from the youths he sees, we find the imagination able to offer an aesthetic recompense, an atonement, for the burden of self-awareness experienced by the speakers. The epitaph exists for future readers, both inside and outside the poetic situation, to be reread, and the college exists for future scholars, both inside and outside its registry, to be reexamined. Historical inquiry, manifestly traumatic in the speaker's aesthetic process, emerges as recompense in the poem. The speaker encounters something much like what Odney describes, the "interweaving of myth and history" that is "deliberately distanced from immediate and fixed notions of national identity."[101] The physical site of commemoration exists as a statement of national identity that the speaker increasingly realizes—as Williams elucidates—cannot be "fixed."

The problem of origins remains particularly rich when reading Gray, as scholars continue to debate the commemorative purpose behind the "Elegy." Contention still exists concerning the individual to whom the "Elegy" is directed. Such questions lead scholars through the revisionary history of the poem, attempting to identify a chronology for the composition of the text. As Robert Mack details, part of the allure of the "Elegy" exists in piecing together a timeline of its creation, pulling together evidence found in correspondence between Gray and Walpole, as well as in the Eton Manuscript, the copy of handwritten poems owned by Eton College. In addition, Gray also included a version in a commonplace book, and yet another was sent in a 1750 letter to Thomas Wharton. Ultimately forced to publish his poem to prevent an unlicensed version from appearing in print, Gray dismissed the poem's virtues, only glad that he had finally completed it. As he wrote to Walpole, he hoped it would be viewed as "a thing with an end to it," words that clearly do not anticipate the overwhelming fame it brought to Gray.[102]

Gray's tedium for the "Elegy" certainly does not coalesce with the enthusiasm with which it was greeted by its readers. The anxiety to pinpoint the exact individual to whom the poem is addressed, as well as the circumstances under which it was written, suggests the importance of the poem's history and the way that history connects to the eighteenth century. The "Elegy" is very much aware of itself as engaging in and deviating from the standard conventions of pastoral elegy. As such, it consciously considers exemplary narratives while emphasizing introspection as necessary for a stable England, one built on a variety of voices, both elite and rural. As with *The Dunciad* and *Clarissa*, the "Elegy" relies on the reader to perform those acts typically reserved for exemplars: identifying social ills, deliberating solutions, and, hopefully, enacting meaningful change. By shifting responsibility away from heroic examples of virtue and vice, the "Elegy" reconstitutes recompense, implicating the general public in the crimes and victories enshrined by the poem. England, as Gray imagines it in the "Elegy," is forged from meditative prowess and historical awareness. Rather than standing in contrast to Gray's overtly historical Pindaric odes, the "Elegy," alongside "Eton College," marks history as constituted by forms other than the exemplar, such as the longue durée and burial practices. In so doing, Gray indicates his commitment to, not retreat from, public meditations, upsetting his legacy as the "pensive poet" isolated from worldly concerns.

Perhaps Gray was eager to wash his hands of the poem, but the reading public was not so willing. The zeal with which so many readers embraced the "commonplace emotions" of the poem indicates the desire to map onto it their own desires, ambitions, and needs. By reading themselves in the "Elegy," the audience could immerse themselves into the text in ways not available in traditional exemplary works. Instead of reading it solely for moral-didactic gain, the reader could *feel* the poem and experience its resonance in their own lives, marking empathy as integral to historical self-consciousness. Rather than "artless," then, the tale the "Elegy" tells is one that narrates the interconnectedness of various forms of genre, as well as the intricate—and intimate—role of the reader in its legacy.

Another Epitaph, Another Historical Subject

Before moving on to the discussion of Richardson's *Clarissa* in chapter 3, I find it important to consider Gray's further use of the epitaph later in his career, most evidently in his 1758 poems "Epitaph on a Child" and "Epitaph on Mrs. Mason," as well as his 1775 "Epitaph on Sir William Williams." The epitaph as figured in these later poems does not stand as the culminating testimony to a speaker's struggle with alienation from poetic forms, and it does not offer aesthetic representations of the collision between individual and collective, as in the "Elegy" and "Eton College." However, reading Gray's "Epitaph on Mrs. Clarke" (1758) alongside Pope and Richardson enhances the connections between historical inquiry and literary recompense available from burial rituals and the attendant issues of temporality.

Since "Eloisa to Abelard," "Epitaph on Mrs. Clarke," and *Clarissa* offer male-authored literary imaginings of female suffering and contemplate the recompense available to females, we might find it surprising that all three texts meditate on *ruptured* domesticity. Eloisa's secret marriage to Abelard does not result in a fertile domesticity, nor does Clarissa's experiences with Lovelace. Similarly, Mrs. Clarke's attempt at procreation does not produce a happy familial setting. If stable domesticity indicated a healthy national identity for the eighteenth century, then it is curious that Pope, Gray, and Richardson would figure the suffering female as the subjects of their texts.[103] For convenience, I include the "Mrs. Clarke" poem in its entirety here:

> Lo! where this silent marble weeps,
> A friend, a wife, a mother sleeps:
> A heart, within whose sacred cell
> The peaceful virtues loved to dwell.
> Affection warm, and faith sincere,
> And soft humanity were there.
> In agony, in death, resigned,
> She felt the wound she left behind.
> Her infant image, here below,
> Sits smiling on a father's woe:
> Whom what awaits, while yet he strays
> Along the lonely vale of days?
> A pang, to secret sorrow dear;
> A sigh; an unavailing tear;
> Till time shall every grief remove,
> With life, with memory, and with love.[104]

Typical formulations of eighteenth-century femininity describe the "Mrs. Clarke" figure, such as "peaceful virtues" (l. 4) and "soft humanity" (l. 6)—in contradistinction to Pope, who provides us with a glorious investigation into Eloisa's female passions. Mrs. Clarke's death is framed in domestic terms: the loss sustained by her role as a wife and mother, not surprisingly, considering the event that engendered the poem has been assumed to be the death of Gray's mother.

Yet the privileging of the "silent marble" proves most striking in this "Epitaph," the positioning of the grave foremost in the initial line of the poem rather than a gesture to the warmth and "affection" (l. 5) of the deceased. The poem as a site of commemoration initiates the speaker's musings, and the "memory" (l.16) inherent to that commemoration closes the poem. The first and last lines structure a reading of the poem that involves more than lament for the passing of an individual; issues of historical consciousness ground the poem in its lament.

Certainly, there seems to be a redemptive quality to the final two lines of the poem: "Till time shall every grief remove / With life, with memory, and with love," suggesting that "life," "memory," and "love" prevail over the suffering involved in death, wherein "every grief remove[s]" from both the pain felt while dying (here, during childbirth) and the pain felt by those left to grieve the loss of the dead. Mack frames the poem as a response to Gray's memory of the loss of his own mother, using the text as the means of discussing Gray's own apparent symptoms of depression.[105] Mack's final summation of the poem rests on Christian beliefs in the succor of faith, offering a spiritual recompense along the lines of Weinbrot's reading of the "Elegy": "Gray's lines look to dwell with gently dignity on the eventual recovery of that individuality which would otherwise seem to have been lost in the moment of death; the dissolution of mortality at once disperses and encapsulates the individual, rendering her mortal remains static but open to that temporal multivalency which is the result of the defining, personal relationships of this world."[106] Mack's reading seeks to rescue the Mrs. Clarke figure from the death as leveler trope mentioned earlier in my reading of the "Elegy" and to impose upon the corpse a "gentle dignity" that "Eton College's" barrage of misfortunes inflicts upon all individuals. Death, for Mack, rather than indicating a loss of self, renders the individual static, granting the individual an unchanging status free from the vulnerabilities of chronological time while simultaneously remaining available to memory.

The emphasis on "time" as the power responsible for obliterating grief—when combined with the poem's initial emphasis on the grave—suggests, instead, an apocalyptic time in which the various "griefs" of "life," "memory," and "love" are "removed." True, this could support Mack's religiously invested interpretation, wherein this apocalyptic time refers to a Christian Judgment Day inviting the godly to enter heaven. However, there is a strain of trauma that undermines the "gentle dignity" of the deceased individual's transposition into memory, particularly within the line "She felt the wound she left behind." This line occurs directly in the middle of the poem, separating the initial description of Mrs. Clarke's "soft humanity" from the latter description of the effect her death will have on her husband and infant; this aesthetic division within the poem mirrors the temporal division between life and death, and earth and afterlife. Line 8—"She felt the wound she left behind"—involves an overlapping in temporality, though, that defies the poem's apparently easy division.

"She felt the wound" indicates the suffering Mrs. Clarke endured during childbirth, reinforced by the "agony" mentioned in line 7; she literally felt the wound that would cause her death. "She left behind" refers to the wound of grief suffered by her family after her death; the wound "resigned" (l. 7) is replaced by another, less easily assuaged, wound imparted to others. The infant left behind additionally functions as this traumatic wound, that which has literally pained her, but that nonetheless brings love, in a collision of life and death that upsets easy temporal distinctions. The second wound is the wound of significance because it outlasts death, it influences more than the deceased, and it is not easily healed.

When the two phrases are combined, though, an easy interpretation of temporality crumbles: the moment when Mrs. Clarke feels the wound she imparts to others is phrased in the past tense—not "leaves behind" but "left behind"—suggesting that the moment when she felt the pain of her loved ones was *after* she was deceased. Pain, then, particularly emotive pain, continues even in death. This pain, not the pain of her husband or infant, focuses the poem and forms the object of commemoration "weeping" in the first line, upsetting causal recompense. The poem considers the disjunction between the warmth of family surrounding Mrs. Clarke posed in the beginning of the poem and the "lonely vale of days" (l. 12) that is her future (not her family's) in death. As in the end of "Eloisa" and the "Elegy," there is a "tear" shed upon the reanimation of the grave's story; here, though, the tear is "unavailing" (l. 14)—that is, incapable of articulation and of making intelligible to the family left behind the emotive connection the deceased desires. Eloisa and the "Elegy's" speaker are able to imagine recompense within the song of the "future bard" who will weep at their tales, much like the future reader of Clarissa's correspondence that her editor, Belford, amasses. The figure of Mrs. Clarke, though, can envision no such compensatory repair.

Curiously, the tear described in Gray's "Mrs. Clarke" poem resembles the tear that is absent from Pope's *Elegy*:

> No friend's complaint, no kind domestic tear
> Pleas'd thy pale ghost, or grac'd thy mournful bier;
> By foreign hands thy dying eyes were clos'd,
> By foreign hands thy decent limbs compos'd,
> By foreign hands thy humble grave adorn'd,
> By strangers honour'd, and by strangers mourn'd! (ll. 50–54)

Pope emphasizes, repeatedly in these lines, the disconnect between the deceased lady and familial comfort, poignantly manifested by the lack of "domestic tear." As we find in Gray, the tear mentioned is not generative of adequate emotive agency or narration, unable to articulate the story of the deceased to future anonymous readers. Both poems prove impotent, in contrast to the fertility and vitality of the two female figures celebrated.

When describing the treatment of the lady after her suicide, Pope transforms a private act into one of national importance. The handling of her corpse, like that of Clarissa, assumes national meaning. The repetition of "foreign" further reinforces the poem's insistence on the lady's estrangement and separation from the people in her life. Pope, like Gray and Richardson, suggest that moral certitude in domestic, private, and nonmale circumstances forms the scaffolding of a nation, and the mishandling of those circumstances performs a critique upon that nation. Reading the "Mrs. Clarke" poem provides another instance of these writers contemplating nonexemplary individuals as possessing—and having the right to—historical visibility and the recompense available from this status. Anxiety over determining an adequate mode for representing Englishness existed in cross-generic endeavors beyond that found in *The Dunciad* or "Elegy Written in a Country Churchyard," prominently challenging the assumptions of exemplar narratives in *Clarissa*.

3

"She Has Now a Tale to Tell"

THE EPISTOLARY NOVEL AND GENDER IN *CLARISSA*

THE *DUNCIAD* and the "Elegy" rely on the role of the reader in their legacies. The conclusions of these two texts, disparate in genre as they might be, encourage nonexemplary voices to confront, indeed annihilate, the national atrocities depicted. Pope's apocalyptic vision of dullness consuming England cries out to readers to prevent its further spread, while Gray's epitaph pleads for readers to recognize the rural and the poor. Heroic figures of incomparable might and bravery do not—*cannot*—charge into battle in the final lines, slaying the embodiment of evil. Instead, Pope and Gray heave exemplary action onto the anonymous audience reading, reciting, or listening to their poems and suggest that vice is more pervasive than a specific name attached to a discrete individual. Consequently, the recompense that emerges from these texts eliminates linear causality while broadening historical consciousness.

Likewise, Richardson forefronts the role of the reader in enabling a more capacious English nationhood in *Clarissa*. As an epistolary novel, *Clarissa* undermines the assumption of exemplary narratives that historical change is inherently linked to the ethos of a single exemplar. Richardson, like Pope with verse satire and Gray with pastoral elegy, uses the genre to challenge the integrity of the moral-didactic insularity of the exemplar. A series of letters, the epistolary exchange creates a conversation wherein multiple individuals are given space to discourse, not solely that of Clarissa. The letters become a form of archive, a collection preserved after Clarissa's death to be read, commented on, and learned from by the other characters. *Clarissa* becomes the subject of national discourse as many extant eighteenth-century readers debated its ending. Notice that in letter 177 Anna attempts to reassure Clarissa that "to all who will know your story, you will be an excellent example."[1] Anna does not write "to all who know *you*" but rather "to all who will know your *story*," phrased in the future tense. The distinction emphasizes Clarissa not as woman or sufferer but as a "story," one that is not simply private but historical, intended for a future reading public, grounded in moral instruction.[2]

Scholarly interest in Clarissa as a character typically draws on a religious argument, on a narrative stance, on an ethical compass, as political victim, as exegete.[3] In this chapter, I will emphasize Clarissa's role as letter writer founded on historical inquiry: her letters reveal her poignant attempts to articulate history and establish a relationship with historical time. As such, Richardson reimagines traditional exemplar narratives by granting historical status to an individual usually considered by eighteenth-century ideology to be peripheral to history, that of the white gentlewoman. Richardson positions Clarissa's capacious reflection on her own experience as her defining characteristic, as that which makes her an exemplary historical subject, rather than overt heroic deeds.

Clarissa's proficiency with the genre of epistolary writing provides her with narrative and didactic visibility. In the early volumes of the novel, Clarissa and Lovelace, both adept at letter writing, engage in a battle for control over the narrative that is being created. Typically, scholars argue that Clarissa's exceptionality arises from her virtue, what Laura Runge has termed "the feminine standard" governing constructions of femininity in the period, such as the morality that she expresses in her letters and the virtuous manner in which she conducts herself during Lovelace's scheming.[4] As Terry Castle points out, "The Preface, first of all, is a fairly ponderous attempt to condition our understanding of the letter sequence that follows."[5] Like Pope in his extraction and publication of his critics' own words on satire as part of the prefatory material to *The Dunciad*, Richardson frames his novel in order to ensure a correct reading; the introductory apparatus of both Pope and Richardson reveal the basic aesthetic assumptions of the texts, such as the folly of those satirized in *The Dunciad* and the virtue of Clarissa.

Clarissa's acute awareness of her position as moral exemplar fosters her narrative. When discussing Clarissa as Christ figure, Peggy Thompson notes that Clarissa follows the Christian tenets of self-suffering and self-denial: "Clarissa's well-known adherence to Puritan conduct-books *exemplifies* a life lived in the spirit of Christ as called for in this interpretation of atonement. But by so living, Clarissa not only follows his [Christ's] *example*, she becomes an *exemplar* herself, thus reinforcing her identification with Christ."[6] Thompson's words are critical here because they emphasize—three times in two sentences—Clarissa's exemplarity. Anna certainly reminds Clarissa of this from the start of the novel, twice reiterating it in letter 1: first writing, "My mama, and all of us, like the rest of the world, talk of nobody but you," and shortly after repeating, "Every eye, in short, is upon you with the expectation of an example" (40). Those who read Clarissa's narrative (her intimate domestic circle, her friends, and those gaining access to the letters edited by Belford) assess her actions and her morality.

Despite the novel's easy assignment of virtue to Clarissa, her letters reveal her historiographic struggle—as in *The Dunciad* and the "Elegy"—to find a mode of representation capable of adequately conveying her narrative and maintaining her virtuous reputation. Clarissa's epistles demonstrate her reliance on various strategies for articulating herself when confronted with the restrictive ideologies of her family and of Lovelace. The forging and dissemination of historical knowledge motivates *Clarissa* as Clarissa explores a multitude of ways of knowing history, marking time, and establishing a meaningful relationship between the past, present, and future. The epistolary letter allows Richardson to look beyond narrated events as valid sources of historical knowledge, particularly using the rape and Clarissa's "mad papers" to critique extant historical data. Instead, Richardson charts the inward movement of historical consciousness, away from named, blamable individuals, to other areas such as commemorative objects (Clarissa's coffin and mourning rings), legal discourse (Clarissa's will and the possession of her corpse), and religiosity.

Clarissa's genre choices demonstrate that she is not a static exemplar, incapable of ambiguity or misdeed. Richardson crafts her exemplary status as arising *because of* her missteps and charts a history that privileges inner meditations rather than outward action and event. As we find in *The Dunciad* and the "Elegy," *Clarissa* reimagines exemplar history by considering the moral intentionality behind official choices and outcomes. Pope uses verse satire to expose the secret follies and vices of specific individuals, traits that influence their political and moral ineptitude. Gray imagines history as involving fantasies of alternative endings, where moral integrity dictates historical worth rather than overt exemplary status. Richardson likewise positions Clarissa's turmoil as the means of deliberating the relationship between inner contemplation and outward action.

Richardson not only challenges the assumptions inherent to exemplary narratives but also participates in the long eighteenth century's experimentation with the prose novel as a new genre.[7] A glance at only a handful of period novels reveals the instability of the form across the century, as well as the heated conversations orbiting the conventions of the novel and its relationship to past models—questions that *The Dunciad*, the "Elegy," and *Clarissa* all explore in their respective texts about their unique genres. *Clarissa*, published at mid-century, is positioned well to incorporate and comment on many disparate theories of the novel as a legitimate form of literature. As Margaret Doody writes, "The Richardsonian novel, observing at once the tempo of outer life and the flux of inner consciousness, begins a new tradition in English and Continental fiction."[8] Brean Hammond and J. Paul Hunter both point out that mid-century novel writers did not always consider that they engaged with a new form of genre, with the exception of Richardson and Fielding, who "actually *knew* that it was novels they were writing and began to theorize consciously about the process."[9] This theorization marks the 1740s as a period of crucial development for the novel as a genre. *Clarissa* offers the illusion of historical reality in its profession to be "A *History of a Young Lady*," seeking to authenticate itself through association with verifiable, historical writing. At the same time, it also hearkens to Restoration amatory plots of scandal and erotic temptation. Moreover, *Clarissa* anticipates end-of-the-century emphases on the fictive interiority of characters, characters who seem "real" because they possess a complex moral and ethical code and who edify through sentiment rather than wholly exemplary feats.

Richardson is cognizant of the novel's status as *novel*, as a new form of prose under scrutiny to prove itself as a valid form of literature. Just as the speakers in *The Dunciad* and the "Elegy," as well as Clarissa herself, deliberate the modes of self-representation most adequate, so too does Richardson in his novel. As Hunter intimates, "The contemporary recognition" of Richardson's "achievement[s] provided perhaps the firmest sense in the 1740s that something new had happened."[10] Although, together with Fielding, Richardson's work "became a kind of double-barreled answer to the literary and moral objections raised by the Augustans against innovation and novelty," we can see that *Clarissa* profoundly joins Pope's verse satire and Gray's pastoral elegy as immersed in historical inquiry.[11]

Lennox's 1752 novel *The Female Quixote; or, The Adventures of Arabella* might seem a more obvious choice for study in this book. After all, Lennox's novel famously tampers with the relevancy of amatory romances to the historical realities of contemporary England. However, Lennox's novel lacks *Clarissa*'s epistolary style, the form that specifically enables Richardson's introspection into history and genre. Other novels like Fielding's *The History of Tom Jones, Foundling* (1749) or Sarah Fielding's *The Adventures of David Simple* (1744) likewise maintain their focus on the linear journeys of their named protagonists. After a series of comical mishaps, both Tom Jones and David Simple end up with their birthrights, perpetuating stability into the future. As with Arabella, these characters realize their mistakes, move on from them, and ultimately become moral citizens. Laurence Sterne's 1760 *The Life and Opinions of Tristram Shandy, Gentleman* stands out from Richardson's milieu as a text that is also interested in the interweave of historical time similar to *The Dunciad*, the "Elegy," and *Clarissa*. In its iteration of the various stories connected to the birth of Tristram, it enacts the problems of linear chronology and originating events. Its persistent digressions provide a version of the cacophony Richardson performs in his epistolary novel, but the first-person narration firmly marks Sterne's text as *Tristram's* story, albeit challenging the insularity of the exemplar.

The didactic function of Richardson's contemporaries reinscribes continuity and causal effect in ways that Richardson denies, thereby separating his vision of English nationhood from them. In *Clarissa*, Richardson purposefully refuses his readers the happy ending many sought, turning away from linear recompense as a valid literary representation of English life and people. *Clarissa* unrelentingly insists on the historical realities of Richardson's England: the legal and political power of the great white male, the abuse suffered by women, and the enshrinement of vice by those supposedly responsible for English moral and civic virtue (such as lawyers and those destined for the House of Lords). In *Clarissa*, Richardson intentionally destroys the affable and redeemed England he had constructed in his 1740 *Pamela; or, Virtue Rewarded*, shattering his earlier depiction of a jocund, fertile nation able to thwart expectations of social class and birth. *Clarissa* invalidates *Pamela* as an authentic representation of historical time and national identity, reminding us that "while the 1730s had ended in financial success [for Richardson], the story of Richardson's emotional life is harsher and sadder. Richardson had experienced great sorrow" by the death of eleven people in two years and "his health had been settled into a lifelong malady."[12] We often think of Pope as the champion of his own disabilities, but the Parkinson's disease that afflicted Richardson from the mid-1730s until his stroke in 1761 certainly complicated his successes.

In turning to novel writing as a second career, Richardson seems to be conforming to his public persona as a careful, cautious thinker, willing to ingratiate himself into a wide range of discourse so that he may assist in building and ensuring English morality.[13] His general investment in judgment, sober living, hard work, diligence, and acknowledgment of one's limitations points to his knowledge of the world. As the breadth of Richardson's lively personal correspondence demonstrates, his acquaintances were vast and he was implored by many, of differing ranks and stations, for advice on an assortment of topics. Yet Doody asks us to consider that lingering behind Richardson's literary creations is the traumatic losses he endured. Writing specifically of Richardson's 1733 *The Apprentice's Vade Mecum*, Doody states, "Amplifying his earlier letter of advice" to his deceased nephew, who had been his apprentice for two years prior to his death, "into a booklet for the benefit of numerous young men seems to have been Richardson's way of dealing with his loss" of a person potentially viewed as his substitute son. "In his instructional work," Doody writes, "he could make rational and assert control over a harsh world. He could act as a father, giving advice to young men who would themselves rise to the position of master. Richardson is not really addressing inferiors, but passing along social, moral, and practical wisdom to his own kind."[14] Regarded as the "first of Richardson's known compositions," the *Vade Mecum* not only serves as a guidebook for aspiring apprentices, providing essential practical knowledge, but it also discourses on the larger tenets of Christian philosophy in opposition to skepticism, potentially a means for Richardson to work through the lingering pain associated with the death of his first wife, all six of their children, and his fifteen-year-old nephew.[15]

The publication of Richardson's 1741 *Letters Written to and for Particular Friends* (often referred to as the *Familiar Letters*) continues to confirm his persona as moral guide. In this epistolary collection, he offers his advice, assisting others with decisions regarding the formation of their characters, their livelihoods, and ultimately their happiness. He uses the preface to the collection to advocate for a reading of the letters as didactic, interested more in the "judgment" it gives than in its imaginative prowess.[16] He writes that the aim of his collection is "to inculcate the Principles of *Virtue* and *Benevolence;* to describe *properly,* and recommend *strongly,* the SOCIAL and RELATIVE DUTIES; and to place them in such *practical* Lights, that the Letters may serve for Rules to THINK and ACT by, as well as Forms to WRITE after."[17] The curated collection includes letters written with practical purposes, such as to suggest possible professions or to warn against the allure of gaming and clubs, but others read almost like an epistolary novel itself, following the courtship of individuals, or giving insight into domestic life (such as the frequency with which a sister should remain in communication with her brother or how to apologize for disrespect against parents). The variety of these letters show Richardson's vast knowledge of the world, from maids and servants to merchants and tradesmen, lawyers, chaplains, and physicians, as well as the gentry and lower aristocracy, both in the Town and in the country. In letter 62, for instance, we find the beginnings of a *Clarissa*-like snare, the potential entrapment of a young lady just arrived in London by a procuress.

Richardson declares in his title to this collection that these are *familiar* letters written on *important* occasions—a curious descriptive pairing if we consider it as rendering the familial, the common, and the personal as inherently important. In this way, he inserts into historical record those issues that are not "important" along exemplary lines, but that Richardson deems as fundamental, needing to be widely circulated via the printing advancements of his trade. Moreover, he views this collection as serving an instructive purpose for an anonymous reading public, unconnected to the people narrated, as intimated by one of the last letters in the collection. Letter 173 demonstrates that Richardson intended for the ideas in his letters to be replicated by the reading audience. Although the subtitle of the letter states that this letter is "To a Widow on the Death of Her Husband," Richardson notes below that "With Small Variations, the Same Arguments May Be Used to a Husband on the Death of His Wife, and on Other Melancholy Occasions of the Like Nature."[18] As Doody notes, "Such compilations of sample letters had been common since the Renaissance" and would have been seen by Richardson to be an "unpretentious project."[19]

These *Familiar Letters* form a crucial backdrop to our reading of *Clarissa* because they indicate, not only his awareness of a diverse reading audience but also the constructed nature of Richardson's persona and his hyperawareness of crafting his legacy, on par with Pope's aspirations of gentlemanly status at Twickenham and Gray's visits to his landed friends. Richardson would, of course, be eager to cultivate such a benevolent, worldly, well-informed persona because it could only increase the attractiveness of his own printing business and legitimize his own literary productions, securing him from the tyranny of the booksellers. As letter 173 intimates, Richardson's fame rested on his ability to convince others that the epistle—specifically, *his* epistles—are a form of education. Richardson's collection suggests that there is proper advice to be given on any occasion, a formula that can be followed by the general public. In this reading, Richardson emerges as an exemplary individual because he is a storehouse of useful advice and practical knowledge.

However, perhaps we can read Richardson's confidence more cautiously, as troubled by Richardson's own doubts orbiting the malleability of the epistolary form. As *Clarissa* performs, the problem of origins emerges from a project such as the *Letters*. Does an epistle that borrows the sentiments of Richardson convey the same sincerity and integrity as an original epistle, one that does not rely on Richardson's ideas? How does this impact our understanding of compensatory gestures of repair? Doesn't the replicated epistle, forged from the formula Richardson provides, contain the traces of its predecessor, multiple voices impressed into it, thereby linking the past, present, and future in ominous ways?[20]

By embracing the role of the genre's foremost exemplar, "the progenitor of the English epistolary novel," Richardson suggests that the epistle can indeed perform its moral-didactic work, with *Clarissa* serving as the culminating example.[21] Reading Richardson alongside of Pope and Gray, though, introduces the enticing possibility that Richardson questions the efficacy of the epistle as an adequate mode of representation as well as suggests that he is not the transparent exemplar his canonical status might indicate. After all, as James Bracken and Joel Silver note, Richardson gave few details of his early life, and we have extremely limited knowledge of his activities during his twenties, the period his biographers refer to as his "lost years."[22] Pope and Gray both deliberate whether their genres, verse satire or pastoral elegy, can live up to their pretensions when confronted by the historical realities of eighteenth-century England—even though they are predominantly responsible for securing their genre's conventional status. Similarly, Richardson struggles to believe that the epistle can perform the moral-didactic purpose behind his literary attempts. Consider that this is a man who knowingly published anti-government tracts early in his printing career, who refused a paid position at court offered by his friend in the House of Commons, who omitted 266 fables in his revised version of Sir Roger L'Estrange's 1692 edition of *Aesop's Fables* (because he felt they did not convey a proper moral), and who published, without much success, the "laborious and exacting" collection of *The Negotiations of Sir Thomas Rowe* (1740), seventeenth-century British ambassador (because they contained useful moral and national lessons).[23] This brief biographical sketch emphasizes Richardson's own moral fortitude, even when faced with potential negative financial repercussions. This certitude, though, cannot resist the prowess of his literary imagination; the genre indelibly grafted to Richardson's legacy, the epistolary novel, performs moral *un*certainty.

After all, the multivocal method, what Hunter terms "the epistolary totality of shared circumstances," shapes our reading of Richardson's *Familiar Letters*, as well as *Clarissa*, framing the knowledge that we receive as well as the information circulated amongst the individuals.[24] Clarissa does not simply use the epistle as the means of exploring her status as a historical agent, capable of enacting and witnessing historical change. Richardson, like Pope and Gray, explores the efficacy and authenticity of historical knowledge if that knowledge is disseminated through genre. Richardson challenges the assumption of immediacy inherent to the epistle (does a letter represent unedited, visceral response?), foregrounds the problem of delivery (what if a letter is intercepted by someone other than the addressee?), and undermines words as a stable system of communication (can recipients of letters misapply the meaning of the written words, attributing ulterior motives to them?). Clarissa's search for historical knowledge is tampered with by other individuals in the novel who equally want to craft the narrative in their favor. Rather than a coherent story, *Clarissa* represents a collection of competing voices maneuvering for linguistic space, upsetting a chronological telling of history and potentially alienating Richardson from the genre that connects so ardently to his persona.

The performance of this multivocality is essential for troubling Clarissa as exemplar and for the dissemination of Clarissa's story. Scholars since Ian Watt have debated the function of novel characters as either artificial or abstract forms versus realistic, psychologically developed people, the distinction between categories of social type and emotionally discrete individuals. I suggest that *Clarissa* offers a unique depiction of and comment on the power of the literary imagination to offer, using prose, the complexities of human interconnectedness. Its multivocality in epistolary form enables Richardson to mimic the problems Clarissa faces in the text. *Clarissa* is not the history of Clarissa's epic struggle with

Lovelace only, as Pamela's is against Mr. B, despite the menacing presence of Mrs. Jewkes. Lovelace, in a letter to Belford after reading of Clarissa's death, aptly writes, "The whole world is but one great Bedlam" (letter 497, 1384). Indeed, the qualities of "Bedlam," the apparent disarray of voices and intentions, the often unjust and painful imprisonment of the disenfranchised and unwell, haunt the epistolary genre, forming the problem of historical inquiry in *Clarissa*.[25]

Clarissa's Epistles: Active Interiority

Early in the novel, multiple individuals comment on Clarissa's uncommon "knack," as her brother, James, states, for "letter-writing" (letter 33, 161). Many characters in the novel script letters, but Clarissa's stand apart, evidence of her status as an exemplary individual. Clarissa's intellectual prowess and discursive abilities substantiate her exemplary status. Natalie Roxburgh suggests that Clarissa's epistolary power manifests from the way she uses letter writing as the means to account for her behavior, values, and virtue: "Her writing is a contract to herself, serving a regulatory function" in a way not existent for the other letter writers in the novel.[26] While this is true, Clarissa's letters also demand that other characters account for themselves as well, aligning her with the great Homeric orators of antiquity. Her letters enrapture her audience, motivating them to action and eliciting a variety of emotional responses.

The impact of Clarissa's incessant writing on those around her marks her as exemplary because her writing generates deep emotional investment from her readers in ways that other letter writers do not. In letter 80, Clarissa's mother advises her to read rather than to write, since reading would cast Clarissa as the passive recipient of knowledge, teaching Clarissa her proper "duty." Writing, in contrast, allows Clarissa an active role in events, serving as a call to action for other characters, involving a didactic edge that often incites fear in her recipients. Clarissa's sister, Bella, disparagingly calls Clarissa "a ready penwoman!" (197) in letter 42, a description that hints at the latent energy contained in Clarissa's pen. Bella's words depict Clarissa as a warrior, in complete control of her wartime strategy: Clarissa remains "ready" to do battle, using her pen as other exemplars might wield a sword, restraining her ferocity until the right moment. Like any highly skilled warrior, Clarissa responds quickly to her family's movements; indeed, her relatives often express their surprise at how fast she can write an answer to the letters they send up to her. Clarissa's effect on those around her may be inadvertent, unlike the oratory purposes of Achilles or Odysseus, but nonetheless her words motivate the action of the other characters and the novel. Such speed points to Clarissa's intelligence and wit, while also verifying her as the exemplar of the epistolary genre.

In the scenes leading up to her escape from Harlowe Place, Clarissa's epistolary correspondence with Lovelace also showcases her cleverness, as she proves herself more than capable of engaging in a linguistic battle of wits with him. Although female, Clarissa possesses a strength of articulation equal to that of Lovelace. Such a feat is worthy of praise, as "the desire to control others through language is Lovelace's ruling passion."[27] Indeed, part of Lovelace's attraction to Clarissa arises from her refusal to falter under his masterful epistolary machinations. Clarissa's slightly bantering tone to Anna in letter 22 reveals her own wit in combating Lovelace's attempts to draw her out of Harlowe Place. Letter 22 is the first instance in the novel when Lovelace's actual words to Clarissa are quoted; prior to this, Lovelace is paraphrased, such as by Anna and Mrs. Fortescue in letter 12. In letter 22, Lovelace, after describing Solmes boasting of his upcoming marriage to Clarissa, again offers Clarissa marriage and the protection of his family, primarily that of Lord M. Clarissa's interpretation of his offer reveals her distaste for his assumption that their clandestine correspondence indicates a greater intimacy than she has desired: "Really, my dear, were you to see his letter, you would think I had given him great encouragement and were in direct treaty with him; or that he were sure that my friends would drive me into a foreign protection; for he has the boldness to offer, in my Lord's name, an asylum to me should I be tyrannically treated in Solmes's behalf" (117). Clarissa recognizes Lovelace's scheming nature early on in the novel. Here, she laughs to Anna about his presumptuous offer, but the fact that she can discern his arrogance marks Clarissa as possessing an exemplary intelligence, not just exemplary virtue or beauty, capable of seeing beyond Lovelace's personal charms: his handsome physique, the honor of his family name, and his wealth and connections—all evidence of his own elite, exemplary status. Rather than trusting him *because* of the trappings of elitism that he bears, Clarissa (like Pope and Gray) wonders if those trappings conceal less than virtuous qualities.

Clarissa's use of political terms in letter 22, such as "treaty," "foreign protection," and "tyrannically," elevates her predicament beyond the private and feminine, casting her domestic dilemma in terms usually associated with exemplary strife: warfare, imperialism, and monarchical rule—much like Pope does in his *Elegy*, with his own invocation of the "foreign" as a critique of the nation, discussed at the end of chapter 2. Clarissa gestures to an exemplary lineage, framing her situation using the same terms as traditional sources of historical knowledge would provide. Her relationship with Lovelace, then, becomes equivalent to an exemplary feat or heroic journey of self-discovery and testing of the exemplar's moral strength. By conceiving her familial and marital struggles along exemplary lines, Clarissa indicates her nonacceptance of the rigid boundaries between public and private, as well as intimates that domestic circumstances implicate national identity. Clarissa writes her struggles as if they were public events, such as the signing of a treaty or the declaration of war. The problem with this, for Clarissa's family members, rests on how this strategy makes her personal history accessible to those outside of her immediate family. Public, occasional history writing invites a mass audience to read, reflect, and critique. The Harlowes endeavor to keep their domestic disputes in the confines of Harlowe Place, but Clarissa's attitude toward writing threatens to allow the public to gaze at (and perhaps condemn) their actions. The Harlowes, one could imagine, fear becoming the members of the household Pope derides in his *Elegy*, with the public gathered outside their gate, jeering and calling out opprobrious names, because of their treatment of the virtuous lady.

In making visible the failings of her family, Clarissa brings into the public record private family disputes and the private traits of each family member, those "secret histories" mentioned in chapter 1. As Castle points out, "In the early parts of *Clarissa* there is much to suggest that the grotesque resentment of the heroine which surfaces among her relations is as much as anything a fear and envy of her remarkable power of articulation. (What they really fear, of course, is the 'construction,' couched in language, which she might make of their own invidious actions.)"[28] Jennifer Wilson concurs with this observation, noting that, "at this stage in the conflict, no one wants to correspond with Clarissa or even see her. Her father, the authority who supposedly presides over her trial, angrily avoids his daughter; her mother, aunt, and uncles shun her as well because they know that they will be made into fools by her rapier wit."[29] Clarissa also meditates on the public exposure possible from her private narration, writing, with a voice that quickly shifts from first to third person, "But whither roves my pen? How dare a perverse girl take these liberties with relations so very respectable and whom she highly respects?—What an unhappy situation is that which obliges her, in her *own defence* as it were, to expose *their* failings?" (letter 13, 82). Curiously, we see the Harlowe family—and Clarissa herself—fearing Clarissa-as-Pope: writing with the intention of exposing ridicule and vanity in supposed authority figures.

Scholarship tends to regard the radical element of Clarissa's epistles as her refusal to acquiesce to either Solmes or Lovelace and the differing patriarchal constraints they represent. Katherine Binhammer, for instance, emphasizes Clarissa's ability to imagine an alternative place for women, outside of the gender-defined roles of wife or whore.[30] I will add that, in rethinking the gender-defined spaces of public and private, Clarissa reimagines the principles of exclusion typically involved in historical knowledge.[31] Like the novel itself, which represents the domestic publicly, Clarissa's desire, expressed through her epistles, to envision an alternative outcome for her dilemmas reinvents the assumptions inherent to exemplar writing in particular, the topics, individuals, and problems seen as historical issues. Clarissa's family feels threatened by Clarissa's writing because she, in their opinion, *mis*uses the epistle: approaching letter writing as if it were narrating the lives and deeds of an exemplary figure, rather than the defiance of a gentlewoman.

Clarissa proves herself quite capable of emulating the oratory prowess of standard exemplars, but part of her epistolary strategy involves the use of silence. Unlike her epistolary foe, Lovelace, whose loquaciousness Clarissa sometimes bemoans, Clarissa knowingly refrains from speech at purposeful moments. This silence, like her active writing, motivates those around her to action, prompting conversation and decision-making even when she herself remains discursively quiet. Kathryn Steele identifies this "pattern of deliberate diffidence" as evidence of Clarissa's clever manipulation of her family.[32] Steele notes the dual function of silence for Clarissa: "By remaining silent, Clarissa resists being read by others, and simultaneously, by remaining silent she persists as a model of femininity and filial piety."[33] Clarissa's reticence to argue directly with her father and her anguish over leaving her father's household points to her extreme virtue *and* acts as form of resistance, often leading others to misinterpret her silence.

Although Steele successfully argues that Clarissa's reliance on silence ultimately signals her desire for communion with God, I posit that Clarissa's silence serves as a further way that Clarissa reimagines her relationship with historical inquiry. Clarissa's refusal to write suspends her physical action, much like a warrior who withholds using his sword. Usually, we associate the exemplar with action, physical movement, and busy activity rather than extended periods of contemplation aimed at moral purity. The purpose of the exemplar in traditional exemplary accounts is to act, to perform a series of deeds that manifest change and that mark him as beacons of either virtue or vice. Yet Clarissa transforms her inaction into a profound reinvention of exemplary visibility. Rather than heroic action marking the exemplar as visible to historical discourse, Richardson locates action in areas outside of typical exemplary feats. As discussed in chapter 2, Gray, with his image of the "heaving" graves, undermines the notion of silence as devoid of articulation; similarly, Richardson offers Clarissa's silence as an alternative, less obvious, means of generating movement and precipitating action. For both writers, silence does not reference vacuous space but is teeming with energy and potential.

Although silence opens her behavior up to misinterpretation by others, as does her refusal to adhere to typical codes of feminine behavior, her epistles speak for the purity of her intentions. Her silence pulsates with meaning, performing certain moral-didactic work, even if her family cannot recognize this. When her mother demands to know if Clarissa's affections are engaged to Lovelace, Clarissa chooses to remain silent because, as she transcribes to Anna, "I knew what the inference would be, if I had said they were not" (letter 16, 90). Fearing they will infer that Clarissa has compromised herself without securing an engagement with Lovelace, Clarissa refuses to speak. Although knowing her family will view her silence as inaction and as a blatant disrespect for their authority, Clarissa prioritizes moral clarity, not overt action. Her family may cast her silence as petulance or as immaturity, as Clarissa performing an epistolary tantrum, but Clarissa views her silence as a fertile means of protest, actively resisting the inferences her words might inspire in the minds of her family. Doing so allows Clarissa to remain a benchmark for moral authority while she subverts eighteenth-century patriarchal expectations: disobeying her family by rejecting Solmes and by escaping with Lovelace.

If the epistle acts as Clarissa's historical register of events, then it is important to note that it is Clarissa as writer (bracketing the fact that "Clarissa" is a narrative construct of Richardson) who conceives her own self as silent within her letters. Clarissa chooses to mention—to make visible—her silence. Silence becomes a form of action that counters assumptions about the type of behavior exhibited by exemplary figures. Clarissa spends most of her time writing—a solitary, contemplative activity, isolated from others, removed from the nexus of power (i.e., the councils her family holds to determine their behavior toward her). Her physical action ceases so that she may meditate and compose. In letter 94, Clarissa writes that she wrote "down to the last hour" (372), meaning, she stopped participating in the events unfolding so that she might record, isolated and removed from the scene of action, everything that occurred since she started writing one hour ago.

In *Clarissa*, the history recorded focuses not so much on action performed by the individual narrated, or on change an exemplar's actions generates, but on the development of that figure's inner consciousness. Although Roxburgh claims that the epistolary form "seems disinterested in part because the writer has no time to manipulate the truth," the time gap between the event and the recording of that event naturally allows for reflection and filtration, halting the forward movement of plot.[34] The illusion of immediacy embedded in the epistolary style disrupts typical ceremonial commemoration, as it allows the writer time to reflect on—and perhaps edit—the action that occurred. While Clarissa retells the events and conversations she has participated in verbatim, her act of letter writing is constructed at a distance from the actual occurrence. The first-person narrative method of "writing to the moment" suggests a subjectivity and "psychological interiority" of "a new secular and modern subject" who is unsure of her own desires and thus utilizes the epistolary space to gain inner knowledge.[35] Richardson constructs an exemplar who needs to learn how to be an exemplar and how to record her history (like Gray's speaker in the "Elegy"). Part of Clarissa's exemplary nature comes from her insecurity and incertitude; unlike traditional exemplars who are confident in their strengths and cognizant of their failings, Clarissa must learn about herself if she is to overcome the pain inflicted on her by Lovelace and her family.

Although Clarissa's intentions are to use her epistles to affirm her virtuous motivations, she, like the other members of her family and Lovelace, exploits the form in order to protect herself and to secure the scripting of her narrative according to her desires.[36] Indeed, Clarissa often utilizes her epistle as the means of *interrupting* the narrative that she is scripting. Writing to Anna in letter 98, Clarissa states, "And here I got two hours to myself; which I told him [Lovelace] I should pass in writing another letter to you (meaning my narrative)" (395). Clarissa considers her letter to Anna as a break from the chronological progression of narrative events, "two hours" to reflect upon and select which events (already occurred) she will transcribe to Anna (and thus to the historical record). She interrupts the action typically required of an exemplar in order to meditate. Binhammer points out that Clarissa chooses to write approximately twenty-one thousand words in two days about her encounter with her mother in letter 16. This surprising figure demonstrates the highly self-reflective nature of Clarissa's meditations that are as crucial to the history of *Clarissa* as are her interactions with Lovelace.

Clarissa's letter writing acts as substitute for face-to-face conversations with her family. At the beginning of the novel, this epistolary exchange offers a form of recompense: a crime has been committed (Clarissa's breach with her family), a pain is endured (Clarissa's removal from her family), and a gesture of repair is offered (Clarissa's willingness to sign over ownership of the dairyhouse). The trajectory of these events follows the linearity inherent to a legal reading of recompense, and indeed the Harlowes view Clarissa's refusal to marry Solmes as a crime against the family for which she must be imprisoned in her bedroom. However, the epistolary exchange that occurs showcases Clarissa's refusal to submit to the punishment ordained by her family. Although desperate to maintain their affections and convince them of her virtue, Clarissa will not marry Solmes. Clarissa privileges her private emotive and sexual desires over the commands of those legally responsible for her person. Compensatory gestures of repair, then, are more complicated than tort law might suggest when individuals involved prioritize the integrity of their own consciousness over that of the collective group.

Clarissa suspects the possibility of a disjunction between what her private history relates and what her public image shows, suggesting the inadequacy of the process of recompense she is involved in as well as the genre she uses to secure that recompense. She fears that her letters can never excuse her from censure: "I have no doubt that I am the talk, and perhaps the byword of half the county. If so, I am afraid I can now do nothing that will give me more disgrace than I have already causelessly received by their indiscreet persecutions: and let me be whose I will, and do what I will, I shall never wipe off the stain my confinement and the rigorous usage I have received have fixed upon me; at least in my own opinion" (letter 85, 349). Her trepidation acknowledges the didactic quality of her narrative, but, unlike typical exemplars, Clarissa questions herself as a model of instruction. In response, Anna provides the novel's first detailed depiction of Clarissa's life before her relationship with Lovelace: "You were immensely happy, above the happiness of a mortal creature, before you knew him. Everybody worshipped you" (letter 177, 578). She depicts the Harlowe family as deferring to Clarissa's opinions and tastes in all things, stating that everyone "looked upon you as one set aloft to be admired and imitated" (579). Clarissa's cousin, Dolly, repeats the words her own mother used to characterize Clarissa, describing her as "the flower and ornament of their family" (letter 78, 308). Because the novel begins after the turmoil in the household has already started, we do not get a glimpse at the tranquility that Anna and Dolly describe.

By constructing Clarissa in this way, Richardson draws on exemplar narratives, positioning Clarissa as a historical subject worthy of being "imitated." Tellingly, though, Richardson imagines Clarissa as able to subvert hierarchy, albeit unself-consciously, proving her exemplary status since she is a woman in a patriarchal society. Not only did elders defer to her opinion before she met Lovelace but her grandfather also overlooked standard inheritors in order to will Clarissa a small estate. These points illustrate just how far Clarissa has fallen—although her virginity is intact. In this way, *Clarissa* manipulates the conventions of amatory fiction preceding it by dislodging notions of the fallen female from a purely sexual context and transporting it into the realm of interiority. In so doing, the novel charts the movement inward of historical visibility, away from external determinants of exemplary status and toward a conception of history writing as focusing on the subjective consciousness.

Moreover, this transition inward suggests the inadequacy of traditional renderings of recompense because of the complex, and often unstable, emotive and philosophical energies structuring human action. Clarissa finds it difficult to move past the wound her family inflicts on her, just as her family finds it impossible to forgive her. Reconciliation involves the integration of the injury into the respective ontologies in order to make themselves legible again; neither Clarissa nor the Harlowes can do this. Painfully aware of herself as historical subject, Clarissa reviews the pattern of her self-representation within the epistles she has scripted to ensure that this history maintains the moral integrity for which she is celebrated. She also reveals moments when mental clarity escapes her, when her intelligence and wit fail to convey her thoughts: "What to do, I know not. The more I think, the more I am embarrassed!" (letter 88, 358). Clarissa reveals to Anna that her uncertainty as to "what I *ought* to do" (letter 82, 332) frightens her, more so than the physical actions she has performed. Clarissa is burdened not by what she has overtly accomplished, but by the moral repercussions of those actions and how that morality links to her identity as a gentlewoman. Clarissa's insecurity, her recognition that she does *not* possess moral certitude, informs her exploration of the various modes of self-representation available. Quite literally, she has consistently been true to her *word*, since it has been through a written genre that she has maintained, demonstrated, and reported her virtue. At the beginning of the novel, she maintains her secret correspondence with Lovelace despite the wishes of her family, one reason being because she is reluctant to break her word with him (both in the sense of promise and written word) until she is satisfied it will remove him from her life.

Such adherence to genre makes Clarissa's refusal to see Lovelace on the morning after the fire, much later in letter 226, striking. Clarissa promises Lovelace that if he leaves her room she will forgive him for the liberties he took with her and will see him in the morning "as if nothing had passed" (727). Lovelace eagerly anticipates their meeting and imagines her "all sweetly blushing and confounded" (728). However, Clarissa informs him that she will not see him for at least one week, despite swearing "upon her honour" (727). Lovelace clearly understands that her motive lies in postponing a union with him, but her blatant disregard for her promise puzzles him. He states: "But what vexes me of all things is that such an excellent creature should break her word—Fie, fie, upon her!—but nobody is absolutely perfect!" (731). Lovelace is truly perplexed by her action, as it is certainly not in keeping with her previous behavior. Although it is true that Clarissa's decision could indicate her desire to take over the role of plotting in the novel, I posit that Clarissa's decision pointedly challenges traditional narrative renderings of exemplary figures, where the didactic hero possesses no moral ambiguity. Clarissa's "change of heart" reveals, instead, a character lacking moral certainty, unsure of the virtuous course of action.

Clarissa's behavior in letter 226 suggests that Clarissa's exemplary status derives from her ability to assess and subsequently alter her behavior when she finds it in violation of the didactic qualities she envisions her historical record as transmitting. This letter illustrates that something written in a previous letter could be ignored or overruled by a later decision. Epistles appear to exist individually, rather than as a coherent narrative that progresses, in linear fashion, toward an end. Clarissa may not treat her decision lightly, but nevertheless her actions imply that promises recorded in an epistle are not necessarily binding, able to be utilized and discarded at will. Clarissa is unsure how to use her knowledge of the past to script the present moment and her futurity, generating her uncertainty. Typically, the exemplar possesses no moral ambiguity, or even a complex private, inner life substantially explored by the text. In privileging intentionality, Richardson, like Pope and Gray, challenges the substance of historical recording, suggesting that inner (private) meditations hold historical value—perhaps more than outer (public) demonstrations of acquiescence, fortitude, compromise, or valor. The maid, Betty, points out, "Everybody takes notice, miss, that you can say very cutting words in a cool manner, and yet not call names, as I have known *some* gentlefolks, as well as others, do, when in a passion" (letter 63, 266), words that curiously echo Dryden's description of effective satire in *A Discourse Concerning the Original and Progress of Satire:* "To spare the grossness of the names, and to do the thing yet more severely, is to draw a full face."[37] Clarissa's writing may be so proficient as to conceal her true affections or intentions toward Lovelace and thus to deceive her family, further weakening their authority over her.

Clarissa's ambition to preserve the record of events through her epistles places her in a position of control that is uncomfortable for her family, who cannot approve of Clarissa possessing any agency outside of their authority, such as the property granted to her by her grandfather's will. Ultimately, this concern prompts them to remove all ink and paper from her bedroom. Significantly, Clarissa names this an "act of violence" (321), suggesting that the separation of herself from her correspondence involves a violation that is more painful than the physical abuse she has suffered downstairs at the hands of her brother and Solmes. Not only has the security of her physical space of confinement been eliminated but also her means of speech, pleading, and persuasion are eradicated. In silencing her writing, her family is attempting to silence Clarissa, taking away her means of action. Specifically, Richardson frames their action as an attack on *genre*, on Clarissa's access to the tools that will allow her to disseminate historical knowledge through epistolary writing. Alpers, discussed in the previous chapter, claims that "some sort of violence" is necessary for the promulgation of new literary forms.[38] Although Alpers writes with the pastoral directly in mind, we could apply his logic here to consider how violence initiates Clarissa's search for alternative modes of writing her narrative and performing historical inquiry. Her family's tactic to eliminate her epistolary writing eventually leaves Clarissa no other choice but to assume a more traditional role as exemplar: overtly performing action by escaping with Lovelace.

Like a heroic exemplar, Clarissa boldly decides to escape further familial persecution and imagine an alternative to the fate they had constructed for her; unlike such an exemplar, though, her daring and bravery propel her into more intense indecision rather than closer to heroic accomplishment. As Clarissa indicates in her letter informing Anna that she has run away with Lovelace, the emotive and meditative components of decision-making are of greater importance than the actual deed performed. Clarissa emphasizes her "self-accusation" and the moral component of her choice to leave Harlowe Place rather than the practical, material concerns she now encounters:

> They cannot, however, say worse of me than I will of myself. Self-accusation shall flow in every line of my narrative, where I think I am justly censurable. If any thing can arise from the account I am going to give you, for extenuation of my fault (for that is all a person can hope for, who cannot excuse herself), I know I may expect it from your friendship, though not from the charity of any other: since by this time I doubt not every mouth is opened against me; and all that know Clarissa Harlowe, condemn the fugitive daughter. (letter 94, 372)

Despite the fact that this is ostensibly the first time Clarissa has left the overt protection of her family, thrusting herself into the unknown, her thoughts betray her moral ambiguity rather than fear for her bodily comfort and safety. Either way, staying at home or escaping with Lovelace, Clarissa's options seem doomed to moral uncertainty.

This must seem curious to us, especially if we read Clarissa's moral ambiguity alongside of Richardson's own moral fortitude. As a text such as the *Vade Mecum* shows, Richardson believed in the universal ability, at least of young male apprentices, to follow certain standards of behavior. His earlier work implies that an individual does not need to be exemplary to attain a valuable reputation; indeed, the honest and sober character of an industrious tradesman should be the goal, rather than the lofty, heroic aspirations of exemplary figures. If we contrast this with Richardson's portrayal of Clarissa, we see Richardson as unsure of whether there exists a similar guidebook for women and for domestic circumstances, thereby troubling his own legacy as the caretaker of what Hammond terms "the responsible novel as written by Richardson."[39] Of course, by the time of *Clarissa*'s publication in the late 1740s, Richardson surprisingly resembles Pope at Twickenham: both men, upon earning a sizeable fortune, occupy a pseudogentlemanly retreat—Richardson leasing the North End estate. Perhaps the slight distance from the hands-on work of his trade allowed Richardson to trouble the moral certainty upon which his own reputation was built.

Conflicting Voices in Epistolary Writing

Richardson puts pressure on intentionality as integral to moral history, but Clarissa's words to Anna in letter 53 reveal the emotive quality to writing that could potentially trouble its didactic function: "If you think, my dear, that what I have related, did not again fire me, you will find yourself mistaken when you read at this place the enclosed copy of my letter to my brother, struck off while the iron was red hot" (226). Clarissa describes her writing as arising from her emotions, "while the iron was red hot," rather than as the result of calm assessment. The epistolary style of *Clarissa* presumably allows insight into a character's inner deliberations, but often these insights showcase rhetorical duplicity, linguistic wordplay, and intentional abuse of language—ultimately scripting an understanding of history as destabilized from any system of logic or rationality.

For *Clarissa*, the outcome of an event is less important than the emotive and meditative preliminaries, those unseen, closeted, private contemplations that traditionally remain invisible from public gaze. Yet Clarissa fears that even her closest friend, Anna, will misinterpret her actions, a fear that calls attention to the discrepancy between intention and action, and what Castle terms the "appalling physical malleability of the letter."[40] Castle writes, "Letters open themselves, promiscuously, to distortion by readers, who, out of naiveté or unscrupulousness, disregard the intended meaning of the letter writer. . . . We can compare actual letters with the fictional readers' interpretations. Characters show themselves (and Lovelace is a classic, disturbing example) reading according to whim alone. . . . Every reading thus becomes in some sense a misreading, in that it is an imposition on the text, and may or may not coincide with the writer's intended meaning."[41] Castle focuses on the way that the potential "distortions" arising from the reading of letters presents difficulties for the characters, primarily Clarissa, who takes the letters she receives at face value, assuming they represent authorial truth.

Clarissa's opponents are not just the characters themselves (i.e., the outward vestiges of historical visibility, the power they wield, the cultural prejudices they represent), but also their finesse with moral ambiguity, the degree to which they are conversant with manipulating what is visible and what is concealed, a dilemma that curiously mirrors chapter 1's definition of verse satire. Tom Keymer discusses "the assumption about epistolary self-revelation," the collision of artifice and intimacy upon which the epistolary method is built. Keymer questions whether it can "be assumed that a unitary and describable self is in place prior to its articulation in language, or that the relation between writing and the self is simply descriptive (rather than also constitutive)."[42] Clarissa reads the letters she receives as if they were indicative of an authentic self, not realizing that the letter could only be a performance of self, a version supplied in order to get the desired action rather than to be transparently honest. When considering Clarissa's brother, James, Wilson gestures toward this problem: "The text implies that if James can assume the false role of filial obedience within the close confines of his family who know him well, then all social identities might be performances and evade the control of traditional hierarchies."[43] Such upheaval does not allow "traditional hierarchies" of good and evil, honorable and dishonorable, to be transparently represented in historical knowledge, aligning *Clarissa* with Pope's and Gray's attacks on the traditionally great.

Clarissa is aware of the potential for alteration inherent to the epistolary form and she gestures toward the effect of the "physical malleability of the letter" on her historical record. In a letter to Anna, Clarissa writes, "I know not by what means several of [Lovelace's] machinations to ruin me were brought about; so that some material points of my sad Story must be defective if I were to sit down to write it" (letter 379, 1163). Earlier in the novel, before her departure from Harlowe Place, Clarissa complains to her uncle of the mishandling of her letters: "I find I am a very sad creature, and did not know it. I wrote not to my brother. To *you*, sir, I wrote. From *you* I hope the honour of an answer" (letter 61, 257). As the novel progresses and Clarissa's dilemmas escalate, Clarissa learns that a moral history is a much more fragile document than a standard history written to convey action and outcome.

Part of Clarissa's struggle across the novel involves learning how to be an epistolary player in her war with Lovelace and her family. Clarissa protects her letters as extensions of her virtue (both morally and physically), and as such regards them as evidence, even weapons, to be used in her self-defense: "On my aunt's and sister's report of my obstinacy, my assembled relations have taken an *unanimous* resolution (as Betty tells me it is) against me. This resolution you will find signified to me in the enclosed letter from my brother, just now brought me. Be pleased to return it, when perused. I may have occasion for it in the altercations between my relations and me" (letter 50, 217). Like the speaker of Gray's "Elegy," Clarissa worries that her moral intentionality cannot retain its integrity: "I fear, I very much fear that my unhappy situation will draw me in to be guilty of evasion, of little affectations and of curvings from the plain simple truth which I was wont to value myself upon" (letter 135, 484). Clarissa acknowledges that even the best of intentions can be manipulated by genre, human emotion, or unconscious guile.

Each character in *Clarissa* possesses intentions, often depicted as strategies for self-aggrandizement, that come into conflict and sometimes overlap with the intentions of other characters. The multiple-correspondent method of the epistolary form challenges the privileging of overt action and outcome as indisputable signs of virtue or vice, as well as the reliability of the historical knowledge conveyed. As disparate versions of events arise in *Clarissa*, a chronological development of plot falters, disrupting a sense of historical time. Castle explicates the result of this multivocal method:

> Clarissa's "Story" is what never really gets told in *Clarissa*; it is that text which is always interrupted, suspended, fragmented by the texts of others. That which we might at first assume to be her "Story"—the vast collection of letters, the fiction itself—is obviously no story in any conventional sense. Rather, it is a contradictory, roiling, multivocal system: more a concatenation of possible narratives told by different tellers, of whom the heroine is only one. The multiple-correspondent epistolary text is not a simple discourse—never, as Richardson himself held it to be, the transparent "History of a Young Lady," but a congeries, a cluster of disparate discourses.[44]

The novel's showcasing of various epistolary voices ultimately, for Castle, distances the reader from truly apprehending the "Story" that Clarissa seeks to write.

However, *Clarissa* is not interested in a linear accounting of a sequence of events, where an exemplar battles a foe and enacts change, or in a linear trajectory of recompense with an easy assignation of guilt and innocence, but in the way that linearity unfolds as a result of much inner, moral turmoil. Rather than portraying them as one-dimensional beacons of either virtue or vice, Richardson purposefully constructs both Clarissa and Lovelace with a nuanced moral code that speaks to their psychological and emotional complexity, positioning them as more intricate characters than simply the damsel in distress and rake. For instance, Lovelace increasingly uses his letters to insist on the "correctness" of his intentions with Clarissa. Letter 31 justifies his actions toward her based on the material circumstances she finds herself in with her family: "And she, withstanding them all, is actually confined and otherwise maltreated by a father the most gloomy and positive; at the instigation of a brother the most arrogant and selfish" (142). Lovelace emphasizes himself as rescuer rather than as seducer. He showcases the discrepancy between his outward action (saving Clarissa from a tyrannical family) and his inner intention (enticing Clarissa away from her family so that he may fulfill his desires for her). While Lovelace's intentions cannot completely "purify" his deeds, Richardson nonetheless scripts them into his narrative, granting them space alongside Lovelace's public maneuvers in *Clarissa*.

Richardson's earlier work, *Pamela*, might seem a stronger choice for inclusion in this book. After all, in *Pamela*, Richardson grants a maidservant titular status, endowing her with traits usually associated with exemplars: chastity, honesty, cleverness, and beauty. Her consistent virtue, despite the sexual advances and worldly temptations of Mr. B, assist her in developing as a character over the course of the novel, so that when she finally accepts the role of Mr. B's wife, we feel that she bestows greater integrity on the position than it has possessed before. Certainly, *Pamela* depends on the trajectory of linear recompense in its constitution of Pamela's responses to Mr. B. The novel must convince readers that Mr. B has reformed, and that Pamela, a low-born maid, is worthy to transcend social restrictions through marriage. Eighteenth-century readers generally applauded the "virtue rewarded" plot of *Pamela*, generating the penning of Richardson's sequel to it, but, as Fielding's *Shamela* (1741) indicates, many doubted the sincerity of Pamela's humility and scoffed at the novel's disruption of traditional class barriers. Richardson may have heeded, perhaps unconsciously, Fielding's attack as he wrote *Clarissa*, where Clarissa refuses the recompense Pamela embraces in her marriage.

Moreover, although *Pamela* also uses the epistolary form, it lacks the problems arising from a multivocal method. The novel's actions are primarily recounted through Pamela's epistles to her parents, with a few others scattered throughout. The single self-centered voice of *Pamela* directs the novel and provides "an utterly uncomplicated view of the relation between self and text."[45] Pamela's letters aim to support her claim to virtue, under attack by the lustful Mr. B, despite the misgivings of other characters (and readers of the novel itself) who evaluate and scrutinize her actions. Castle iterates the basic structural distinction operating in *Pamela* and *Clarissa*; in *Pamela*,

> the letters of a single character (usually the heroine) tend to dominate the sequence [so that it] comes to resemble that of simple

first-person narrative.... When the letter upon letter follows with the "X—in continuation" heading and the replies are omitted, the reader's impulse is to read the letters as a continuous narrative, disregarding the breaks between them. To the degree that it approximates in this way a first-person memoir, the single-correspondent epistolary novel makes a far more successful vehicle for ideological statement than does the multiple-correspondence type. The dominant correspondent seems to speak with a special privilege and insistence—so much so that we tend almost invariably to identify his or her views with the real author's.[46]

By centering the novel in Pamela's epistolary voice, Richardson encourages readers to accept Pamela's statements of her intentions as genuine; he allows Pamela's motivations to prove productive of the narrative. Pamela explores what it means to control and disseminate the epistle, and thus the record of her thoughts and actions, such as when she attaches her letters to her body to prevent their falling into Mr. B's hands, an act that attempts to fuse the narrative with the narrator. The letters that she receives from others, such as Mr. B, are copied by her and included as part of her narration, so that they seem to continue her voice rather than assert their own. Again, it is curious to note that *Shamela* performs its critique of *Pamela* through its use of multiple correspondents, including Parson Oliver, Shamela's mother, and Mrs. Jervis.

In *Clarissa*, though, it is precisely the befuddling of intelligibility that interests Richardson and that generates the novel's historical inquiry. When Clarissa despairs over the mishandling of her letter to her uncle ("I wrote not to my brother. To *you*, sir, I wrote"), she laments the network of foes operating against her. Rather than a single enemy, such as Mr. B, Clarissa faces a whole score of individuals who manipulate the discrepancy between visible, declared action and concealed, inner desire.

The Problem of Naming in History Writing

Coupled with the instability of intention as presented by the epistle is *Clarissa*'s complication of naming. As discussed in chapter 1, Pope fundamentally disagrees with Swift on the satiric power of naming, rejecting Swift's opinion that satiric reformation could occur through allusion rather than directly targeting specific figures as emblems of cultural degradation. Likewise, in Gray's inability to identify his unnamed rural dead, he emphasizes the authority that names typically possess.

The rural inhabitants fall outside collective norms precisely because they lack names with which to classify them properly, such as family names that indicate genealogy, social status, and economic situation, or even pastoral names that would gesture to certain pastoral types.

Richardson also challenges the assumption that proper names are synonymous with authority. He, like Pope, invokes names only to demonstrate the opacity of their given status, to dismantle the legitimacy they supposedly espouse as stable referents for a particular individual. Catherine Gallagher famously explores the transformation in the eighteenth-century novel towards "nonreferentiality," claiming that "novels are about nobody in particular, that is, proper names do not take specific individuals as their referents, and hence none of the specific assertions made about them can be verified or falsified."[47] Although not writing with exemplar narratives in mind, Gallagher nonetheless gestures to the assumption inherent to exemplary texts that named individuals, immanent to historical data, motivate action and are responsible for large-scale change.

Primarily through Lovelace's machinations, the practice of naming in *Clarissa* becomes an exercise in wordplay and deceit, revealing the same problems of veracity as the epistle itself.[48] Lovelace, in a letter to Belford, boasts of his power in manipulating Clarissa's understanding of events through the malleability of names, here specifically with the creation of a "Captain Mennell" who is actually a nephew of one of Lovelace's friends: "I have changed his name by virtue of my own single authority. Knowest thou not, that I am a great name-father? Preferments I bestow, both military and civil. I give estates, and take them away at my pleasure. Quality too I create. And by a still more valuable prerogative, I *degrade* by virtue of my own imperial will, without any other act of forfeiture than for my own convenience. What a poor thing is a monarch to me!" (letter 174, 569). Lovelace's manipulation of names threatens the stability of identity, of what it means to possess subjectivity and value in a historical record. Recall to mind Gray's invocation of Milton and Cromwell when trying to invest the rural dead with historical worth: he, like Lovelace, deliberates the value a name holds. Both Gray and Lovelace bestow a name upon an individual in order to grant economic and social status on them, conveying virtue or vice. Lovelace "places" individuals by attaching to them a particular subjective space with an appropriate degree of visibility. Unlike in the "Elegy," though, Lovelace's name games reveal his belief in his powers to subvert even the authority of "a monarch," who is, as the head of the nation, the proper disseminator of cultural meaning, ultimately responsible for the extant historical record. Lovelace, through his ability to manipulate and indeed rewrite reality, acts more like Cibber in *The Dunciad*, upsetting the meaning of historical veracity and the inherent worth of proper names.

Lovelace's invention of fictions, his embrace of imagination and performance, compete against Clarissa's desire for historical transparency and moral integrity. Binhammer reads Lovelace as bound by his knowledge of the conventions of amatory fiction: "His minute knowledge of the way the amatory plot of seduction conventionally unfolds allows him to manipulate the action in the novel *ad nauseam*. . . . Lovelace sees the plot so clearly" that he cannot fashion an alternative beyond that of amatory fiction.[49] Yet I wonder if Lovelace's manipulation of names in fact demonstrates his proficiency with imagining and scripting countless narrative versions of his desires. Lovelace draws on the literary and experiential history he embodies to direct his actions and to formulate new possibilities for narrative success—fantasies on par with Pope's and Gray's imaginings.

As a proficient, self-celebrated "name-*father*," Lovelace, of course, couches his proficiency in chauvinistic terms, as part of the strategies that enable him to dupe repeatedly Clarissa into believing his version of the narrative he envisions once she runs away from Harlowe Place. Lovelace's invocation of "name-father" recalls Gray's use of "forefathers" discussed in chapter 2. In contrast to Gray, Lovelace does not eradicate the name in order to help the larger community but instead creates names—false names—that end up shattering Clarissa's world. Gray uses a masculine noun but fuses it with the feminine, refusing the reversal of the cottage-door scene, in order to show that the bulwark of English identity is the countryside and the quiet alternatives to exemplary history. In contrast, Lovelace promotes himself as the exemplar of name change, the master manipulator. As Lovelace's name games begin, Clarissa finds herself unable to compete with Lovelace, unable to discern his stratagems, as she had at the beginning when she was in Harlowe Place. Clarissa is bombarded with names that in fact have no material connection to identity, such as is the case with the so-called Mrs. Sinclair, as Castle aptly points out: "The actual identity of the woman running the house on Dover Street is never made clear in *Clarissa*, even in Lovelace's letters."[50] Instead, Lovelace boasts to Belford, "Ay, SINCLAIR, Jack!—Remember the name! SINCLAIR, I repeat. She *has* no other" (letter 131, 473). By stressing the word "*has*," Lovelace ironically degrades names as possessions and as markers of individual identity and instead fashions them as authorial constructs that can be revoked at any time and replaced by others when necessitated. Moreover, Lovelace emphasizes the verb tense: "has," not "had." In stressing the present tense, Lovelace refuses to acknowledge the individual "Sinclair" was prior to his maneuvers, rejecting the past as a stable referent of self-identity. The continuity that Gray imagines from his forefathers cannot exist in Lovelace's schemes, as Lovelace's interest rests with the same changeability, theatrical spectacle, and immediate gratification found in *The Dunciad*'s nightmares.

Lovelace views the names he bestows as protection against potential litigation concerning his treatment of Clarissa. I replicate his words here, lengthy as they are, in order to capture the increasing self-confidence and hauteur that Lovelace depicts as his imagination runs away with him:

> Well then; here are—let me see—how many persons are there who, after Monday night, will be able to swear, that she has gone by my name, answered to my name, had no other view in leaving her friends, but to go by my name? Her own relations not able nor willing to deny it. First, here are my servants; her servant Dorcas, Mrs. Sinclair, her two nieces, and Miss Partington. But for fear these evidences should be suspected, here comes the jet of the business. No less than four worthy gentlemen of fortune and family, who were all in company such a night particularly, at a collation to which they were invited by Robert Lovelace of Sandoun Hall, in the county of Lancaster, Esquire, in company with Magdalen Sinclair widow, and Priscilla Partington spinster, and the lady on a multitude of occasions, as *his* lady; as they and others did, as Mrs. Lovelace; everyone complimenting and congratulating her on her nuptials; and that she received such their compliments and congratulations with no other visible confusion, might be supposed to express upon such contemplative revolvings as those compliments would naturally inspire. (letter 158, 539)

Notice that by sentence 5 Lovelace is overstimulated by the imaginative potentials of his stratagems; indeed, punctuation cannot contain his almost orgasmic exuberance. Lovelace anticipates, if ever called on to defend himself in regard to his usage of Clarissa, that the names he has positioned within the story of Clarissa's adventures will stand as evidence of his own moral purity—especially because the men he names come from "fortune and family," and the women are classified as either a "widow" or a "spinster," two nonthreatening (because of the sterility granted them by social expectations) categories. Lovelace assumes that subjectivity remains the provenance of elite, white European men, a stance that infuses exemplar theories with a troubling depth of misogyny and xenophobia, casting doubt on their efficacy for a progressive, enlightened nation.

Clarissa's predicament becomes even more striking when we consider how considerably it alters Richardson's strategy as used in *Pamela*. Throughout Pamela's trials, she consistently finds ways to remind her tormentors of her self-identity, specifically by refusing to change her name. When she arrives at the Lincolnshire estate, she begs, "Pray, Mrs. Jewkes, said I, don't Madam me so; I am but a silly poor Girl, set up by the Gambol of Fortune, for a May-game; and now am to be Something, and now Nothing, just as that thinks fit to sport with me."[51] Pamela grows increasingly frustrated by the name games she finds herself involved in with Mrs. Jewkes, who calls her "Lambkin"; in turn, Pamela disparagingly refers to her as "Wolfkin." This verbal sparring turns physical, directly tied to the practice of naming, as Pamela bemoans: "But I durst not call her Names again; for I dread her huge Paw most sadly."[52] Pamela recognizes the significance that names possess, and part of her struggle focuses on maintaining her identity as "Pamela." She continues to sign herself as Mr. B's servant at the close of her letters to him, continually reminding him that she is not a gentlewoman, mistress, or wife.[53]

In startling contrast, Lovelace's machinations dupe Clarissa, as she "finds her own identity, confusingly enough, revised by his naming. At Sorling's, she becomes [Lovelace's] 'sister' for a time; at Sinclair's, she becomes his betrothed, 'Mrs. Lovelace.'"[54] Lovelace's version of Clarissa's " confusion" at receiving wedding congratulations scripts a historical record vastly different from that maintained by Clarissa. Lovelace shows that names do not indicate substantive reality, an assumption inherent to exemplar writing. In Homer or Virgil, for instance, names bestow power, indicate worth, and embody discrete characteristics; names constitute clear boundaries between virtue and vice, fixed in the reader's mind as emblems for certain tropes. In *The Odyssey*, Penelope represents the patient wife, never to be confused with a siren. In *Clarissa*, though, Lovelace successfully convinces Clarissa that Mrs. Sinclair, a proprietress of a den of iniquity that tempts men as did ancient sirens, is a respectable widow. Lovelace undermines the surety with which we read the verifiable facts of *Clarissa*.

To a less dangerous extent, other characters also deliberate the efficacy of names in establishing dominance and conveying meaning. Clarissa's family pointedly constructs the manner in which they phrase their greetings and close their letters, reflecting their changing relationship with Clarissa. Notice that James and Arabella no longer address Clarissa as their sister but as a nonrelation, such as James's salutation in letter 24, "Miss CLARY," and his formal close of "Ja. HARLOWE" (120). Clarissa's father addresses his letter to "Undutiful and perverse Clarissa" and signs it "Your incensed father" (letter 41, 190–91). The ease with which various characters assume and discard names explores the assumption inherent to historical knowledge that names remain stable markers of identity, unchanging beacons of explicit virtues or vices, capable of being, to use Gallagher's words, "verified or falsified."

Making Visible the Traumatic in History Writing

Perhaps the most poignant moment in the novel when historical knowledge and temporality is challenged occurs after the rape. Clarissa's cry of "I don't know what my name is" (890) most clearly attacks the exemplar emphasis on verified referentiality. Clarissa has no idea what function her rape has served, beyond fulfilling Lovelace's desires, and she cannot assimilate it into the history she has thus far been recording. As such, Clarissa cannot identify herself by name because that name has been involved in an event that traumatically deviates from everything it initially indicated, such as virtue, filial obedience, and chastity. Scholars have shown that Clarissa's inability to locate her proper last name stems from the precise legality of her situation: as a rape victim, should she identify as the property of Lovelace, who expects, according to common eighteenth-century practices and traditional linear recompense, that she will now marry him and officially assume his name, or is she still able to use her father's last name because she has not technically married Lovelace? While these readings do an excellent job of focusing on the practical implications of Clarissa's cry, I will add that Clarissa expresses how deeply ambiguity is entrenched in her as a character, ambiguity that compromises her position as exemplar while, simultaneously, heralding her as a new type of historical figure. In considering the way Clarissa reimagines the exemplar after the rape, I will comment first upon the initial "mad papers" period before discussing Clarissa's subsequent commemorative practices that are, I posit, intimately linked to her regaining control over historical inquiry and historical time, as well as reconceiving what recompense entails.

Clarissa returns to her pen as the means of working through the trauma of rape, but her writing emerges as unintelligible fragments, "torn" and "scattered" (890). These fragments represent disparate historiographic attempts to elucidate Clarissa's suffering, all demonstrating that the violence of the rape is ongoing in the process of seeking historical knowledge and finding an appropriate genre. Kathryn Steele, when considering the manner in which readers are acquainted with the rape, writes, "The structure of the novel, thus, works with delicate readers' needs by deflecting and distancing the event, and allowing readers to adjust to the idea before encountering the details, just as Clarissa herself must recover from it before describing it."[55] Steele's concern rests with the relation of this passage to the volition that silence affords Clarissa at other moments in the novel, but she additionally shows how chronology is tellingly subverted at this moment. In the face of female suffering, the historical register crumbles into fragments. The text of *Clarissa* resonates with the impact of the rape, as the mad papers appear disjointedly on the page and in unusual fonts. The violence of rape seeps through the frame of the novel, disrupting readers' reception of the plot, as they must navigate the physical presentation of Clarissa's trauma. Clarissa, in her grief, searches for a discursive mode capable of fully explicating her devastation; in finding none, genre seems to fail her. The mad papers provide a profound textual moment of male-authored female introspection, linking Richardson to the despair articulated by Eloisa and Mrs. Clarke.

Clarissa cannot record the event not only because she does not know what happened but also because the rape exceeds the physical penetration of her body. Her inability to write it as part of her history proves the ongoing nature of the assault, the continuing violence done to her even after the physical possession is completed. As Castle writes, "The violence that Clarissa, in her madness, wreaks against her writing—tearing, gapping, halving—recapitulates a phantasmic imagery of sexual violence. In light of the rape, her behavior has the quality of hysterical repetition."[56] The event of rape does not cease and thus cannot be contained in a specific narrative time-space in a typical chronological progression. Her genre, the epistolary style that Clarissa had utilized in exploring herself as exemplar, proves ineffective—and it is *this* silence, indicating the loss of her active voice in her own narrative, that is of the most significance in the novel and most deeply shatters traditional renderings of recompense. In Clarissa's initial response to the rape, Richardson suggests that a new kind of history writing is necessary, one that makes the inner life of the individual a new historical object. The rape of Clarissa manifests the physical and affective rupture of the text—that is, the knowledge that available modes of representation prove terrifyingly inadequate.

Richardson represents trauma as ongoing action, where there is no cease to the replay of the event. As in chapters 1 and 2, here I offer that it might be useful to consider Caruth's work in *Unclaimed Experience* in order to understand more fully how trauma breaks with a straightforward progression of time, where events and names no longer embody the referential specificity of exemplar narratives but continue to torment the individual. Unlike traditional subjects of historical knowledge, Clarissa cannot escape the rape, as Steele intimates above. By placing his exemplar in a domestic and sexual crisis, Richardson subverts the expectation that the exemplar's inner worth will be enough to propel him beyond the monsters that hunt him. Clarissa's monsters cannot be expelled with a sword, both practically and metaphorically. Clarissa cannot murder Lovelace in retribution because that is not in keeping with her moral code; she is still a construct of eighteenth-century patriarchal conventions, and she knows that, realistically, Lovelace will always have the upper hand in society. Richardson's Clarissa is not the elite exemplar, connected to the nexus of power and in full command of all the resources of the privileged white male; therefore, she does not have access to the means of securing legal compensatory gestures of repair.

Likewise, she cannot evict Lovelace from her thoughts because the trauma he has inflicted is ongoing. He has not performed a *single* action; he has not inflicted a *single* wound. Instead, he has ruptured Clarissa's sense of chronology through the *repetition* of pain (although the action of intercourse occurred only once). As Caruth writes, trauma results in "a break in the mind's experience of time."[57] We could perhaps see the length of the novel, the longest in English literature, as a tangible reminder of that traumatic repetition: the novel cannot end quickly because it needs to perform, over and over, and in new ways, the trauma inflicted that escapes immediate comprehension. Sequential history disintegrates, and linear progression crumbles, when Lovelace rapes Clarissa. Clarissa loses a sense of time, certainly, caused by her drugged state when raped. But her mad papers show the disruption of time beyond the action and the inability of causal recompense to occur. Clarissa now literally *breaks* her word as she tears her writing, fracturing the temporal linearity of genre, of historical progression, and of linear recompense. Combined with her fragmentation of writing embodied by the mad papers, the rape destroys Clarissa's control over the history she has written, which has become not "history" but "his story." In so doing, Richardson reimagines the historical figure as victim rather than hero, as vulnerable and female rather than invincible and male. Moreover, he claims that the domestic and sexual are legitimate sources of historical knowledge and, indeed, should be made visible to a mass reading audience because, like exemplar texts, there is a didactic element that should be read and replicated by succeeding generations.

Commemoration, Burial Practices, and the Coffin

Once Clarissa regains the ability to write cohesively, her history—physically manifested as fragments—alters, showing that a change has occurred in the scripting of *Clarissa* and in Clarissa's relationship to history and time. Binhammer's focus on Lovelace's realization of the "ultimate impotence of his plot" after the rape and the "limitations of his way of knowing" the world as outlined by libertine discourse certainly is apt, yet Clarissa, too, experiences the shock of realizing her "way of knowing" cannot function.[58] By assuming control of the rituals surrounding her death and burial, Clarissa builds on a reflection she expressed early in her relationship with Lovelace: inundated with Lovelace's effusions of adoration for her, Clarissa admits to Anna that "he is too full of professions: he says too many fine things *of* me, and *to* me: True respect, true value, I think, lies not in words: words *cannot* express it" (letter 98, 397). Clarissa identifies an inadequacy of language and genre conventions to convey true intention, particularly of Lovelace's reliance on libertine and Petrarchan flourishes. Clarissa expresses a new understanding of the discursive authority of words, which become sufficient if they can be stabilized and grounded by other forms of authority, such as the law, religion, funerary arrangement (i.e., last wishes), and commemoration. Clarissa locates other means of recording her history outside of the epistolary form, such as through the legal discourse of her will and the visual images of her coffin. Significantly, Richardson depicts Clarissa as rejecting the genre upon which his own literary success stemmed.

Clarissa never fully escapes the trauma of rape, but the descriptions other characters provide of her actions reveal the agency she still assumes. In the theatrics that she consequently stages, Clarissa emboldens her own status as exemplar by her hyperawareness of herself as commemorative artifact and by her acknowledgment of the importance of preserving her story after she is dead, as she writes to Dr. Lewen in letter 428: "And for the satisfaction of my friends and favourers, Miss Howe is solicitous to have all those letters and materials preserved, which will set my whole story in a true light.... The warning that may be given from those papers to all such young creatures as may have known or heard of me, may be more efficacious" (1254) than, she claims, an attempt at litigation. Her deliberate use of spectacle and the crafting of her will both point to her desire for complete control over the dissemination of her body as text and the archival collection of her writings after her death. In a letter to Lovelace, Belford chronicles Clarissa's glee in making her funeral arrangements, such as her reaction to paying for an expensive coffin: "She discharged the undertaker's bill after I was gone, with as much cheerfulness as she could ever have paid for the clothes she sold to purchase this her *palace*, for such she called it" (letter 451, 1306). Although she admits that her preoccupation with the arrangements may seem "shocking," she argues that "I must say I dwell on, I indulge (and, strictly speaking, I enjoy) the thoughts of death. For believe me (looking steadfastly at the awful receptacle): believe what at this instant I feel to be most true, that there is a vast superiority of weight and importance in the thought of death, and its hoped-for happy consequences, that it in a manner annihilates all other considerations" (letter 451, 1306).

Here, again, Richardson reinvents the action usually associated with the exemplar. Clarissa does not engage in an overt battle with Lovelace, obviously prevented from dueling by her gender but also with her preoccupation with spiritual retribution. Unlike typical historical figures who would enact revenge on an enemy to seek traditional recompense, Clarissa refuses to act. She does not enter into matrimony, she does not enter into litigation, and she does not reenter Harlowe Place. Indeed, she does not even write; there are no letters written by Clarissa from letter 240 until letter 295. Instead, Clarissa solidifies her role as exemplar by the moral-didactic instruction she provides. Rather than epistolary production, Clarissa arranges the practical circumstances of her death and, more importantly, the promulgation of her memory. In so doing, Clarissa does not represent herself as heroic but as commemorative artifact, transitioning what it means to be exemplary when confronted with trauma in a domestic and sexual setting. The epistolary genre failed her, prompting Clarissa to look to other forms capable of disseminating, accurately, historical knowledge and of providing the compensatory gesture she desperately seeks in order to reestablish a cohesive self.

Like the speakers of *The Dunciad* and the "Elegy," Clarissa encounters the destabilizing awareness that her historiographic modes have thus far proved futile. As Castle points out, "Clarissa's 'Story' everywhere lacks underlying authority. It is without social and material force. Hence it remains a fragmentary, futile utterance subject to the radical incursions of a more potent collective rhetoric—the patriarchal discourse of the Harlowes and Lovelace."[59] Castle elucidates what I have described in chapter 2 as Benjamin's "moments of danger" between the individual and the collective. In rejecting causal history, where discrete actions arise from specific, verifiable instigators, Benjamin locates "moments of danger" as motivating and constituting historical consciousness.[60] History, for Benjamin, does not follow a chronological trajectory but emerges when violence wreaks havoc on an individual's sense of stability, disturbing that individual's relationship with traditional forms of legitimate authority. Castle iterates the disconnect Clarissa feels with the sources of authority in the novel, arguing that her epistolary style after the rape reflects her complete separation from traditional forms of power. Yet, as in Pope and Gray, Clarissa manipulates the outward vestiges of those traditional institutions, such as burial rituals, in order to transform her experience into an act of commemoration that fulfills her desire that "may my story be a warning to all" (letter 458, 1319). This desire reinscribes her status as exemplar while manipulating the assumption that an exemplar is representative of—or, at the very least, connected to—the governing authority.

In staging the spectacle of her death, Clarissa reveals her intention of utilizing different discourses to express her history, including material forms of writing (her collected letters, her will, the writing on the coffin), rather than only intimate utterances subsisting as words between individuals. In letter 314, when Clarissa describes her memories of the rape to Anna, she specifically emphasizes the inability of her speech to enact a change in Lovelace's determination to possess her: "I remember, I pleaded for mercy—I remember that I said *I would be his*—indeed *I would be his*—to obtain his mercy—But no mercy found I! My strength, my intellects, failed me!" (1011). Upon the realization that her active voice holds no power, her faith in herself to effect change, what she calls her "strength" and "intellects," evaporates. Drawing emphasis away from her physical, bodily virtue, which has been ruined by Lovelace, Clarissa instead places the focus on her soul—but I will argue that this focus on her soul's journey toward death, which is beyond Lovelace's reach, is a specifically historiographic journey fundamentally obsessed with maintaining her authorial control over the narrative. Through her assumption of the final arrangements herself, Clarissa insists on controlling the narrative of her bodily death and expressing her history in a myriad of visual and written forms, such as the coffin and mourning rings. Recall to mind that Runia describes the commemorative process as an act of *narration*. Throughout *Clarissa*, Richardson forefronts intentionality as crucial to historical consciousness; Clarissa's extreme involvement in the scripting of her death and commemoration aligns her intentions with narrative outcome in a way she had not been able to do before. Clarissa's story resolves in a similar fashion to that of Gray's speaker; in the "Elegy," the speaker finds compensation for his sufferings through a visual memorial, the epitaph. Again, Clarissa reimagines what it means to be an exemplar by refusing to act publicly (i.e., to demand public condemnation of Lovelace via the court system, or to agree to marry him and thus outwardly ameliorate his actions). Instead, Clarissa makes private burial rituals the provenance of exemplary action and compensatory repair.

Clarissa not only purchases her coffin but she also decides how it will be used and where it will be placed. She utilizes it in such a way as to make it an inextricable part of herself, the object that will contain her physical body so that her soul can transcend the physical and escape suffering. Castle ultimately claims that the "coffin-text is a residue, a sign of absence. As such, it can guarantee no ultimate meaning."[61] For Castle, "It lacks 'authority,' utterly and abysmally—because the author is in fact dead: mute and eternally hidden from view; inside yet inaccessible. All that is left is the inscription itself, the surface—estranged from being, cut off from any human presence, any 'natural' point of origin."[62] While this argument works well within the logic of Castle's interpretation, that the novel gradually works toward the ultimate silencing of Clarissa's voice because "language avails itself everywhere as an instrument of aggression," yet if we place Clarissa in the role of articulating history, the "coffin-text" becomes precisely that: another *text*, another mode of representation that Clarissa appropriates in order to ensure the veracity of her historical record.[63] Castle's observation that Clarissa's body is "inside yet inaccessible" showcases the paradox of the historical visibility entertained by Richardson's novel. The specter of "Clarissa" is present—tangible, actual, physically *placed*—yet she is also nonpresent, buried and misconstrued under the weight of the various modes of representation she explores and that others have applied to her. She is not so much *contained* within the coffin as she is buried *beneath* the coffin's inscriptions, indicating the plethora of self-representations through which she has sought articulation and shifting the meaning of exemplar status.

Certainly, Clarissa's body decays within the coffin, completing the inaccessibility that interests Castle. However, after the rape, the body no longer holds significance for Clarissa. As the object of temptation for Lovelace, as the means of control by the Harlowes, and as the general vehicle for the imposition of others' fantasies, Clarissa rejects her physicality and turns toward alternative modes of self-representation. Clarissa, then, can never be buried, subsumed, or silenced by the coffin; instead, it becomes one more mode along her historiographic journey, one more material object she arranges and makes available as a source of knowledge about her history—such as Eloisa imagines at Paraclete. The body is not the source of Clarissa's narrative authority, nor is it the object of her narrative intention. Her body may decay, but the inscriptions and the way she utilized the coffin will not.

The various similes that Clarissa uses to describe her coffin indicate her search for the right narrative mode in which to place it, and how it can best function to historicize her ending. The coffin, established in her bedchamber, becomes her "harpsichord" and her "house" (letter 457, 1316), two similes with pleasant connotations that act as substitutes for the comfort of her family during her suffering, as pleasant as Gray's pastoral descriptions when articulating the death of the forefathers in the "Elegy." Runge argues that, "with the growth of sentimental values in the later eighteenth century, the image of woman as prey lost favor in popular fiction and the less carnal configuration of the domestic woman took shape."[64] Richardson manipulates *both* constructions of femininity here; Clarissa certainly moves past being the "woman as prey," but her manipulation of the coffin perverts the "non-threatening and pleasing" connotations of the domestic sphere.[65] Moreover, "she writes and reads upon it, as others would upon a desk or table" (letter 457, 1316); she transforms the coffin into the site of her narrative and historiographical composition. The design on the coffin acts as a further manifestation of the narrative Clarissa composes. "The head of a white lily snapped short off, and just falling from the stalk" (letter 451, 1306) signifies herself, and the biblical passages surrounding this image speak to her freedom from her suffering and, more importantly, provide textual clues to the events producing that suffering. The attention to detail that Clarissa brings to the orchestration of her death ensures that the scripting of her death and her entombment afterward will be controlled by her hand.[66]

This array of spectacle clearly gives the voice back to Clarissa that had been wrenched from her by the rape, showing that she conceives of her death as a deliberate and direct means of reassuming authorial power. Clarissa positions her physical body as a commemorative artifact in a manner that indicates multiple meanings of historical subjectivity. Clarissa, like Pope, interests herself in making intelligible for the historical record the specific choices and actions of her individuality, contemplating the use of objects in making meaningful connections between past, present, and future. Like Gray, Clarissa appreciates the historical value of abstract symbols for unifying the discrete figure with a collective narrative, constituting a history in which intentions are absent from the official register but nonetheless are implicated in subjectivity. Clarissa becomes an object of commemoration not because she dies but because of her ability to manipulate the historical record to reflect the continuous present of the rape, an uncontrollable event that she manages to control through her explicit historiographic decisions.

Clarissa desires that the commemorative objects she arranges do not solely memorialize herself but everyone else involved in her history. She structures these objects so that they deliver historical information about her life and her interactions with others, all aimed at providing the spectator with knowledge about the events that occurred. She hopes that the objects will thus edify the audience in a manner similar to the commemorative function Runia describes in terms of public landmarks and memorials. Like Clarissa, Runia emphasizes the didactic purpose of commemoration, the manner by which objects reveal knowledge about ourselves: "Commemorative self-exploration is a confrontation with what we don't like to be confronted with: with the fact that occasionally we behave in utter contradiction to what we regard as our identity."[67] The awareness of "contradiction" provides knowledge, Runia argues, that alters spectators, forcing them to come to terms with traumatic events they would rather not claim as part of their past. Yet, by recognizing such moments as part of the past, the commemorative object imbues the present with new meaning, allowing for the creation of a more stable, cohesive futurity. For Clarissa, her attempts at narrating the history of her suffering through objects aim at instructing individuals such as Anna, her parents, her siblings, and Lovelace—not only providing them with accurate information about her but also helping them to learn from her so that they can change their behavior in the future. In so doing, Clarissa imagines her death as recompense for the suffering endured in the novel because this death educates others, providing them with a moral-didactic frame by which to govern their own lives.

Scholarship rehearses the manner in which Clarissa becomes representative of the transcendent violated female, but Ann Louise Kibbie offers a unique reading of "Clarissa's posthumous self-creation" in terms of the function of the coffin: "This fiction is not contained in the paper trail she leaves in the hands of her executor; instead it is found carved on her coffin. Unable to predict with certainty her 'closing day,' Clarissa revises the record of her life in a way that would transform the entire narrative after her flight from Harlowe Place; by means of her coffin, Clarissa asserts that she has, in effect, been dead all along, a ghost haunting her own story."[68] According to Kibbie, by listing as the day of her death "April 10"—the day she left her father's house—Clarissa's "own eerily ghostly identity" establishes her within a gothic frame of reference.[69] I invoke Kibbie's thoughts in order to point out that Richardson's definite interest in posthumous agency gives rise to a manipulation of the novel's understanding of temporality. Through her reading of April 10, Kibbie suggests that what has been taken for granted in terms of the narrative's time and plot development becomes destabilized, thus sharply undermining any sense of Lovelace's or the Harlowes' ownership of Clarissa. Through the orchestration of her death, Clarissa transcends the violence done to her by Lovelace and scripts her history in the narrative mode she chooses and in a manner that forces her readers to question radically, as Runia encourages us to do, all they thought as stable within the text of *Clarissa*.

The commemorative impulses within her bequests of mourning jewelry stand as Clarissa's final act of historian who successfully manipulates—not just observes—time. Kathleen Oliver, in her study of the significance of mourning jewelry, argues that the object "allows the mourner to communicate with the deceased, to resurrect, to reify, and to remember the dead, while it offers the decedent the material means to demonstrate, one last time, love for the mourner, and to insist upon the mourner's continued remembrance."[70] For Oliver, the "continued remembrance" fostered by the "repeated reunion" of the dead with the living through a piece of mourning jewelry positions Clarissa as fetish, as a spirit that can be summoned in order both to connect the living to the exemplary conduct of Clarissa and to reify Clarissa as a saintly being.[71] I argue that the fundamental purpose behind mourning jewelry negates causal human understandings of time, in which death functions as the ultimate leveler, reached by a chronological progression of events. Rather than occurring "one last time," mourning jewelry replays the relationship between the deceased and the living, influencing the life of the living, with the deceased standing as exemplar. Through the intercession of the fetish object, Clarissa ensures that she remains a part of the historical memory.

Again, we might find it curious that Richardson involves objects in his narrative, considering that both Pope and Gray likewise deliberate the value of objects in establishing a significant relationship between past, present, and future. As discussed in chapter 1, new Enlightenment emphases on objects aimed at categorizing and systematizing the individual's relationship to historical time, suggesting the ability of the present to decode the past. Pope performs a satiric nod to such processes by vilifying the actions of virtuosic collecting, while Gray belittles the elite for their reliance on burial objects as affirming historical value. Clarissa's decisions either to bequeath or withhold access to a piece of mourning jewelry signifies the control that she insists on maintaining over the temporal relationship between past and present. Clarissa punishes or rewards individuals in a maneuver seeking to transcend the finality of death wherein her voice would be silenced. As Oliver points out, Clarissa controls the distribution of her mourning jewelry, thus separating "the living into two groups: the blessed and the damned."[72] This emphasis on categorization mimics Enlightenment empirical tactics. She is simultaneously the individual who dies and the individual who records that death, but, I will point out, she also casts these individuals in their final configurations for the reader, greatly influencing who is remembered favorably after the novel nominally concludes (much like Pope's commemoration of the dunces in *The Dunciad*). Resurrected from within the pages of the novel come individuals who are not only granted a ring and a blessing but also narrative importance. For instance, Clarissa's desire to gift rings to members of Lovelace's family recalls them to the reader's mind and suggests that since Clarissa finds them worthy of remembrance by *her*, then the reader should favorably remember them as well. In this way, Clarissa continues to act as exemplar, as the "pattern" (175) for others, morally sanctioning those who were kind to her and thus preserving their memory in her historical record.

Acts of memorialization sanctioned by Clarissa, such as mourning rings, perpetuate what Kibbie terms her "eerily ghostly identity," troubling fixed boundaries between life and death. This is particularly evident in Clarissa's bequeathing of her personal items to her cousin Dolly. Not only does Dolly receive a mourning ring but she also receives Clarissa's watch, dresses, harpsichord, and books. The array of items, while certainly able to lessen Dolly's grief by bringing her pleasure, succeeds in collapsing definitive limits between the dead and the living and illustrates how objects are imbued with historical meaning. They "allow Dolly, in a way, to become Clarissa herself, to enjoy those very things that gave Clarissa pleasure and informed Clarissa's mind, to become one with the deceased Clarissa in ways that others cannot."[73] In Dolly's donning Clarissa's clothes and accessories as well as having access to the means of her accomplishments, an act of substitution occurs. Kibbie, while not addressing this particular moment in the text, states the issue clearly: "The problem is not so much that the dead refuse to die; it is that death itself may only perpetuate their hold on the world."[74] Clarissa bestows on Dolly the material objects associated with the myth "Clarissa": the accomplished and beautiful female who displays her accomplishments in order to enhance the prestige of the Harlowe family. Readers, of course, realize that Clarissa is not this myth, that she refuses to promote herself in this fashion. Yet Clarissa's gifts to Dolly include the danger that Dolly will act as the substitute for the dead Clarissa; by dressing herself in the signs of bourgeois accomplishment, Dolly potentially inherits the legacy Clarissa vacated by choosing to die. This replacement suggests that the exemplary narrative power of Clarissa could perhaps be reduced, by the Harlowe family, to external expressions of wealth rather than as the moral-didactic impetus for change.

Biographers often refer to Richardson's nephew, Thomas Verren Richardson, as his substitute son. Indeed, the historical realities of Richardson's milieu, with its high infant mortality rate, certainly substantiate such a reading. Richardson, having lost all six of the sons he fathered, would most likely have developed strong affectionate bonds with his nephew, who survived into his teenage years. Serving briefly as Richardson's apprentice before his death would have likewise strengthened that relationship. When Thomas died at age fifteen, Richardson turned to composition to work through his grief, publishing the *Vade Mecum*, recasting the specific advice he shared with Thomas in a personal letter to him two years prior into a more general guidebook. The grief, incredulity, and frustration attendant to the loss of his "potential successor" haunts Clarissa's bequeathal to Dolly, or, at the very least, invites a reading of her actions clouded by unease.[75] As in *The Dunciad* and the "Elegy," issues of succession in *Clarissa* involve more than the passage of tangible fortune, such as the bequeathal of personal objects or of estate (dairyhouse or even Richardson's own fourteen thousand pounds at his death). Succession involves ethos, the passage of virtuous action and moral integrity to a new generation. Dolly-as-Clarissa substitute potentially threatens the legacy Clarissa works diligently constructing. After all, Dolly is no Clarissa, and so may prove incapable of resisting the machinations of the Harlowes.

Certainly, Richardson would likewise have no way of ensuring that the anonymous readers of his *Vade Mecum* would benefit from his text in the ways he intended, a predicament enshrined by Anna's reaction to Clarissa's corpse. Anna, Clarissa's closest friend, does not understand the import of Clarissa's narrative use of her corpse, as indicated by her exclamation in letter 502: "This cannot, surely, be all of my CLARISSA's story!" (1403). Although Anna throws herself on Clarissa's corpse in an attempt to unite her presence with that of Clarissa, I posit that Anna, unlike Clarissa, cannot distinguish between Clarissa's corpse, the victim of violence, and Clarissa's narrative body, the historiographic legacy Clarissa leaves behind. Sadly, it seems that Anna does not become a spectator of Clarissa's commemoration in the way described by Runia: she receives—at least in the letters we are offered by Richardson—no edification from the commemorative objects arranged by Clarissa.

Nonetheless, by permanently fixing her body as commemorative artifact, Clarissa rescripts her physicality from the sexual (the potentialities as lover and mother existing within her womanhood) to her physicality as discourse—that is, the historical inquiry contained within her epistles. Clarissa fixes her body as both a visible presence in the narrative and a nonpresence. Clarissa's body is certainly not her private possession in the legal sense; as a woman, her body is not protected, legally or culturally, from surveillance or encroachment, as Clarissa is well aware (consider her realization that despite her attempts Lovelace will undoubtedly gain access to her corpse). Richardson, though, by denying the primacy of Clarissa's physical body in *Clarissa*, makes a claim to privacy for females, for the self-possession of their physical selves. Clarissa reevaluates issues of chastity, modesty, and virtue in women, dislocating them from the physical, masculine-controlled space—and from the narrative of rape scripted onto that body by Lovelace. She recasts what it means to be an exemplar of a text when that exemplar purposefully removes herself from that text (physically, at least) and yet refuses to relinquish, through her bequests, influence in the world.

Legal Discourse as Historiography

I offer that it is in the writing of her will that Clarissa most fully transcends the violence caused by the rape and assumes final mastery over her narrative body since, as she claims, "a will of my own has been long denied me" (letter 401, 1191). Eighteenth-century legal history fostered and participated in patriarchal codes, wherein females had no legal presence outside of that granted to them as possessions of their male guardians (fathers, husbands, brothers, other male relatives). Clarissa both adheres to and repudiates the historical subjectivity arising from such a legal system. By bequeathing Clarissa the dairyhouse, her grandfather subverts traditional patriarchal expectations in which his son (Clarissa's father) would inherit, thus keeping the property in male hands. More than this, her grandfather bestows on Clarissa traditional landed presence, usually reserved for males or for a minor number of widowed females, identifying her as capable of bearing the responsibility of maintaining, both practically and legally, the property.

Clarissa's decision to reject her inheritance by returning control to her father stabilizes the terms of historical subjectivity once more; she denies herself the historical and legal agency that her inheritance represents so that she may placate her family and retain her place within the family dynamics, offering a compensatory gesture of repair. She retreats from the public status that her grandfather offers—that is, the insertion of herself into the public domain of landownership, estate management, and inheritance. In so doing, Clarissa does not utilize the law for her living self, but, I argue, relies upon it as a historiographic mode of self-representation for her posthumous self.

Doing so remakes her relationship to history. Rather than assuming a public role as landowner, Clarissa retreats inwardly, like Gray's speaker, concerned with her private moral certitude. Such a retreat, of course, does not register as cowardly for Clarissa as, say, Sir Thomas Hanmer's retreat in *The Dunciad* appears, but more in line with a mid-century shepherd's retreat from overt historical concerns as described by Sitter in chapter 2. Clarissa refuses public visibility and the traditional trappings of historical status, indeed, all those material possessions that Lovelace flaunts in order to tempt Clarissa to marry him: land ownership, independent wealth, and the security such property offers. A traditional exemplar would welcome the physical rewards granted him in the aftermath of his epic journey. Clarissa, though, is not attracted by the allure of material security. Evidence of her exemplary status arises from her inner stability rather than outward displays of plenitude and success.

Clarissa consistently refuses to make public the story of her rape, to seek recompense for it in a standard causal way. Despite the prodding of Anna and others, Clarissa does not seek redress through the law, the public avenue normally entrusted with settling private disputes. Clarissa knows that in a rape trial Lovelace would succeed in convincing the jury of his version of the narrative. Lovelace boasts to Belford, "So thou seest, Belford, that it is but glossing over *one* part of a story, and omitting *another*, that will make a bad cause a good one at any time. What an admirable lawyer should I have made! And what a poor hand would this charming creature, with all her innocence, have made of it in a court of justice against a man who had so much to *say*, and to *show* for himself" (letter 443, 1287). Lovelace, like the law, emphasizes wit and material possessions (physical charm, land ownership, social rank) as the rhetorical tools of persuasion. His status in society, as well as his gender, grant him exemplary status. Moreover, as Roxburgh points out, "the rape is framed so that legal culpability cannot be measured because its very definition depends on the account, which is not represented here."[76] As at different moments in *The Dunciad* and the "Elegy," Richardson disrupts the notion of origins, a single originating event as the basis for recompense. The rape cannot be made visible in the legal record because of its unintelligibility, its obscure details, so characters such as Anna collect Clarissa's letters in the attempt to form the correlative of a legal defense substantiating her claims.

Given Clarissa's past refusals to utilize the law as a discursive mode capable of rendering her private struggles publicly—either with her family regarding the dairyhouse or with Lovelace regarding the rape—it is curious that she embraces legal discourse in order to reassert her authorial control in her last will. Rather than finding solace within the narrative sphere of the epistle, or even in the self-effacing allure of spirituality, Clarissa turns to human law as the final enshrinement of the expression of her *will*—the final resting place for the dissemination of her story. As a result, she shifts the meaning of legality in recompense from one of straightforward transaction, as in tort law, to one of self-reflection and retribution. Clarissa appropriates legal language as a historiographic mode capable of articulating herself (her wishes, her opinions, her commitment to historical veracity) beyond the self that is commemorated by her corpse and coffin (her body as site of physical, emotional, and psychological suffering). In the fossilized and unchanging documents of the law, Clarissa finally finds the genre for which she has looked, one that stabilizes the historical knowledge she wishes to generate. Clarissa turns away from more traditional forms of exemplary expression, such as ceremonial verse, epic poetry, Pindaric ode, or Homeric oration. Instead, Clarissa finds solace in the fixed language of the law, language accessible to and applicable to all individuals, regardless of socioeconomic status or gender identity. Unlike exemplary texts, with their exclusionary emphasis, the personal will can be utilized by any English subject; Clarissa, fallen woman and morally unsure of herself, nonetheless finds such a document available to her.

Simultaneously, the existence of the will within the provenance of legality thrusts Clarissa's story into the public register, available for widespread review. Clarissa rejected the visibility offered by her inheritance and a trial, two situations where she was maneuvered into legality by masculine figures in her life. By choosing to use legal discourse, Clarissa recognizes the way it can activate her voice—her voice that would have had to compete for intelligibility against the patriarchal codes embodied by inheritance and trials. Belford's dissemination of her letters after her death certainly enters Clarissa into the public gaze, but the will allows Clarissa to speak free from interference or editing from others. For Clarissa, public forms of knowledge typically reinscribe the patriarchy that denies her subjectivity, but the will provides safekeeping for the intimate disclosures of her private story.

The will is not a typical legal document in that it is full of Clarissa's digressions and auxiliary thoughts that are not directly connected to the simple act of bequeathing. Rather than simply stating her bequests, she *mis*uses the will as the means to assert her voice after being silenced for so long by her family and by Lovelace, thereby simultaneously misusing the genre to convey certain knowledge. Thus, the will is long, and it takes hours for the family to read; Morden writes to Belford that the reading of the will "took up above six hours" (letter 508, 1422). She excuses the style of her will: "For I have heard of so many instances of confusion and disagreement in families, and so much doubt and difficulty, for want of absolute clearness in the testaments of departed persons" (letter 507, 1412). She claims that she takes liberty with the genre in order to avoid "confusion" and "disagreement" in the interpretations of the will, but I argue that she constructs the novelistic length of her will purposely in order to grant herself the visibility denied her by her family, Lovelace, and patriarchal codes in general.

Crucially, not only does Clarissa's will lodge her voice within the inviolate space of legality but it also disrupts notions of chronological narrative time, or a sense of the novel as moving steadily toward rape. As Kibbie points out, "The documentary evidence she leaves behind"—specifically the will—"leads us backwards, rather than forwards, to a kind of dead end. Her textual remains lead the reader away from reproduction and succession and towards Clarissa's speaking, in perpetuity, from the grave."[77] Clarissa's will challenges the assumption that historical figures must physical *act* in order to motivate change or perform moral-didactic work. Clarissa wields great power, yet she does not engage in exemplary feats of strength, tests of fortitude, or epic battles. However, Clarissa demonstrates that even the simple act of writing can possess an energy equivalent to that exhibited by typically masculine heroes.

Most importantly, in her will Clarissa finally addresses the rape in a public form. By inserting her private trauma into the publicness of legal discourse, Clarissa validates her suffering as a proper topic of history writing and registers the rape as a historical event. Specifically, Clarissa transforms the narrative from one of youthful indiscretion (the way that Colonel Morden initially views Lovelace's actions) in which Clarissa is cast as a nonsensical girl who does not know the value of patching up a seduction with Lovelace through marriage—the comedic ending so many of Richardson's readers, such as Lady Bradshaigh, desired. Instead, Clarissa rescripts the narrative as a narrative of trauma, directly setting in motion the events that lead to Lovelace's death: "But if, as he is a man uncontrollable, and as I am nobody's, he insist upon viewing *her dead* whom he ONCE before saw in a manner dead, let his gay curiosity be gratified" (letter 507, 1413). Clarissa had previously rejected taking Lovelace to trial because she feared the lack of evidence against him, but in the will there is no room for his public charisma. By charging him with rape in the will, Clarissa denies Lovelace the opportunity to use those aspects of himself that make him exemplary—and hence believable—to the law, such as his rhetorical eloquence and his landed status. Clarissa strips the typical benchmarks of power and visibility as she refuses them space within her will.

The great triumph of Clarissa's will is that it forefronts only her voice, disentangled from the contentions and machinations arising from the multicorrespondent epistolary form. The declaration of her rape, the narrativizing of it into the historical record, is protected by the safety of the will from any degradation by Lovelace's schemes. Clarissa assumes, then, a triumphal tone that celebrates her volition and that indeed corresponds to Lovelace's own self-deprecating assessment of the narrative: "A *jest* I call all that has passed between her and me; a mere jest to die for!—for has she not, from first to last, infinitely more triumphed over me than suffered from me?" (letter 453, 1308). Lovelace's words convey the embedded disbelief that a written document could activate the conclusion of the story, rather than typical markers of resolution and the traditional compensatory ending (such as a forced marriage, pregnancy, or disgrace). Clarissa refutes his notion of their being husband and wife through the use of her family name, "Harlowe." Denying the union between her and Lovelace recalls her description of her burial clothes as "wedding garments" and her identification of herself as a "bridal maiden" (letter 466, 1339), which positions her as a virgin preparing for her sacred marriage with God, not as a victim of rape.

Traditional linear recompense did not arise in the story of Clarissa. The wound inflicted proved too traumatic to be repaired with a single instance of compensation; the crimes involved more than two clear opposing parties, attributed with simple assignations of guilt or innocence; and the origins of the wound manifest as too complex and astonishing to be assuaged with one compensatory deed. How, then, can recompense ever fully materialize when the injury sustained violates all assumptions regarding historical time and exceeds the capacity for expression?

Clarissa's will admirably represents her attempt to produce a cohesive narrative of events but in one instance she reveals the ongoing nature of traumatic assault. Clarissa distances herself grammatically from the presentation of the corpse when she imagines Lovelace viewing it; he will view "her" corpse rather than "my" corpse. The obliqueness of "whom he ONCE before saw in a manner dead" stands in stark contrast, written in the third person, to the rest of the will in which Clarissa adopts the first-person voice. Although it is clear that the referent is her rape, Clarissa chooses to use a simile to express her drugged condition. Moreover, her knowledge of him as "uncontrollable," "gay," and "curious" suggests an intimacy that collapses that distance between them that she wishes to erect with her language. Emerging from her mode of representation, legal discourse, comes the epistolary and the sentimental, a joining that suggests that Clarissa's historical veracity depends on the affective as well as the explicative; Clarissa preserves the private characteristics of Lovelace alongside of her public condemnation of him. The ostensible desire of her assumption of death and hence the scripting of her will is to transcend Lovelace's presence in her life, yet in revealing the truth of the moment of their conjoined narrative, the rape, Clarissa can only find expression through a distancing act, the third person, that reveals their intimacy. In seeking to control the actions of Lovelace at the moment of viewing her body, Clarissa's words reveal a residual stain from the rape that enters into her discourse.

Here we find Clarissa experiencing what Caruth describes as trauma, invoked in chapter 2 in the discussion of the "Elegy's" epitaph: "It is always the story of a wound that cries out, that addresses us in the attempt to tell us of a reality or truth that is not otherwise available. This truth, in its delayed appearance and its belated address, cannot be linked only to what is known, but also to what remains unknown in our very actions and our language."[78] Caruth's words help us to understand the significance of the will as a type of historical document granting Clarissa and her story visibility and historical value. Clarissa's will represents her ability to acknowledge the rape as an event of historiographic importance, and it tellingly reveals the "delayed" and "belated" quality of that achievement. Lovelace, in his disbelief that his "jest" has led to such a conclusion, cannot appreciate that what he has performed is not a single action—a single originating event of physical intercourse—but, instead, an ongoing assault that penetrates Clarissa's "very actions" and "language." Clarissa's initial response to the rape, the mad papers, showcase the unfathomable nature of Lovelace's attack, and the will demonstrates Clarissa's heartbreaking attempt to "tell us of a reality or truth" that defies intelligibility.

This moment of linguistic anxiety in the will, when Clarissa's first-person voice is lost to a third-person "her," occurs only when Clarissa considers Lovelace's access to her physical body after Clarissa has ceded control of it. Her concern to protect her body from any further brutality inflicted by him prompts her memory of the rape and the lack of authorial control connected to it. She is aware that even as she seeks to punish him by revealing the rape, she is also commemorating the rape, positioning it as the key event in her relationship with him and in her decision to stage her death. The act of violence upon which the will is founded arises from a painful paradox of dependence between victim and aggressor, an occurrence that Runia anticipates: "Coming to terms with a historical trauma is the free by-product of a sustained attempt at commemorative self-exploration" because it "demonstrates that it is impossible to come to terms with a past event as long as we evade the question 'who are we that this could have happened?'"[79] Clarissa's commemorative practices force her to examine her past, reevaluate the tortuous events that occurred, and create a memorial to that legacy. Her linguistic anxiety reinstates the inevitable trauma of repetition, threatening Clarissa's ability to articulate her own story and proving how difficult it is to engage in the process of "commemorative self-exploration" and recompense.

Once Clarissa moves past the moment of narrating her rape, her language again assumes the agency and control that is at the heart of her act of writing the will. She dictates how Lovelace should view her body, thus anticipating any scheme he could devise in order to retain control: "Let some good person, as by my desire, give him a paper whilst he is viewing the ghastly spectacle, containing these few words only: 'Gay, cruel heart! behold here the remains of the once ruined, yet now happy, Clarissa Harlowe!—See what thou thyself must quickly be—and REPENT!'" (letter 507, 1413). Clarissa invokes writing as a kind of motto that might be inscribed under effigy on her tomb, as if she is visualizing her body already as a monument performing the didactic function Runia ascribes to commemorative objects, thus collapsing the present moment in the future. Clarissa realizes that upon death her physical body cannot escape Lovelace, who indeed reveals to Belford his desire for possession of the corpse. Kibbie writes, "Lovelace is motivated not simply by the desire to memorialize Clarissa but, more importantly, by the desire finally to own her."[80] Lovelace's desire, which Kibbie reads as evidence of eighteenth-century anxiety surrounding the legal possession of deceased bodies, raises important questions concerning the relationship between commemoration and ownership. Put on display as essentially spectacle, the corpse, like a commemorative artifact, is the site of both private self-dissolution and public, collective mourning. Lovelace's desire to "own" Clarissa's corpse reveals his inability to break free of linear recompense and his failure to see himself as *part* of collective grieving rather than as Clarissa's foremost mourner.

Rather than being a passive testament of her bequests and desires, voiced through the objective and dispassionate language of the law, the will embodies Clarissa at her most brutal. Clarissa, often angry, uses her will to enact vengeance on those who hurt or abandoned her, as is evidenced by her desire that only if it is "required" should her narrative be shown to her Aunt Hervey, rather than to her mother or father, and only if certain "restrictions" are enforced. Her vengeful tone arises specifically when she addresses the deposition of her Meditations: "As for the book itself, perhaps my good Mrs Norton will be glad to have it, as it is written all with my own hand" (letter 507, 1417). Instead of leaving it to her mother, Clarissa leaves it to her *second* mother, to the woman who raised her and infused her with her values and did not exile her after her escape with Lovelace. Clarissa must know that this will be a source of contention with her mother, and so her bequest acts as the means by which she can inflict suffering on others, retaining control of the intimate dissemination of herself while relying on a public mode of explication.

On her deathbed, in the moment of final assimilation with the spiritual, Clarissa may speak her forgiveness, but in this last piece of her narrative discourse she is the most open about her revenge. Indeed, at the very end of her will she includes a final diatribe against her family's unwillingness to give her the voice she desperately sought. She asks for pardon if any part of her will seems "doubtful or contradictory" (letter 507, 1419) since she was forced to forbear writing until "very weak and ill" as she waited "in hopes of obtaining the last forgiveness of my honoured friends; in which case I should have acknowledged the favour with a suitable warmth of duty" (letter 507, 1419–20). Hurt from the silence of her "friends" informs the texture of the will and strips it of "a suitable warmth of duty" to them. The will makes visible the vengeful side of Clarissa and the private disputes manifesting her anger, emphasizing her as suffering *woman* before her transformation into public, commemorative *artifact*. Such emotion reminds the reader that Clarissa is not a traditional didactic exemplar but one who has spent the majority of her journey embodying moral ambiguity.

Through Clarissa's preservation of herself into perpetuity by means of mourning rings and her last will, Clarissa challenges what it means to possess historical consciousness as she is both present and nonpresent, neither concretely alive nor completely dead. The volition Clarissa asserts through her assumption of legal discourse as the structure for her historical record positions her as historically self-conscious, yet Richardson challenges what counts as a historical event by taking as his subject the trauma of a female, a figure typically disassociated from public concerns. *Clarissa*'s history is a history of an individual denied visibility in the public sphere that not only takes as its subject—its particularly *historical* subject—the disenfranchised female but also the private dispute of sexual violation and the succeeding refusal of compensatory marriage and legal action. In so doing, Richardson destabilizes what is public and what is private, and consequently upsets the formulation of rape as either a private or a public history.

Archiving the Collection

Lovelace boasts to Belford, "The methods taken with her have augmented her glory and her pride. She has now a tale to tell, that she may tell with honour to herself" (letter 279, 943). Lovelace assumes responsibility for the narrative that is *Clarissa*; in his mind, according to his formulation, he has bestowed on Clarissa a "tale" worth telling, one that brings her "honour" because it reinforces her "glory" and "pride." By the end of the novel, though, Clarissa emphasizes that it was pride that led to her undoing, rather than benefiting herself, as she writes to Lady Betty Lawrence: "Glad if I may be a warning, since I cannot be an example: which once (very vain, and very conceited as I was!) I proposed myself to be!" (letter 306, 985). Clarissa refutes the idea that she could be an "example"—that is, a traditional moral exemplar. In her mind, a "warning" is antithetical to "example," and she views her history as nothing beyond a piece of instruction that might dissuade others from the same path of ruinous moral incertitude, thus recasting the knowledge she bestows.

Despite the power that Clarissa asserts in her will, she declares that "I am nobody's" (letter 507, 1413). Here, we find Clarissa rejecting the language of the traditional historical figure itself. Rather than declaring herself an "example," Clarissa absents herself from all connection. "I am nobody's" speaks to the same sense of dislocation emphasized by her fragments after the rape, but now she has assumed that dislocation and makes it the triumphant mark of her transcendent nature.[81] She belongs to nobody, neither her family nor Lovelace, which allows her to leave the world operating under her own volition, motivating what Kibbie terms "the turn from Clarissa's corpse to her literary corpus."[82] She has assumed control of her body and her fate and thus proclaimed that nobody else controls her: not familial authority or other centers of power.

Since Clarissa's sense of selfhood has been inextricably linked to narrative formation, it is not surprising that even her will identifies her as a narrativized being, an individual written as text:

> Having been pressed by Miss Howe and her mother to collect the particulars of my sad story, and given expectation that I would, in order to do my character justice with all my friends and companions: but not having time before me for the painful task, it has been a pleasure to me to find, by extracts kindly communicated to me by my said executor, that I may safely trust my fame to the justice done me by Mr Lovelace in his letters to him my said executor. And as Mr Belford has engaged to contribute what is in his power towards a compilement to be made of all that relates to my story, and knows my whole mind in this respect; it is my desire that he will cause two copies to be made of this collection; one to remain with Miss Howe, the other with himself; and that he will show or lend his copy, if required, to my Aunt Hervey, for

the satisfaction of any of my family; but under such restrictions as the said Mr Belford shall think fit to impose. (1418)

Twice Clarissa refers to the circumstances of her suffering as "my story," a story of which she is intent on controlling the propagation. In her will, she prescribes the exact number of copies of her narrative to be created, "two," as well as who may have access to them, Mr Belford and Miss Howe, and how they are to be used, to do her "character justice." The emphasis is not the death of Clarissa but "a compilement" or a "collection" of a story, a *history*, that will survive into the future despite the physical decay of her body, thus distorting the private, intimate suffering of the individual into a document to be circulated within the public sphere. Consider the connections here to Gray's speaker who fashions an epitaph for himself in the "Elegy": both the speaker and Clarissa imagine their stories as useful for an anonymous future reading audience. Kibbie describes Clarissa's collection of letters as the novel's "final act of substitution" in which "Richardson diverts attention from his heroine's dead body to the text that will become *Clarissa* itself."[83] This "diversion" from Clarissa's corpse echoes Richardson's act of substitution in recasting his personal letter to Thomas as the *Vade Mecum*, an attempt that potentially distances himself from the reality of the death of so many of his sons.

Clarissa obsessively controls the use of her physical body after her death, and she continues this work in determining the use of her narrative body to ensure that it is memorialized according to her vision. She even polices the extracts from Lovelace's letters that are to be included in the "collection," as an editor might in order to assure herself that her "fame" is correctly presented, that the narrative reality she chooses to exist will not be compromised by the inclusion of Lovelace's letters (his attempts at controlling and directing the narrative). Her hyperattention to anticipating the collection of her letters echoes the anxiety Pope expresses regarding the archive in *The Dunciad*, particularly his concern that objects in an archive might lose their especial meanings, lumped together and thus unable to edify. Once satisfied that nothing will pollute the purity of her historical conception, Clarissa finds "pleasure" in knowing her story will be retained not only in memory but also in physical form. Clarissa's "pleasure" rests in the satisfaction of having historical recompense for the personal violence she suffered.

In emphasizing the history of herself, Clarissa reinvents historical status, remaking the action typically associated with exemplary figures.

Clarissa does not worry about concluding her story with one grand finale, an action of great purport that can change society or impact culture on a large scale. Instead, Clarissa focuses on her private, domestic relationships. She considers the influence her actions will have on those closest to her. Most importantly, she condones the preservation of her moral ambiguity in her history, choosing not to edit her indecisions, her missteps, and her foibles. Clarissa allows her history to narrate all of her—not just the typically exemplary.

Richardson is not alone in emphasizing the domestic and the emotive as valuable components of history writing. Later in the eighteenth century, David Hume, too, invoked what Donald T. Siebert terms "domestic emotion" to create empathy between the exemplary personages and the reader, such as in his depiction of Charles I. Siebert quotes Hume, writing to his friend William Mure, to showcase the emotive urgency of Hume's historiographic endeavor, particularly his desire that if "Mrs. Mure be not sorry for poor King Charles, I shall burn all my Papers."[84] For Hume, history writing becomes "interesting" when it contains an emotive response in the audience—in other words, a moral involvement. For Siebert, this interest is what separates Hume from Gibbon: both historians write from "a superior, almost Olympian perspective—a point of view that is detached and often ironical," but Hume often invokes the emotive where Gibbon does not.[85] Richardson, writing earlier in the century, shows how turning away from the "detached and often ironical" exemplar produces a more capacious history, one that showcases not only outward actions but the thought processes and incertitude informing those actions. Both Hume and Richardson—and Pope and Gray—seem to suggest that historical knowledge emerges authentically, across genres, from those moments when the reader feels most connected to the individuals and events narrated, and that those moments arise through humanizing and emotive practices that are at odds with exemplary standards.

Writing the Nation in Clarissa

Through the means of spectacle and the composition of her will, Clarissa regains mastery over her narrative and the use of the voice she lost in the rape, the voice of virtuous exaltation in the face of trauma. The history of Clarissa seemingly ends, then, with Clarissa firmly in control of the dissemination of her story and remaining as an exemplar of virtue to all. Yet there is a tension between Clarissa's obsessive need to control the ending of her story and the framework of the narrative text itself. Whereas the impulse behind Clarissa's actions is to reassert her control over the promulgation of her text into perpetuity (such as the presence maintained by the mourning rings and the last will), Richardson's *Clarissa, or, The History of a Young Lady*, reveals an anxiety about the notion of a "complete" story, despite its assertion that it is a "history." The further editions, the added letters, the sentiments, and the postscript attached to the end of the text, all point to the inability of the text to complete itself and to exist as a singular unity. Although Oliver argues that "Richardson bequeaths metaphoric mourning rings in the form of moral missives and/or aesthetic gems embedded, enclosed, and encapsulated within the massive text," such additions, such repetitions, serve as fragments rather than as crucial additions to the text, excerpts only that refer the reader back to the larger text for contextualization, much like the copious footnotes attached to *The Dunciad*.[86] Indeed, Hunter's description of Richardson could equally be written about Pope: "For Richardson, no secrets of the mind dare remain secret, and when his epistolary method fails to give him enough room to display the intricacy of the secrets, he resorts to footnotes, glosses by other personae, cross references, and other direct authorial intrusions to be sure that real motives are bared and the ultimate ends of confessional (as he understands them) achieved."[87] Like Pope, Richardson explores the secretive, the hidden, rather than public expressions of identity, begging the question: How much is sufficient? At what point is the text adequately formed? What number of additions finally make the text complete? When is the story whole?

Richardson's concern over the quantity of letters in his text offers a direct contrast to the officiousness of Clarissa's handling of her affairs. The obsessive footnoting of the text interrupts the reality of the novel, indicating the presence of a Richardson figure who edits the story. The additional apparatus to the novel exceeds Anna's original desire for Clarissa's recording, as it points to an editor obsessing over the construction of the novel and proves that Clarissa's history cannot be confined to a circle of intimacy but extends much farther (as Clarissa's handling of the will also demonstrates). Richardson crafts *Clarissa* as an archive, complete with various prefaces, appendixes, index of instructive sentiments, postscript, and letters of correspondence. Richardson's anxiety over the proper narrative "package" of his novel reflects Clarissa's struggle to locate the proper mode of writing her history. Like Pope, whose anxiety about the interpretation of his own *Dunciad* reveals itself through his obsessive notes and correspondence, what Castle has termed "an ongoing, petulant babble at the bottom of the page," Richardson's novel suggests the inability of a history being told, despite the temporal markers within the epistles and despite the intense revisionary process.[88] Richardson demonstrates a reluctance for finality at odds with the successful close of his novel and the specific calendrical dating system marking the passing of time in the text.

Richardson provides a didactic, moral piece of "instruction" (1499) through his outright rejection of the term "fairy tale" (1499) and its connection to the conventions of medieval romances—and, indeed, the assumptions inherent to tort law. Crafting a marriage between Clarissa and Lovelace, the expected comic "happy ending," would prevent, Richardson acknowledges, the emergence of "poetic justice" in accordance with a "Christian system" of punishment. Richardson describes the "general depravity" existing in the period, in both secular and sacred avenues, as "Skepticism," "Infidelity," and "the Gospel brought into question." These sins necessitate his "attempting something that never yet had been done." As Castle notes, "In a letter to Aaron Hill soon after the third and fourth volumes of the first edition appeared in 1748, Richardson complained of the tendency of his female readers in particular to yearn—inappropriately, he thought—for a 'happy' ending: Lovelace's reformation, Clarissa's change of heart, marriage between them."[89] Richardson writes, "I intend another Sort of Happiness . . . for my Heroine, than that which was to depend upon the Will and Pleasure, and uncertain Reformation and good Behaviour of a vile Libertine, whom I could not think of giving a Person of Excellence to."[90] His need to deny a "happy ending" to his novel, in contrast to his earlier *Pamela*, showcases his critique of his contemporary milieu (and implies a critique of linear recompense), placing blame on period practices for the fate of Clarissa, an accusation that bridges the fictive world and that of the audience. Such a concern also recalls to mind the Beggar's initial desire to construct the ending of *The Beggar's Opera* as "poetic justice."

As seen by the intense public interest in the outcome of Clarissa's fate by her readers, and the immense quantity of correspondence Richardson received concerning the resolution of *Clarissa*, the personal trauma of Clarissa becomes a national trauma as well.[91] As Terry Eagleton notes, Richardson's novels enter into the register of "public mythology," or what I term "the collective historical record": "The literary text is not merely to be read: it is to be dramatized, displayed, wielded as cultural totem, ransacked for moral propaganda or swooned over as love story, preached from the pulpit and quoted in the salons. Pamela, Clarissa, and Grandison are public property subject to strategic uses, lynchpins of an entire ideological formation. Around the fictions they inhabit, an enormous body of writing begins to proliferate: letters to and from the author, savage spoofs and denunciatory pamphlets, bawdy rhymes and poetic encomiums, imitations and translations."[92] The novel's invitation to its readers to participate in the world of Clarissa is evidenced by the insertion of sheet music into its original editions (such as to accompany the "Ode to Wisdom" in letter 54), intended by Richardson as didactic exercises. As Eagleton's thoughts intimate, the fanfare surrounding Clarissa well exceeds the control she longs for over the dissemination of her story.

The possibility for alternative endings as imagined by the reading audience and the continued conversations generated by the novel is openly encouraged by Richardson. As Binhammer writes, "The desire of Richardson's female readers for the novel to end differently is, in fact, an alternative ending that the text propels its readers toward through the discourse of Clarissa's story and that to prioritize an ending that fixes meaning in terms of a restrictive bourgeois femininity is to ignore the other endings that the novel makes possible."[93] Likewise, Eagleton emphasizes Richardson's attachment to his readers: "He sent the manuscript of *Clarissa* in frequent lengthy instalments to his friend Aaron Hill for editing, and circulated it constantly among friends during its three or so years' gestation."[94] Moreover, Eagleton continues, "Richardson invited his women friends to contribute scenes and prefaces, occasionally showed them each other's critical comments."[95] The triumph of the text, then, lies in its ability to excite alternative endings within the imaginations of its readers. Rather than simply encapsulating the oppositional friction between libertine discourse and bourgeois domesticity, Richardson's novel (like Clarissa's desires) exceeds the limitations of eighteenth-century femininity in order to discover *what else* could exist for women and for the novel genre generally.[96]

Clarissa provides a forum for Richardson's readers to discuss the social ills plaguing eighteenth-century England, many of which orbited around assumptions regarding exemplary figures such as Lovelace. The novel challenges the expectation that elite birth, wealth, and connections to centers of power inherently possess virtue and honesty, welcoming discussions about the foundations of English political, economic, and social power. Richardson, a man who earned his fortune through diligence, hard work, and candor, represents a different class of men than that of Lovelace, yet his novel does not summarily dismiss Lovelace as an outdated mode of elite privilege, in opposition to Enlightenment principles of science and nascent revolutionary democratic ideals. Instead, Richardson presents his reading audience with nuanced characters struggling, like themselves, to determine the meaning the past can hold for the present, and how those choices impact English futurity. Seen in this way, the intense scrutiny of *Clarissa* by a vast readership endows the novel and its revisionary history with the same hopeful potential as offered by *Pamela*. *Pamela* gives readers the potential for social mobility attained through moral integrity and linear recompense, a trajectory that *Clarissa* certainly denies. Yet *Clarissa* entices the reader to consider alternative endings where that recompense perhaps could occur, or where other nonwhite, nongentle, non-Anglican Clarissa-like figures could triumph.

The bulky additions to *Clarissa* suggest that a novel, like human life, can never be transparent or narrativized completely. Richardson's earlier *Familiar Letters* offers an orderly rendering of human experience, a series of responses to typical circumstances that can be replicated for general public use. Rather than similarly prescriptive, *Clarissa* invites the readership to construct their own amendments to the text, acknowledging that human interaction is messy, often fragmented, and typically multivocal. Most importantly, *Clarissa* challenges the assumption grounding the *Familiar Letters* that personal experiences can be authentically and sincerely transcribed in a single-voice epistolary style. Instead, the literary imagination provides the stimulation for other conversations in a myriad of forms, both verbal and written.

We might recall to mind Pope's question in his *Elegy*: "What can atone" for the death of the lady? In *Clarissa*, as with Pope's *The Dunciad* and Gray's "Elegy," we see an individual who struggles with the burden of writing history under the pressure of apparently insurmountable human pain. The demands of the story, of the history, seem at odds with the rupture experienced by the speaker who must heal the violence suffered. In the cases of Pope and Gray, the recompense offered by the literary atones for these acts of violence—so, too, in the case of Clarissa. Philosophical questions of the self, augmented with concerns about the female voice and narrative structural formation, spark within readers the desire to script for themselves the proper conclusion to Clarissa's story.[97] The reader becomes the storyteller in this exchange, aesthetically constructing their own imagined endings much like Gray's speaker with his epitaph. Runia envisions individuals as participating in a national rescripting each time they view a commemorative artifact, and indeed the manner in which *Clarissa* involves itself in and is enhanced by its readership suggests that a similar commemorative transaction occurs. It is telling that both the heroine and the novel share the same title, as this enacts the collapse of private and public upon which the success of the novel and its attendant commemoration is predicated. Steele writes, "The resolution of the novel reveals conflicting interpretative strategies centred on the way it tells, or refuses to tell, stories."[98] *Clarissa* serves as the springboard for aesthetic imaginings outside of the fictive community, instigating an act of ongoing storytelling, the repetition of a rescripting process that continues the historiographic impulse ultimately left unfinished (albeit unknowingly) by Clarissa herself.

One Last Burial

At the conclusion of chapters 1 and 2, I offered the burials of Eloisa and Mrs. Clarke as examples of Pope and Gray's historical inquiry that challenge the assumptions of exemplary narratives, specifically because they imagine the discontinuity of historical time and the commemorative impulse of the grave. Now I would like to consider for a moment Richardson's construction of his own burial. Doody, in her biography of Richardson, notes that "he was buried at last in St. Bride's Church—the church of William Caxton—which has been called the Cathedral Church of English printing."[99] This certainly reinscribes Richardson's exemplary status as printer, able to build a career that eventually saw him as master of the Stationer's Company with a fortune, at his death, of fourteen thousand pounds.

Richardson's grave marks a profound similitude as he places himself literally into the same common ground as his forebearers, much like Gray's forefathers. In so doing, Richardson assumes their identity and their status, the individual becoming the anonymous, as we see in the "Elegy." But, as in Gray's poem, the collective significance of the dead constitutes Englishness itself: by choosing to be buried with other landmark printers, Richardson reifies printing, mass dissemination, and large-scale dialogue as fundamental to Englishness, as inherent to Englishness as death itself. Like Pope, he sees the print trade as specifically English, even when dangerous, such as his brush with the law by printing explicitly Tory tracts in the 1720s. As he writes in his *Vade Mecum*, England is a "Great Trading Kingdom," wherein "the most numerous and useful

Members of the Commonwealth are derived" from the lower orders of servants, tradesmen, and merchants.[100] Richardson buries himself in the past alongside Caxton while perpetuating their memory and their influence on future generations. The location of Richardson's grave argues that printing is as much a part of the English landscape as the dirt itself. It is an incredibly powerful statement of his belief in the significance of commemorative practices, echoing Clarissa's own volition, and the nature of English nationhood beyond the elite exemplar.

CODA

"Building a Monument, or Burying the Dead"

THE CHAPTERS in this book offer three different examinations into articulating history and constituting time in the eighteenth century. The poetic speakers of Pope's *The Dunciad* and Gray's "Elegy," as well as the central female voice of Richardson's *Clarissa*, encounter self-alienation, "moments of danger" (to use Benjamin's phrase), that dislodges them from their historical complacency and precipitates new relationships with temporality and historical knowledge.[1] These new strategies reflect the broadening of historical inquiry beyond narrative modes, producing a more expansive conception of the historical subject and historical time than that traditionally offered by the celebration of specific, named figures and events immanent to historical data. The literary text acknowledges—and indeed mourns—the limitations of genre conventions in disseminating history, incorporates that loss, and produces an original mode of expression: the compromise of attribution in verse satire, the recognition of the embedded cultural traditions of the longue durée in pastoral elegy, and the appreciation of moral intentionality in the epistolary novel.

Each of these texts constitutes the historical subject in differing ways and grants historical awareness to those typically disassociated from historical status. In so doing, the potential to be an exemplum extends farther than the limitations imposed by the traditional exemplar model. Although the elite white male still emerges in historical inquiry, Pope, Gray, and Richardson offer alternatives that enrich our conception of eighteenth-century Englishness. The exemplar, like the English nation, is not a static figure in eighteenth-century writing; while certainly used as a tool for political propaganda, the exemplar could also provide the means of meditating oneself as an agent of either historical continuity or change. Such concerns shift the focus of the exemplar away from public expressions of moral-didactic power to an introspective examination of an individual's relationship to historical narration and national identity.

Pope, Gray, and Richardson recast what it means to be exemplary, moving historical inquiry away from the actions and ethos of elite heroes and locating it in one's ability to imagine alternatives, to acknowledge the need for change, and to break with traditional patterns while still not denying one's past. While, in their own ways, *The Dunciad*, the "Elegy," and *Clarissa* bury the past, they each use that burial act as the means of incorporating a wound and moving forward, paving the way for the official historical tomes of Hume, Gibbon, and Macauley. As Hume famously remarked to James Boswell, "I shall leave that history, of which you are pleased to speak so favourably, as perfect as I can."[2] In order to attain that level of perfection, Hume obsessively revised and edited his work, searching, much like Pope, Gray, and Richardson, for the proper mode of expression. Slater points out that "in a comparison of the volume published in 1754 and the parallel portions of the 1778 edition I have traced 2692 alterations."[3] Slater's numeric tallying provides a sense of the exhaustive attention to detail with which Hume regarded his *History of England*. Pope, Gray, and Richardson, as well as Hume, demonstrate an English capacity for contemplating its own relationship to the past, its cultural and ideological ancestors, and discerning how that past could provide the touchstone for a stable futurity.

The publications of *The Dunciad*, the "Elegy," and *Clarissa* stand as literary events, granting their authors celebrity status and providing a sense of Englishness, a literary object around which to celebrate. The texts inspired historical artifacts in the form of souvenirs that provided the reader with a physical memento, a connective link, to Englishness. Moreover, *The Dunciad*, the "Elegy," and *Clarissa* offer recompense through their canonical positions, providing across time a mythology of Englishness retrospectively imposed by readers. Perhaps Henry Crawford says it best when speaking about Shakespeare in Jane Austen's *Mansfield Park*: "Shakespeare one gets acquainted with without knowing how. It is a part of an Englishman's constitution. His thoughts and beauties are so spread abroad that one touches them everywhere; one is intimate with him by instinct."[4] Similarly, Pope, Gray, and Richardson are stitched into the fabric of Englishness, deepening the contours of English national identity, sustaining continuity between the English past, present, and future. Consider, for instance, how often lines from their works are quoted, appropriated as taglines for various purposes, often by those who have little knowledge of their origins.

Yet we cannot help but remember the Beggar's disappointment when forced to rewrite his intended ending to *The Beggar's Opera*, or Richardson's frustration at some of the suggestions he received for *Clarissa's* conclusion. The revisionary histories of *The Dunciad*, the "Elegy," and *Clarissa* suggest an unease with the act of writing an adequate history at all. The need for revision brought on by the pressure of correspondence and the repercussions of periodical reviews reveals an anxiety over the ability to write history properly, one broad enough to appeal to all readerly tastes yet rich in its historical specificity. Hume certainly took "undeniable pleasure" in the act of correcting, over a twenty-year period, the details of his history, as did Pope, but behind such fanaticism potentially rests the fear that a comprehensive and authoritative text can never be completed, as it proves impossible to appease the whims and demands of a diverse reading audience.[5] The revisionary histories of both historical and literary texts during the long eighteenth century point us to a list of dreadful apprehensions: What is a nation without a legitimate history? What is a nation with a misrepresented history? What is a nation that cannot write its own history?

The celebrity and canonical status of *The Dunciad*, the "Elegy," and *Clarissa* should not obscure the trepidation surrounding historical narration in the period. The achievements of these three texts heighten in retrospect when we consider the inability of prior English writers to complete a history of England. Sir William Temple, for example, "who criticized the state of English historiography, attempted but failed to write a comprehensive national history, producing only an *Introduction to the History of England* in 1695 that proceeded as far as the Norman Conquest. His secretary, the renowned poet Jonathan Swift, continued the work, but only to the mid-twelfth century."[6] Daniel Woolf observes that the histories written after the Restoration often take the form of memoirs relating personal experiences of the recent civil war and regicide, such as by the royalist Sir Philip Warwick (1701), or translations of French histories, such as Dryden's 1684 translation of the French Jesuit Louis Maimbourg's *History of the League*, or collections of historical documents, such as are found in *Historical Collections* produced by the former parliamentary official John

Rushworth (1659–1701, vol. 8, 1721). The great historical annals of Hume, Gibbon, and Macauley do not emerge until the later decades of the eighteenth century, finally "rais[ing] Britain to the stature of France and Italy, as a country that could write about the past—and importantly its own past."[7] Denys Hay, in his oft-quoted 1951 article, likewise points to the office of English Historiographer Royal as little generative of significant historical inquiry. With the first official instated in 1661, James Howell, to the expiration of the office in 1837, Hay marks the post as political patronage, not stemming from historical aptitude or interest. This general unease with regard to articulating a legitimate historical rendering of the English nationhood crosses genre divides, impacting historical and literary attempts at substantiating the meaning the past holds for the present. We can view Pope, Gray, and Richardson as part of a long and complex struggle to pen, regardless of discipline, Englishness as a discrete and especial identity.

Gay's *Opera* comes to mind again: although the Beggar alters his ending, a sense of gratitude does not emerge from the play. Part of the viciousness of the satire rests on the disregard with which the other characters treat the Beggar's predicament. Macheath's satiric response to learning he is to live mocks the Beggar's historiographic dexterity: "So, it seems, I am not left to my choice, but must have a wife at last."[8] Macheath does not esteem the Beggar for sparing his life, emphasizing instead his own helplessness. Macheath seeks exemplary visibility at the conclusion of the play through death; preferring hanging to marrying undermines the apparent harmony promised by the ending and troubles the Beggar's decision to bow to the demands of genre. Moreover, the lively dance concluding the play, with its invocation of "the Turk" with his large harem of slave women, locates Englishness as dissipation rather than the middle-class domesticity inherent to the Beggar's revised ending. The historiographic change enacted by the Beggar affects no continued security, nor does it bring lasting moral change to the criminal community. The Beggar's endeavor remains subservient to marketplace demands for entertainment—and Macheath's commitment to pleasure—marking England as a nation that can only be scripted through the invocation of non-English customs.

Joseph Priestley's *Lectures on History and General Policy* (1788) argues "for history as both an eradicator of national prejudice and as a virtual form of experience: it provides, he said, an 'anticipated knowledge of the world' which is a 'better guide to us, than anything we would have learned from our own random experience.'"[9] Yet Priestley's optimism and Bolingbroke's certitude on the value of "teaching by examples" do not register with the real sense of trauma underlining the conclusion of *The Beggar's Opera* and the works of Hume, Pope, Gray, and Richardson. Part of the revisionary anxiety arising in the period stems from writerly acknowledgment that the exemplar model does not adequately represent the diversity of England. Much like Pope, Gray, and Richardson, Hume recognized himself as a partial outsider as a Scotsman writing a history of England. "Acutely aware of his provincial and provisional status in the English community of letters," Slater writes, "Hume strove for a perfect 'correctness' of register. There was a sense in which his audience was foreign, and all Hume's efforts to attain 'perfection' only emphasised his marginal position."[10] Individuals whom we might see as exemplars of literary form—such as Pope's legacy with verse satire, Gray with pastoral elegy, and Richardson with the epistolary novel—often witnessed, like Hume, the effects of marginalization, feeling like "foreigners" in their own country. Such tremors reverberate throughout their iconic texts, creating the urgency to perfect their writing, absolving it of the moral incertitude enshrined by such a text as *The Beggar's Opera*.

And so we end as we began: with the threat of Bolingbroke's rhetorical showmen, only now we use that term to describe Pope's, Gray's, and Richardson's worse fears about their own literary productions. To glance briefly at Pope's preface to his 1717 *Works*, we find a surprising self-awareness of the "crushing presence" of history for the individual disengaged from processes of exemplary narration:[11]

> I fairly confess that I have serv'd my self all I could by reading; that I made use of the judgment of authors dead and living; that I omitted no means in my power to be inform'd of my errors, both by my friends and enemies. But the true reason these pieces are not more correct is owing to the consideration how *short a time* they, and I, have to live....
> In this office of collecting my pieces, I am altogether uncertain, whether to look upon my self as a man building a monument, or burying the dead?[12]

Such a question must seem striking, coming as it is in 1717, when Pope was twenty-nine and assembling his first collection of his works, surely feeling the weight of his own importance. We might instead believe that it dates from the *end* of Pope's career, the morose thoughts seeming better allied to an older man approaching his death at age fifty-six, decades of vitriolic verse satire and crippling physical ailments behind him. Although in 1717 Pope was fully into his adulthood, he, of course, had no way of knowing that half his life was over. Yet Pope in this preface represents himself similar to Gray's self-fashioning in his letter to West excerpted in the Introduction: "When you have seen one of my days, you have seen a whole year of my life; they go round and round like the blind horse in the mill.... I may, better than most people, say my life is but a span, were I not afraid lest you should not believe that a person *so short-lived* could write even so long a letter as this."[13] Both Pope and Gray articulate the "shortness" of time that they possess to complete their literary and contemplative work and, significantly, to situate their own historicalness.

Although we could read Pope's thoughts in the preface as merely propaganda, written to ward off impending detractors, his self-construction must nonetheless seem striking, perhaps more so if we consider it as deliberate. Pope's early autobiographical prose sketch in the preface stands in remarkable distinction from his later self-portrayal as enshrined by the *Epistle to Dr. Arbuthnot*, where he depicts himself as the beleaguered and abused poet, constantly importuned by others. In the preface, though, he reveals himself as unsure of his position as either exemplary poet or rhetorical showman. His question about whether he is "building a monument, or burying the dead," anticipates, as early as 1717, Runia's 2007 conception of public commemoration as an act of private burial. Pope recognizes his work as an artifact in public archive, yet, rather than purely laudable, he considers his achievements as potential *conclusion*, an intentional turning away from the past in an irrecoverable manner.

Pope's pairing of "building" and "burying" resonates with the self-alienation described by Gray in his letter to West, particularly his acknowledgment of own stilted poetic production. It is striking that the same individual who could pen the magnificent "Elegy," a monument of sorts, could also be considered "disappointing" because of his "relatively small and reluctantly published" body of work.[14] Indeed, in a letter to Wharton in March 1758, Gray explicates his awareness of his disconnection from prevailing attitudes on productivity:

> To think, though to little purpose, has been the chief amusement of my days; and when I would not, or cannot think, I dream. At present I find myself able to write a Catalogue, or to read the Peerage book, or Miller's Gardening Dictionary, and am thankful that there are such employments and such authors in the world. Some people, who hold

me cheap for this, are doing perhaps what is not half so well worth while. As to posterity, I may ask, (with some body whom I have forgot) what has it ever done to oblige me?[15]

Gray seems to be performing in this letter the same "scattered" activities that define the historical endeavors of Bolingbroke's showmen; not committing himself to one branch of learning, Gray pokes around in a variety of subjects, gathering bits and pieces of knowledge from each, ultimately leaving comprehensive studies "unfinished."[16] Wallace Jackson writes that Gray and his fellow graveyard poets "largely failed to provide English poetry with any especially distinctive period identity," an assertion generally supported by Gray's odes of the 1740s ("Ode to Spring, Hymn to Adversity," and "Hymn to Ignorance") that depict "the poet's quest for his tutelary spirit."[17] Jackson reads Gray as burdened by "the dominant figure" of Pope, but if we remember that the 1740s marks a decade of *coexistence* for Pope, Gray, and Richardson, then we can see Gray as likewise wrestling with "building a monument or burying the dead."[18]

Gray's 1742 "Hymn to Ignorance" particularly reminds us of the connections between Pope and Gray, rather than their dissimilarity. The poem invokes Ignorance, a goddess harkening to Pope's Dulness; indeed, Gray's lines could perhaps be mistaken for lines from Pope: "Fierce nations owned her unresisted might, / And all was Ignorance, and all was Night."[19] Both Dulness and Ignorance draw their power from exemplary centers, the "fierce nations" that control "all," initiating the poem's lament for a past golden age:

> Oh! sacred age! Oh! times for ever lost!
> (The schoolman's glory, and the churchman's boast.)
> For ever gone—yet still to Fancy new,
> Her rapid wings the transient scene pursue,
> And bring the buried ages back to view.[20]

In these lines, Gray's speaker cries out, painfully cognizant of the "rapid wings" of historical time over which he has no control. His lament signals that a closure has occurred, relegating the past as relic.

Richardson's call to action in the preface to his *Vade Mecum* also echoes the sentiments of Pope, especially when he bemoans the "Depravity, . . . the Degeneracy of the Times, and the Prophaness and Immorality" of the age. This lament seems to suggest, as does Gray, that "sacred" times are past.[21] As with Pope and Gray, we find in Richardson the same balancing act between "building a monument" and "burying the dead," the utility of both a backward and a forward-looking gaze. In a July 9, 1754, letter to Lady Bradshaigh, Richardson writes, "I really do think myself in a manner worn out; and as one proof, begin to loath the pen; yet know not how well, such is the Mill-horse habit, to employ my supererogatory Time."[22] Curran deliberates Richardson's conception of "supererogatory Time" at length, considering its theological connotations of performing good works beyond the common muster. Curran concludes that "the possibility of publishing from his correspondence led him to consider what beneficial effect, both literary and moral, preparing his letters for public consumption might promise."[23]

Notice, though, the similarity between this letter to Lady Bradshaigh and Gray's description of himself as "the blind horse in the mill" penned to West. In both letters, the writers express a sense of dissatisfaction with their discrete relationships to historical time. Significantly, the invocation of the mill horse emphasizes monotony, repetition, and inalterability for both Gray and Richardson, a shared sense of doubt that their literary productions affect substantiative and lasting change beyond the transitory wit of "labour'd nothings" and rhetorical showmen. Read alongside of Pope's question posed in the 1717 preface, the fear of the mill horse lurks behind the archival attempts at monument building undertaken by all three writers: Pope's collected works, Gray's various aborted histories, Richardson's assembled correspondence. Their endeavors are founded on an exemplary moral-didactic impulse, but their doubts suggest conclusion, the fear that something (literary period, genre convention, national identity, a golden age) is buried or subsumed beneath rhetorical showmanship.

Perhaps thinking about Benjamin's interpretation of the angel of history might prove useful here:

> A Klee painting named Angelus Novus shows an angel looking as though he is about to move away from something he is fixedly contemplating. His eyes are staring, his mouth is open, his wings are spread. This is how one pictures the angel of history. His face is turned toward the past. Where we perceive a chain of events, he sees one single catastrophe which keeps piling wreckage upon wreckage and hurls it in front of his feet. The angel would like to stay, awaken the dead, and make whole what has been smashed. But a storm is blowing from

Paradise; it has got caught in his wings with such violence that the angel can no longer close them. The storm irresistibly propels him into the future to which his back is turned, while the pile of debris before him grows skyward. This storm is what we call progress.[24]

The angel of history wishes to reanimate the dead, to negate the effects of burial, so that he may triumph as an exemplar, forging from the "wreckage" a monument to his own volition. Yet, for Benjamin, the angel of history is essentially impotent: "fixed" in place, he cannot act. He cannot "stay," "awaken," or "make," nor does he possess control over his own body. He cannot "close" his wings, thereby moving himself and ending the "catastrophe unfolding." Benjamin imagines the angel as suffering from ideological and physical restraint, locked in traumatic repetition.

Strangely, this might be the ordeal iterated by Pope's 1717 question and likewise intimated by Gray and Richardson. We find in their writing, as in Benjamin's interpretation, the struggle of private individuals to reconcile themselves to their own historicalness and to enact meaningful change in the public world. Aware only of the past, these individuals cannot foretell the future, becoming, like the angel, a poignant mix of wound and resilience, a similarity that performs the collapse of heaven into hell that haunts Pope in *The Dunciad*. When we consider the Klee painting alongside of the images of burial in *The Dunciad*, the "Elegy," and *Clarissa*, we might deliberate the distinction between "awakening" and "burying" the dead. The latter connotes closure, the sealing off in the earth of the lifeless body, while the former suggests hopefulness, the sparking to life of the dormant body. Notably, Benjamin envisions the angel as desiring to "awaken" the dead, but this angel does not reflect further on them or their origins: Who buried them, who are they, how are they interred? This lack of narrative buries the dead in historical obscurity, a closure far more frightening than actual entombment because it casts them as passive victims, negating any visibility that the angel's desire to awaken them might confer. In this conception, the angel of history remains isolated, the lone exemplary participant struggling throughout historical time.

Recalling to mind Runia's description of commemoration as a national act of *narration* and history as a form of burial is essential here. Runia insists that both history and burial are never committed in isolation, and that private and public self-identities are indelibly fused, mutually sustaining and encouraging the other. This forces us, I think, to reevaluate Benjamin's implication that the dead remain unresponsive to the angel of history, and that the angel exists as a singular, exclusive being. Moreover, if we remember Gray's image of the "heaving" graves in the "Elegy," as well as the orchestration of Clarissa's coffin and corpse, then perhaps we can read the angel's apparent impotence as generative, and Pope's positioning of monument building and burial in a less oppositional way. As Runia states, commemoration involves both "closure and perpetuation," a process by which the individual frankly acknowledges the discomfort the past brings, accepts the past as their own, and forges a more nuanced identity, one that intertwines the personal with the public.[25] Historical time is not built on segregating the past in a temporal container, one that is closed and inaccessible, or on ignoring the discomforting past altogether; rather, historical time infuses the past in the present through the historical self-awareness of individuals.

"Building a monument" and "burying the dead" are not antithetical activities, nor are the angel's struggle and the dead's passivity. Commemorative acts do not mark the past as irrecoverable or outdated, but celebrate what *could be*, the possibilities that could emerge when individuals use their own historical consciousness to rescript their identities based on the moral-didactic lessons of the past. We may read in the Klee painting, then, the potential for narration rather than its silence. The same claim is made by *The Dunciad*, the "Elegy," and *Clarissa*: the literary imagination proves capable of breaking chronological time, of "bring[ing] the buried ages back to view," as Gray iterates in the "Hymn to Ignorance." Pope, Gray, and Richardson dismantle the closure seemingly inherent to burial, attributing to literary production the commemorative impulses that Runia describes.

What is striking here is that we see Pope, Gray, and Richardson thinking about their own historicalness well before the advent of psychology or history as explicit, acknowledged fields of study in later centuries. This should seem even more astonishing when we consider that their iconic works emerge during the 1740s, a particularly prerevolutionary decade. Prior to discourses about the rights of common individuals emergent in American colonial writers and the expansion of liberties articulated by Continental political philosophers, Pope, Gray, and Richardson invest in a historical inquiry that moves beyond exemplary assumptions. They do this by positioning their texts as "publick Epitaph[s]," to invoke Pope's description of *The Dunciad*. These writers rely on their anonymous reading audiences and the knowledge that their private meditations will become public artifacts to script their own historical consciousnesses, and to enable others to do the same. Pope, Gray, and Richardson encourage their eighteenth-century audiences to participate in the same self-reflective processes that Runia offers twenty-first century readers.

In so doing, Pope, Gray, and Richardson transform our understanding of recompense. Recompense, as iterated by *The Dunciad*, the "Elegy," and *Clarissa*, is not a linear, straightforward transaction with clear assignations of innocence and guilt, victim and aggressor, and with transparent iterations of originating crimes and compensatory gestures. The traditional binary standard of recompense collapses in a metropolitan and multivocal society, one that is built on brutal contradictions and horrifying disparities between rich and poor, landed and commercial, titled and obscure. These texts embrace this collapse of linearity, insisting that there can still be stability and cohesion even when we cannot rely on the narratives of exemplars to sustain us. Pope, Gray, and Richardson suggest that Englishness is forged from more than just these great men, that it is rooted into the very soil of England itself, tied to the imaginative prowess of English creativity, dependent not on the reified few but on the ethos of every person claiming affinity to England.

Although borne of strife, contention, and, at its worst, prejudice and willful exclusion, the literary recompense articulated by Pope, Gray, and Richardson represents nationalism as its best: the self-conscious examination of one's own relationship to the nation and its history. This self-reflection provides England with its strength, marking it as an especial nation where philosophy and inquiry thrive. The manifold eighteenth-century endeavors in poetry and prose to challenge existing frames, imagine alternative possibilities, and script new options fostered an England built on active investigation and invention, one where the past, present, and future intertwine. Such introspection enabled writers to imagine a richer, more capacious England, one that is truly exemplary.

NOTES

Preface

1. Pope, *Dunciad*, book 4, l. 656. Hereafter cited in-text.
2. See Hughes, "More Popeana," 1093. Hughes discusses the fact that the poet Elizabeth Rowe embraced Pope as "the Darling of my heart" (1090) in a 1719 letter. Writing later, though, in 1734–35, Rowe rejects his work as possessing "something infernal in it" (1093). See also Abrams and Greenblatt, *Norton Anthology*, 2507. For an overview of critical biographical renderings of Pope, see chapter 7 of Hammond's *Professional Imaginative Writing*.
3. As quoted in Seidel, *Satiric Inheritance*, 235.
4. As quoted in Krutch, *Selected Letters*, 10
5. Bolingbroke, *Letters*, 12
6. As quoted in Curran, "Samuel Richardson's Correspondence," 60.

Introduction

1. Bolingbroke, *Letters*, 14.
2. Bolingbroke, 5.
3. Pope, *Essay on Criticism*, ll. 326–32.
4. Bolingbroke, *Letters*, 14. This concern is likewise echoed by Hume, who, as Dray states, believed "one of the chief values of historical study . . . [is] that it provides moral exercise and moral instruction" as "the moral point of view finds its touchstone not in interest, but in social utility" ("David Hume on History," 739). At the heart of exemplar theory rests civic investment and improvement, public power and national aggrandizement.
5. Bolingbroke comments on the actions and decisions of such elite men. He specifically critiques the ode of Horace and the work of the historian Polybius, both of whom describe the Roman statesman and general Marcus Attilius Regulus.
6. See Mack, *Literary Historicity*, who points out that "it is widely agreed that the philosophy of history in the eighteenth-century context is not a new intellectual innovation but the end of a long reign of the classical idea of exemplar history . . . which advocated the imitation of the actions of great men in history for the current, reading man's political life" (5).
7. As Siebert notes, "The emphasis in ancient history tends to be on battles in the field and on the subtler battles for power among the great" ("Hume's History," 553). Such thoughts register in John Rushworth's Restoration-era *Historical Collections*, a hefty document outlining the events of the English

Civil War. In both of these, the great men of history provide the examples that anchor future generations, regardless of country or culture.

8. History is often personified as the goddess Clio, one of the nine ancient Greek Muses. Commonly depicted holding parchment scrolls or tablets, Clio preserves the memory and records the actions of the great. The translation of the original Greek establishes Clio as "the Proclaimer" who celebrates momentous deeds and individuals. As Hume writes, "History charges herself willingly with a relation of the great crimes, and still more with that of the great virtues of mankind, but she appears to fall from her dignity when necessitated to dwell on . . . frivolous events and ignoble personages" (as quoted in Siebert, "Hume's History," 550).
9. Scholars have examined the exemplary as a genre of history writing proper, a task that is beyond the scope of this project. See Looser, *British Women Writers*; or Phillips, *Society and Sentiment*.
10. See West-Pavlov, *Temporalities*, 66.
11. Bolingbroke, *Letters*, 17.
12. Johnson, *Rambler*, no. 60.
13. O'Brien, "English Enlightenment," 521–22.
14. Woolf, "Historical Writing," 486.
15. In her study of the law of strict liability in the seventeenth to the nineteenth century, Macpherson (*Harm's Way*) considers the relationship between personal interest and crime, particularly the way that the law conceives of selfhood as external to the priorities of adjudication.
16. Caruth, *Unclaimed Experience*, 61.
17. For a comprehensive study of the intersection of trauma theory and literature, see Kurtz, *Trauma and Literature*.
18. Sharp, "Elegy," 5
19. Milton, *Lycidas*, ll. 180–83.
20. Wordsworth, "Tintern Abbey," l. 92.
21. Wordsworth, ll. 84–89.
22. For more explanation, see my previously published work "Returning to Eton."
23. Tonson, *Works*, 30, my emphasis. A longer excerpt from this letter is discussed in chapter 1.
24. Colley provides perhaps the foremost explication of nationalism as imagined by the Act of Union, arguing that "Britishness was superimposed over an array of internal differences in response to contact with the Other, and above all in response to conflict with the Other" (*Britons*, 6). Colley points to patriotism and a shared national antagonism against France as the unifying factor capable of suturing together the disparate countries of England, Scotland, and Wales. Colley writes, "Great Britain did not emerge by way of a 'blending' of the different regional or older national cultures contained

within its boundaries as is sometimes maintained, nor is its genesis to be explained primarily in terms of an English 'core' imposing its cultural and political hegemony on a helpless and defrauded Celtic periphery. As even the briefest acquaintance with Great Britain will confirm, the Welsh, the Scottish and the English remain in many ways distinct peoples in cultural terms, just as all three countries continue to be conspicuously subdivided into different regions. The sense of a common identity here did not come into being, then, because of an integration and homogenisation of disparate cultures" (6). Newman and Brown ultimately herald the ways that the rule of the German monarchs "deeply affected modern ideas and styles" (*Britain in the Hanoverian Age*, vii).

25. For further reading on the conception of the collective as an imagined historical object, see Edward Said's description of "imagined geographies" in *Orientalism*.
26. Anderson, *Imagined Communities*, 50.
27. Sitter best describes this position: "Whether by decision or default, from the 1740s on, most of the younger poets avoid direct historical treatment of the events of their day, even of their century. We can best appreciate how fundamental a shift occurs here by recalling that one of the deepest connections we can find between Dryden and Pope—and many of the contemporaries of each—is the shared sense of the poet's role as historian of his own times" (*Literary Loneliness*, 83).
28. As quoted in Seidel, *Satiric Inheritance*, 235.
29. Jackson, *Vision*, 11. As noted by Griffin, initial enthusiasm for Pope's literary canon proved weak in the two decades immediately following his death in 1744, especially when figured alongside of John Dryden's late seventeenth century poetry, despite the efforts of the Wartons: "The debate over Pope's position as the latest and best thing in English began shortly after his death with the Wartons in the 1740s and 1750s, but they convinced a very few. The debate heated up in the 1790s with, among other thing, a two-year-long exchange of letters in *The Gentleman's Magazine* disputing who was superior, Pope or Dryden. When the dust settled in the 1820s it was generally accepted that Pope was indeed very accomplished, but that the Elizabethans were of a higher rank" (*Wordsworth's Pope*, 6). The Romantics, particularly Lord Byron, granted Pope lukewarm praise, acknowledging his incredible rhetorical constraint, control, and organization while dismissing such technique as outdated. David Nokes writes of the "blend of civilised disparagement and polite neglect" afforded Pope through the early twentieth century, with the critic Lytton Strachey disparagingly remarking in 1925 that "Pope's poetic criticism of life was, simply and solely, the heroic couplet" (both quoted in Nokes, *Raillery and Rage*, 99).
30. Hughes, "More Popeana," 1093.

31. Hughes, 1090.
32. Jackson, *Vision*, 170.
33. Sitter, *Literary Loneliness*, 83–84.
34. Foxon and McLaverty, in their book-length study of Pope's relationship to the print trade, note that "Pope first appeared in print in the sixth and last volume of the series of poetical miscellanies produced by Jacob Tonson" in 1790 (*Pope*, 18).
35. Sitter, *Literary Loneliness*, 85, 214, 96, 84.
36. Sharp, "Elegy," 24.
37. In addition to these, see the work of David Fairer, including *English Poetry of the Eighteenth Century*.
38. Sitter, *Literary Loneliness*, 96.
39. Gray, "Bard," l. 21.
40. Hinnant, "Changing Perspectives," 321.
41. Odney, "Thomas Gray," 260.
42. Odney, 248.
43. Weinfield, *Poet without a Name*, 7.
44. Of course, it should be noted that Young was a Christian writer with specifically Christian intentions in his poetry.
45. As quoted in Abrams, *Norton Anthology*, 2826.
46. "Ode on a Distant Prospect of Eton College" begins: "Ye distant spires, ye antique towers" (l. 1). In the 1802 *Preface* to the *Lyrical Ballads*, Wordsworth, when commenting on the construction of poetry to resemble prose, writes of Gray's "Sonnet on the Death of Mr. Richard West" that "it will easily be perceived that the only part of this Sonnet which is of any value is the lines printed in italics" (300)—which only comprise five of the fourteen lines.
47. As quoted in Krutch, *Selected Letters*, 10.
48. Sharp, "Elegy," 24. Likewise, Krutch highlights this when he states that "something made him hesitate to write, hesitate to show what he had written, and hesitate above all to publish" (*Selected Letters*, xix).
49. According to Krutch, "Ruling papers into parallel columns, he headed each with the name of a wine known in antiquity and then under each listed the passages from classical writers which mentioned the one or the other. Then he did the same for olives, perfumes, articles of clothing, etc." Further, Krutch writes, "In addition he made a certain number of field observations and he kept, in column form, a record of temperature, phases of the moon, state of the weather, and so forth, with notes on the blooming and ripening of fruits" (xxiv).
50. Curran, "Samuel Richardson," 280.
51. Curran, 283.
52. As quoted in Curran, "Samuel Richardson," 282.
53. Sabor, "Rewriting *Clarissa*," 149–50.

54. Sabor, 150.
55. Doerksen, "Editorial Mediation," 223.
56. Doerksen, 223.
57. Doerksen, 225–26.
58. Hammerschmidt, "Print, Proximity," 287.
59. Hammerschmidt, 296.
60. This was indeed an ending favored by many of *Clarissa*'s readers, including Lady Echlin.
61. Sabor, "Rewriting *Clarissa*," 142.
62. Gay, *Beggar's Opera*, 3.16.
63. Gay.

1. "Another Phoebus, Thy Own Phoebus"

1. Wilkinson, "Decline of English Verse Satire," 222.
2. Wilkinson, 232.
3. Hammond, *Professional Imaginative Writing*, 6.
4. Hammond, 11.
5. Weinbrot, "Pattern of Formal Verse Satire," 401
6. Brown, *Essay*, l. 333.
7. As quoted in Wilkinson, "Decline of English Verse Satire," 399.
8. Nicholson, "Illusion," 181.
9. Thomas's "Pope and his *Dunciad* Adversaries" and Erskine-Hill's "Pope and the Poetry of Opposition" offer insights into Pope's engagements with his specific adversaries.
10. Hammond, *Professional Imaginative Writing*, 10.
11. Rumbold notes that the younger Pope befriended Whigs, such as the dramatist and Shakespeare editor Nicholas Rowe and Addison, coauthor of the *Spectator*. After the death of Queen Anne in 1714 and the consequential ascendancy of Whig power, political differences solidified, increasing Pope's Tory proclivities and leading to the end of his friendship with Addison.
12. West-Pavlov, *Temporalities*, 74.
13. Bolingbroke, *Letters*, 20.
14. For a more general reading of Pope's troubling of the hero, see Broich's "Pope Menippean Satire."
15. Wilkinson, "Decline of English Verse Satire," 222; Lockwood, "Relationship of Satire and Poetry," 393.
16. Lockwood, 393.
17. Cowper, *Task*, ll. 315–21.
18. Pope, *Epilogue to the Satires*, ll. 110–15.
19. See Butt's editorial notes to the condensed Twickenham edition of Pope's collected works (699).

20. Pope, *Epistle to Dr. Arbuthnot*, ll. 95–104.
21. Lockwood, "Relationship of Satire and Poetry," 399.
22. Sitter, *Literary Loneliness*, in particular 108.
23. Hammond, *Professional Imaginative Writing*, 13, 291.
24. Hunter, *Before Novels*, 99.
25. Hunter, 97.
26. Hammond, *Professional Imaginative Writing*, 292.
27. See Fairier, "Thomas Warton"; Hawley, "Romantic Metropolis"; and Griffin, *Wordsworth's Pope*.
28. As quoted in Rogers, *Alexander Pope*, 310.
29. As quoted in Rumbold, *Alexander Pope*, 30.
30. Rumbold, 30.
31. Black, "Ideology," 186.
32. Dryden, *Discourse*, 2121.
33. Dryden, 2121.
34. Thorpe, *18th-Century*, 143.
35. Mack, *Literary Historicity*, 5.
36. Woolf, "Historical Writing," 485.
37. For a book-length study of satire's connection to secrecy, see Rabb, *Satire and Secrecy*.
38. Even David Hume, in his *History of England*, attempted to move beyond the merely celebratory in his descriptions of the various great men populating his work. As Slater traces over the course of his substantial work on the revisionary nature of the *History*, Hume gradually included "humour" ("Hume's Revisions," 134) or what could be termed "historical colour" (134) into his work, ultimately revealing the "humanity" (155) of his subjects. Obviously, verse satire does not endeavor toward the same aim, as its interest does not lie in creating empathy toward individuals through humanizing moves; yet, the same general impulse toward rethinking public personas exist in Pope's poem, Hume's history, and Woolf's secret histories.
39. See Hunter's chapter on "Private Histories" in *Before Novels*, particularly 304.
40. Pope, *Epilogue to the Satires*, ll. 6–9.
41. Pope, ll. 10–12.
42. Pope, l. 23.
43. Swift, "Verses," ll. 460–64.
44. McLaverty, "Naming and Shaming," 161.
45. Nokes, *Raillery and Rage*, 102.
46. Pope, *Epistle to Dr. Arbuthnot*, ll. 75–80.
47. Pope, l. 83.
48. Rumbold, *Alexander Pope*, 3. Curiously, Colley Cibber's *An Apology for the Life of Mr. Colley Cibber* (1740) also reveals a belated quality. Unlike the

more formal autobiographies attempted during the period, such as Gibbon's *Memoirs of My Life and Writings* (1796), generally considered to be one of the first modern autobiographies, Cibber's text encapsulates his own personal self-confidence, vanity, and comedic talent. Lacking Gibbon's intellectual control and honesty, Cibber reveals himself as tactless, often rude, and self-aggrandizing. Rather than apologizing in a modern sense, Cibber invokes the Latin *apologia*, derived from the Greek term meaning the defense of one's actions or decisions. As such, Cibber depicts himself as the wounded actor, surviving the bitter insults of his opponents as he valiantly attained glory as an actor. Despite his self-serving interests, Cibber's autobiography provides ample historical information on early eighteenth-century theater, rivalries between theater companies, and characters of other actors at the time. Yet his autobiography presents an intriguing view on history writing, since Cibber writes of events that happened nearly five decades earlier. As a result, his *Apology* is often inaccurate, based on personal memory and anecdotes rather than verifiable evidence.
49. Halbawchs, *On Collective Memory*, 47.
50. For a recently published book on memory, narrative theory, and historical time, see Eron's *Mind over Matter*.
51. Although writing specifically on the novel, Gallagher's thoughts in *Nobody's Story* on fictional characters might prove useful here, especially her argument that eighteenth-century characters lack specific referents, not attached to a discrete individual but to a generic representation of a type.
52. Seidel, *Satiric Inheritance*, 238.
53. Bogel, "Dulness Unbound," 847.
54. Lockwood makes a similar point concerning the "fantastic imagery" ("Relationship of Satire and Poetry," 397) in *The Dunciad*, seeing it as a sign of mixed genre rather than strict adherence to verse satire.
55. Tonson, *Works*, 30.
56. As quoted in Lockwood, "Relationship of Satire and Poetry," 397. Jones ("Shelley's Fragment") provides a thorough transcription of Shelley's satire, which exists in fragmentary form.
57. Wilkinson, "Decline of English Verse Satire," 233.
58. Pope, *Preface*, xxvii–viii.
59. Pope, *Discourse*, 123.
60. Hammond, *Professional Imaginative Writing*, 302.
61. See Bolingbroke's description of such showmen in the introduction.
62. Benjamin, "On the Concept of History," 405.
63. Swift first coined the phrase "battle of the books" as the title of his short satire published as part of his *Tale of a Tub* published in 1704. It depicts a literal battle between books in the King's Library, as they fight for supremacy and authority. As Rumbold explains, the battle between the ancient

and the moderns became a personal quarrel for Pope particularly due to his friendship with Sir William Temple. Temple's *Essay upon the Ancient and Modern Learning* (1690), which celebrated the merits of the *Epistles of Phalaris* as representative of the "best" literature existing, drew criticism from the professional classicist Richard Bentley, who, using evidence from dialect and internal references, proved that the work could not be attributed to anyone living near Phalaris. Bentley's critique of Temple's work, for Pope and his friends, stood as an indictment against the taste and knowledge of a classically trained gentleman by a professional (and thereby vulgar) pedant.

64. Rumbold, *Alexander Pope*, 4.
65. Rumbold, 4–5.
66. As quoted in Rumbold, 70.
67. Kalter, *Modern Antiques*, 5.
68. Rogers, *Alexander Pope*, 221.
69. Rumbold, *Alexander Pope*, 133.
70. Rumbold, 13.
71. Both Williams ("Literary Backgrounds") and Sherburn ("Dunciad") trace *The Dunciad*'s connection to various other genres.
72. Rumbold, *Alexander Pope*, 133.
73. Weinsheimer writes, "Pope writes through—he per-scribes, he imitates—the epics of Homer and Virgil, and Milton; he does not write about them. The *Dunciad* is unmistakably indebted to its predecessors" ("Writing about Literature," 72).
74. Erskine-Hill, "Pope," 367.
75. Bogel, "Dulness Unbound," 849.
76. Mack, *Alexander Pope*, 781.
77. Milton, *Paradise Lost*, ll. 1–7.
78. Rogers, *Alexander Pope*, 215.
79. Black, "Ideology," 210.
80. Weber, "Garbage Heap," 11.
81. Eisenstein, *Printing Press*, 93.
82. Rumbold, *Alexander Pope*, 6.
83. Weber, "Garbage Heap," 3.
84. Bullard, "Digital Editing," 59.
85. Bullard, 58.
86. Seidel, *Satiric Inheritance*, 234.
87. Weber, "Garbage Heap," 7.
88. Abrams, *Norton Anthology*, 2576.
89. As quoted in Rumbold, *Alexander Pope*, 324.
90. King, *Gendering of Men*, 89.
91. King, 89.

92. West-Pavlov, *Temporalities*, 67.
93. Bolingbroke, *Letters*, 9.
94. King notes that these included "the Stuart monarchs James I, Charles I, and Henrietta Maria; the powerful courtiers the Earl and the Countess of Arundel and the favorite George Villiers, elevated by James I in 1623 to the rank of Duke of Buckingham; and Sir Henry Wotton, ambassador to Venice" (*Gendering of Men*, 89).
95. King, 92.
96. King writes, in order to illuminate criticism on virtuosic pursuits as trivial, "Judith Drake wrote in her *Essay in Defence of the Female Sex* (1696) that the virtuosos neither increased trade nor discovered anything that had not been deliberately 'unheeded only because useless'" (92).
97. Seidel, *Satiric Inheritance*, 233.
98. Weber, "Garbage Heap," 4.
99. Runia, "Burying the Dead," 317.
100. King, *Gendering of Men*, 93.
101. Runia, "Burying the Dead," 324.
102. Caruth, *Unclaimed Experience*, 61, 62.
103. Caruth, 63.
104. Caruth, 3–4.
105. Rumbold, *Alexander Pope*, 184.
106. Caruth, *Unclaimed Experience*, 62.
107. Bogel, "Garbage Heap," 853.
108. Rumbold, *Alexander Pope*, 184.
109. Rumbold, 205.
110. Rumbold, 278.
111. Dryden, "Astraea Redux," l. 317.
112. Dryden, ll. ll. 320–324.
113. Seidel, *Satiric Inheritance*, 244.
114. Rumbold, *Alexander Pope*, 318.
115. Mack, *Alexander Pope*, 783.
116. Abrams, *Norton Anthology*, 2574.
117. Slater, "Hume's Revisions," 131.
118. Rumbold, *Alexander Pope*, 1.
119. Nokes, *Vision*, 102.
120. Mack, *Alexander Pope*, 775.
121. Rumbold, *Alexander Pope*, 8.
122. Rumbold, 11.
123. Mack, *Alexander Pope*, 778.
124. Rumbold, *Alexander Pope*, 2.

125. Rumbold describes Warburton in *Alexander Pope* as "an ambitious clergyman and former attorney whom he rapidly adopted as his authorised editor and commentator" (2).
126. Foxon and McLaverty, *Pope*, 226–227.
127. Rumbold, *Alexander Pope*, 2. As Rumbold points out, Warburton "very obviously used his friendship with Pope to further his career: aided by his status as Pope's authorised editor, he was to marry an heiress to whom Pope had introduced him, rising to become a bishop and a considerable figure in the world of letters" (2).
128. Weber, "Garbage Heap," 3. See also Nicholson, "Illusion," 192.
129. Kernan, *Printing Technology*, 12.
130. Weber, "Garbage Heap," 8–9.
131. Rumbold, *Alexander Pope*, 1–2.
132. Hammond, *Professional Imaginative Writing*, 302.
133. Hammond, 4.
134. Hammond, 294.
135. As quoted in Todd, "Blunted Arms," 195.
136. Todd, 194–95.
137. Runia, "Burying the Dead," 325.
138. Hammond offers an overview of the critical reception of Mack's rendering of Pope, specifically pages 245–46 in *Professional Imaginative Writing*.
139. Abrams, *Norton Anthology*, 2546.
140. Abrams, 2546.
141. Pope, "Eloisa to Abelard," l. 343. Hereafter cited in parenthesis.
142. Runia, "Burying the Dead," 325.

2. "Their Artless Tale Relate"

1. Kaul, *Thomas Gray*, 4.
2. Pope, *Epistle to Dr. Arbuthnot*, ll. 215–16.
3. In his sonnet, Warton describes Gray as follows: "While slowly-pacing through the church-yard dew / At curfeu-time, beneath the dark-green yew / Thy pensive genius strikes the moral strings" (ll. 4–6).
4. Sharp, "Elegy," 11.
5. Parisot points out that despite the popularity of the graveyard school of poetry in the eighteenth century, a definitive "aesthetic code" by which to understand this body of work falls short, only loosely encompassing texts that together reveal an interest in the macabre, the nocturnal, and the transience of life. Christened such by scholars in the early twentieth century, the graveyard poets, most notably Thomas Parnell, Robert Blair, Edward Young, William Collins, and Thomas Gray, represent a diversity of poetic

forms, making it difficult, as Parisot elucidates, to pinpoint their shared aesthetic conventions. See Parisot, "Piety, Poetry," 175.
6. Weinfield, *Poet without a Name*, 2.
7. Reed, *Background of Gray's "Elegy,"* 246.
8. Parisot, "Piety, Poetry," 184. Starr summarizes the popularity of the "Elegy" by listing the various languages its translations appeared in: "By 1946 there had been over 200 English and American imitations and parodies, besides translations into Armenian, Bohemian, Czechoslovakian, Danish, Dutch, French, German, Greek, Hebrew, Hungarian, Icelandic, Italian, Japanese, Latin, Portuguese, Russian, Spanish, and Welsh. In some of these languages (e.g. French, Italian, and Latin) there appear to have been as many as 25 to 40 different renderings. For a poem of only 128 lines, its impact has obviously been enormous" (*Twentieth-Century Interpretations*, 9).
9. Hammond, *Professional Imaginative Writing*, 294.
10. Sitter, *Literary Loneliness*, 80. Throughout its critical history, scholars have been willing to discuss the historical aspects of Gray's "Elegy"; history in this context, though, manifests as recordable data, such as possible literary sources. For instance, Edgecombe traces a possible literary precedent for the "Village-Hampden" stanza ("Source"). Or conversations center on the poem's literary connections to its commemorative and elegiac predecessors.
11. Sitter, *Literary Loneliness*, 83.
12. Abrams, *Norton Anthology*, 2833.
13. See 54–56 of Thorpe, *Eighteenth-Century English Poetry*, for a full description.
14. Thorpe, 57.
15. See also my previously published work on the "Elegy" in "Historical Representation."
16. For more information on the longue durée, see Braudel, *On History*.
17. Gray, "Elegy," l. 1–4. Hereafter cited in parenthesis.
18. Weinbrot, "Gray's 'Elegy,'" 548.
19. Williams, *Country and the City*, 14.
20. Pope, *Discourse*, 119.
21. Sharp, "Elegy," 11.
22. Williams, *Marxism*, 132.
23. Alpers, *What Is Pastoral?*, 185.
24. Sitter, *Literary Loneliness*, 103.
25. Weinfield, *Poet without a Name*, 59–60.
26. Pope, *Discourse*, 120.
27. Alpers, *What Is Pastoral?*, 174.
28. Sitter, *Literary Loneliness*, 90–91.
29. Parisot, "Piety, Poetry," 181.
30. Alpers, *What Is Pastoral?*, 25.

31. Alpers, 93.
32. Runia, "Burying the Dead," 325.
33. Sharp "Elegy," 3, 4.
34. Goodridge, *Rural Life*, 71.
35. Goodridge, 77.
36. Duck, "Thresher's Labour," ll. 66–69.
37. Collier, "Woman's Labour," ll. 105–16.
38. Thomson, "Winter," ll. 259–260. Hereafter cited in parenthesis.
39. Weinfield, *Poet without a Name*, 60.
40. Weinfield, xi.
41. Weinfield, 15.
42. Sharp, "Elegy," 7.
43. Johnson, "Vanity of Human Wishes," ll. 175–78.
44. Alpers, *What Is Pastoral?*, 12.
45. Benjamin, "On the Concept of History," 391.
46. Benjamin, 391.
47. Benjamin, 396.
48. Pope, *Elegy*, ll. 37–42. Hereafter cited in text.
49. Cole, "Contradictions of 'Community,'" 197, 199.
50. Cole, 198.
51. Weinfield, *Poet without a Name*, 62.
52. Caruth, *Unclaimed Experience*, 62.
53. Weinbrot, "Gray's 'Elegy,'" 551.
54. Weinbrot, 548.
55. Sitter, *Literary Loneliness*, 84.
56. Cole, "Contradictions of 'Community,'" 198.
57. Sitter, *Literary Loneliness*, 95.
58. Williams, *Country and the City*, 35.
59. Weinfield, *Poet without a Name*, 69.
60. Sharp, "Elegy," 13.
61. Weinfield, *Poet without a Name*, 89, 89–90.
62. See Odney, "Thomas Gray's 'Daring Spirit.'" Also worth reexamining in this context is Hinnant's discussion of the way that Gray invokes a different understanding of history from typical eighteenth-century views in "The Bard": "The complexity of Gray's attitude towards the historical mythology of the English Middle Ages grows out of his fusion of antiquarianism and poetry and is quite distinct from the conventional attitudes of historians of his age" ("Changing Perspectives," 326). Hinnant explores Gray's nascent English patriotism, while Prescott in "Gray's Pale Spectre" considers Gray's depiction of Anglo-Welsh relations. For a discussion of Gray's Pindaric odes, see the introduction.
63. Weinfield, *Poet without a Name*, 72.
64. Benjamin, "On the Concept of History," 391.

65. Benjamin, 405.
66. Parisot, "Piety, Poetry," 185.
67. Sharp, "Elegy," 15.
68. Sharp, 18.
69. Milton, *Lycidas*, l. 176.
70. Milton, ll. 182–83.
71. Milton, l. 12.
72. Milton, ll. 152–56.
73. Williams, *Country and the City*, 18.
74. Milton, *Lycidas*, ll. 191.
75. Runia, "Burying the Dead," 324.
76. Sharp, "Elegy," 22.
77. Parisot, "Piety, Poetry," 188.
78. Sharp, "Elegy," 6.
79. Sharp, 24.
80. Haggerty, "Desire and Mourning," 199.
81. Haggerty, 199.
82. Alpers, *What Is Pastoral?*, 349.
83. Sharp, "Elegy," 4.
84. Weinbrot, "Gray's 'Elegy,'" 546.
85. Weinbrot, 550.
86. Weinbrot, 548.
87. Carper, "Gray's Personal Elegy," 462.
88. Runia, "Burying the Dead," 325.
89. Caruth, *Unclaimed Experience*, 4.
90. Williams, *Country and the City*, 12: "What seemed a single escalator, a perpetual recession into history, turns out, on reflection, to be a more complicated movement: Old England, settlement, rural virtues—all these, in fact, mean different things at different times, and quite different values are being brought to question."
91. Sitter, *Literary Loneliness*, 102.
92. Kaul, *Thomas Gray*, 9–10.
93. Alpers, *What Is Pastoral?*, 12. Alpers takes issue with Jameson's conception of literary works as either participating in tradition or performing breaks: "In an essay on generic theory, Fredric Jameson offers a choice between two historical models-one 'based on the identity between its various stages' and the other 'based on difference and discontinuity, thereby projecting a very different view of history itself as a series of irrevocable qualitative breaks.' This absolute division between identity and discontinuity seems to me belied by the history of at least some literary forms" (12).
94. Sharp, "Elegy," 4.
95. Sitter, *Literary Loneliness*, 84.

96. Haggerty, "Desire and Mourning," 186.
97. Sitter, *Literary Loneliness*, 110.
98. For a fuller discussion of the various constitutions of history at play in "Eton College," see my previously published article "Returning to Eton."
99. Gray, "Eton College," l. 60. Hereafter cited in parenthesis.
100. Caruth, *Unclaimed Experience*, 61.
101. Odney, "Thomas Gray's 'Daring Spirit,'" 259.
102. Mack, *Thomas Gray*, 390.
103. Although Armstrong in *Desire and Domestic Fiction* primarily explores eighteenth-century novels, her comments on the interweaving of domesticity and femininity proves useful here.
104. Gray, "Mrs. Clerke," ll. 1–16.
105. Mack notes that Mrs. Clerke was the wife of a friend of Gray's, the physician John Clerke. Mack writes, "Mrs. Clerke had died in childbirth on 27 April, 1757, at the age of only thirty-one ... Gray's epitaph on Mrs. Clerke was eventually inscribed on a tablet in St. George's Church at Beckenham, in Kent, where Clerke's father served as rector" (*Thomas Gray*, 500). Mack also claims that "Gray could not help but recall the death of his own mother" (501) when writing the "Epitaph."
106. Mack, 501.

3. "She Has Now a Tale to Tell"

1. Richardson, *Clarissa*, 158. Hereafter cited in parenthesis.
2. This collective impulse breaks the boundaries of the fictive world, as seen by the intense investment of readers such as Lady Bradshaigh and Mary Delany in the development of the novel's plot—and who in some cases participated in rewriting the ending for themselves, as did Lady Elizabeth Echlin. Castle elaborates on "[Richardson's] pained reaction to what he perceived as misreadings of his book—notably readers such as Lady Bradshaigh, who refused to see Lovelace as the 'blackest of villains' and instead damned the heroine for her 'over-niceness' regarding the marriage proposals" (*Clarissa's Cyphers*, 172).
3. See Thompson, "Abuse and Atonement" (Clarissa as Christ figure); Steele, "*Clarissa*'s Silence" (Clarissa as manipulating silence as a means of assuming control); Lewis, "*Clarissa*'s Cruelty" (Clarissa as a marker of moral authority); Wilson, "Clarissa"; and Castle, *Clarissa's Cyphers*.
4. Runge, "Gendered Strategies," 367.
5. Castle, *Clarissa's Cyphers*, 176.
6. Thompson, "Abuse," 267; my emphasis.
7. See Doody, "Samuel Richardson," who provides an overview of the various conventions Richardson invokes.

8. Doody, 379.
9. Hammond, *Professional Imaginative Writing*, 220.
10. Hunter, *Before Novels*, 19.
11. Hunter, 19.
12. Doody, "Samuel Richardson," 388.
13. Bracken and Silver, "Samuel Richardson," 229.
14. Doody, "Samuel Richardson," 385.
15. Bracken and Silver, "Samuel Richardson," 231.
16. Richardson, *Letters*, 2.
17. Richardson, 3.
18. Richardson, 270.
19. Doody, "Samuel Richardson," 387.
20. Doody, in her biography of Richardson, notes that when he was thirteen he was asked by three girls to write their responses to love letters received. She writes, "The young scribe noticed the difference between what went into the epistle and what went on in the heart" (381).
21. Bracken and Silver, "Samuel Richardson," 229.
22. Doody also mentions the importance of these "lost years," particularly to our assessments of Richardson's theatrical interest ("Samuel Richardson," 387).
23. Bracken and Silver, "Samuel Richardson," 233.
24. Hunter, *Before Novels*, 176.
25. I would suggest that there are connections here to Pope's description of men as monkeys in the noise-making competition of book 2 of *The Dunciad*.
26. Roxburgh, "Rethinking Gender," 426.
27. Castle, *Clarissa's Cyphers*, 86.
28. Castle, 60.
29. Wilson, "Clarissa," 75.
30. Binhammer, "Knowing Love," 868.
31. Lovelace, of course, collapses the two when he adapts a brothel as the domestic space in town in which he holds Clarissa hostage. As Hultquist rehearses in "Matriarchs, Murderesses, and Coquettes," stereotypes of the female figure competed for ideological—and hence aesthetic—space in the eighteenth century.
32. Steele, "*Clarissa's* Silence," 1.
33. Steele, 4–5.
34. Roxburgh, "Rethinking Gender," 412.
35. Binhammer, "Knowing Love," 861.
36. As Castle has pointed out, "Critics often remark, more or less scurrilously, on the apparent disparity between Richardson's own understanding of what he was doing in his fiction—his express intentions—and the uncanny depths of meaning his works open up for the reader" (*Clarissa's Cyphers*, 171).

37. As quoted in Abrams, *Norton Anthology*, 2121.
38. Alpers, *What Is Pastoral?*, 12.
39. Hammond, *Professional Imaginative Writing*, 234.
40. Castle, *Clarissa's Cyphers*, 45.
41. Castle, 44–45.
42. Keymer, *Richardson's Clarissa*, 11.
43. Wilson, "Clarissa," 73.
44. Castle, *Clarissa's Cyphers*, 27.
45. Keymer, *Richardson's Clarissa*, 19.
46. Castle, *Clarissa's Cyphers*, 169.
47. Gallagher, *Nobody's Story*, 341.
48. Richardson also points to the complexity of naming through his naming of both Harlowe father and son as James. Wilson indicates that this shared name references James I and James II: "The names of Clarissa's closest male relatives do, however, suggest tyranny and Catholicism, forces counter to English liberty and its encouragement of the free inquiry of true wit" (75).
49. Binhammer, "Knowing Love," 864.
50. Castle, *Clarissa's Cyphers*, 97.
51. Richardson, *Pamela*, 139.
52. Richardson, 171–72.
53. See particularly *Pamela*, 253.
54. Castle, *Clarissa's Cyphers*, 96.
55. Steele, "Clarissa's Silence," 15.
56. Castle, *Clarissa's Cyphers*, 121.
57. Caruth, *Unclaimed Experience*, 61.
58. Binhammer, "Knowing Love," 865.
59. Castle, *Clarissa's Cyphers*, 25.
60. Benjamin, "On the Concept of History," 391.
61. Castle, *Clarissa's Cyphers*, 145.
62. Castle, 145.
63. Castle, 130.
64. Runge, "Gendered Strategies," 371.
65. Runge, 371. Wilson also looks at the ways that Clarissa "bypasses the traditional paths of domestic power" ("Clarissa," 68) through her rejection of her family's proposed marriage to Solmes.
66. Weber's thoughts on eighteenth-century sculptural representations of femininity offer an intriguing look at visual depictions of the "ideology of sexual containment" that "turns female subjects into effectively paralyzed statues, dubiously exquisite corpses" ("Dreams of Stone," 126). In her reading of various French paintings featuring female sculptures, Weber elucidates the way that those female sculptures serve as overseers of female sexual deportment in scenes in which the female's chastity appears

unstable. Of particular interest here is Weber's description of the Medici Venus as "a body that survives beyond all natural constraints of mortality and matter, in order to gratify the people who have pushed it past those limits" (140). Effectually, Weber situates the sculpture (and the corpse) as the site of commemoration embodying an ideology of femininity that Clarissa encounters throughout Richardson's novel. Like the Medici Venus, Clarissa's corpse is "exquisite" in its ability to survive beyond the violence done to it, although its survival is not intended for the "gratification" of her tormentors so much as for their edification and chastisement.

67. Runia, "Burying the Dead," 317.
68. Kibbie, "Estate," 127.
69. Kibbie, 126.
70. Oliver, "Mourning Clarissa," 42.
71. Oliver, 52.
72. Oliver, 47.
73. Oliver, 50.
74. Kibbie, "Estate," 124.
75. Doody, "Samuel Richardson," 385.
76. Roxburgh, "Rethinking Gender," 427.
77. Kibbie, "Estate," 123–24.
78. Caruth, *Unclaimed Experience*, 4. Caruth's words recall to mind the belatedness of Pope's attacks in *The Dunciad*, discussed in chapter 1.
79. Runia, "Burying the Dead," 317.
80. Kibbie, "Estate," 131.
81. Gallagher's book *Nobody's Story* explores the way the abstract female body transcends the limitations of status as "nobody" in order to expand the nuances of literary prestige and authorial presence within the period.
82. Kibbie, "Estate," 135.
83. Kibbie, 134.
84. Siebert, "Hume's History," 557.
85. Siebert, 558.
86. Oliver, "Mourning Clarissa," 60.
87. Hunter, *Before Novels*, 38.
88. Hunter, 176. Eagleton elaborates on Richardson's ongoing revisionary process following the 1755 publication of *A Collection of the Moral and Instructive Sentiments, Maxims, Cautions, and Reflexions, Contained in the Histories of Pamela, Clarissa, and Sir Charles Grandison*: "Yet even this *summa* is no mere transcription of the original texts: passages are thoroughly rewritten and fresh sentiments added, a preface and appendix supplied, and the whole volume alphabetically arranged. Having completed this labour, Richardson turned in his latter years to arranging, censoring and indexing his voluminous correspondence for publication—that is to say,

reworking texts written about his texts into a new text. He kept up a ceaseless revision of his works (radically so in the cast of *Pamela*) until his death" (*Rape of Clarissa*, 21).
89. Castle, *Clarissa's Cyphers*, 173.
90. As quoted in Castle, 173.
91. See Armstrong's *Desire and Domestic Fiction*, which argues that the middle-class female's influence within the domestic sphere influenced larger historical events and helped shaped centers of power and prevailing notions of identity.
92. Eagleton, *Rape of Clarissa*, 5.
93. Binhammer, "Knowing Love," 874–75.
94. Eagleton, *Rape of Clarissa*, 5.
95. Eagleton, 6.
96. See Binhammer, "Knowing Love," 862, for comments on the alternatives for women. For a further look at changing relations between men and women in the eighteenth century, specifically the manner in which conduct books approached female desire, see Armstrong and Tennenhouse in *The Ideology of Conduct*: "Together with conduct books and other literature that claimed to be directed at women readers, novels helped to redefine what men were supposed to desire in women and what women, in turn, were supposed to desire to be" (11).
97. Lynch, in her book *The Economy of Character*, discusses the collapse of the "public" and the "private" within her study of reader association with fictional characters.
98. Steele, "Clarissa's Silence," 16.
99. Doody, "Samuel Richardson," 383.
100. Richardson, *Vade Mecum*, v.

Coda

1. Benjamin, "On the Concept of History," 391.
2. As quoted in Slater, "Hume's Revisions," 132; the interview with Boswell took place on July 7, 1776.
3. Slater, 132.
4. Austen, *Mansfield Park*, 350.
5. Slater, "Hume's Revisions," 132. Yet contemporary eighteenth-century audiences did not always read Hume's *History* for the history it detailed but rather for the *way* that history is written. The immediate reaction to the first volume published in 1754 was not altogether friendly, with many readers taking umbrage at Hume's depiction of Christianity. Slater points out that both the *Monthly Review* no. 12 (1755) and Daniel MacQueen's *Letters on Mr. Hume's History of England* (1756) accuse Hume of "stepp[ing]

beyond the acceptable bounds of gentlemanly behaviour through his treatment of religion" (141). As he writes in the prefatory piece *My Own Life*, Hume blamed the lack of success on partisan politics. Hume saw himself as the embattled author immersed in the quarrels of Whig and Tory, and other such divisions arising from religion, class, and geographic affiliation.

6. Woolf, "Historical Writing," 488.
7. Mack, *Literary Historicity*, 3.
8. Gay, *Beggar's Opera*, 3.17.
9. As quoted in O'Brien, "English Enlightenment," 522.
10. Slater, "Hume's Revisions," 156.
11. Sitter, *Literary Loneliness*, 84.
12. Pope, *Preface*, xxviii; my emphasis.
13. As quoted in Krutch, *Selected Letters*, 10; my emphasis.
14. Jackson, "Thomas Gray," 168.
15. As quoted in Krutch, *Selected Letters*, 82.
16. Starr, *Twentieth-Century Interpretations*, 4.
17. Jackson, "Thomas Gray," 180, 170.
18. Jackson, 168.
19. Gray, "Hymn to Ignorance," ll. 29–30.
20. Gray, ll. 31–35.
21. Richardson, *Vade Mecum*, v.
22. As quoted in Curran, "Samuel Richardson's Correspondence," 55.
23. Curran, 55.
24. Benjamin, "On the Concept of History," 392.
25. Runia, "Burying the Dead," 324.

BIBLIOGRAPHY

Abrams, M. H., ed. *The Norton Anthology of English Literature: The Restoration and the Eighteenth Century*. 7th ed. Edited by M. H. Abrams and Stephen Greenblatt. New York: W. W. Norton, 2000.

Alpers, Paul. *What Is Pastoral?* Chicago: University of Chicago Press, 1996.

Anderson, Benedict. *Imagined Communities: Reflections on the Origin and Spread of Nationalism*. New York: Verso, 2006.

Armstrong, Nancy. *Desire and Domestic Fiction: A Political History of the Novel*. Oxford: Oxford University Press, 1989.

Armstrong, Nancy, and Leonard Tennehouse. *The Ideology of Conduct: Essays on Literature and the History of Sexuality*. New York: Methuen, 1987.

Austen, Jane. *Mansfield Park*. Edited by Ernest Rhys. London: Everyman, 1906.

Benjamin, Walter. "On the Concept of History." In *Selected Writings*, edited by Howard Eiland and Michael W. Jennings, 389–410. Cambridge: Belking, 2003.

Binhammer, Katherine. "Knowing Love: The Epistemology of *Clarissa*." *ELH* 74, no. 4 (Winter 2007): 859–79.

Black, Jeremy. "Ideology, History, Xenophobia, and the World of Print in Eighteenth-Century England." In *Culture, Politics, and Society in Britain, 1660–1800*, edited by Jeremy Black and Jeremy Gregory, 184–216. Manchester: Manchester University Press, 1991.

Bogel, Fredric V. "Dulness Unbound: Rhetoric and Pope's *Dunciad*." *PMLA* 97 (1982): 844–55.

Bolingbroke, Henry St. John, 1st Viscount. *Letters on the Study and Use of History*. In *Lord Bolingbroke: Historical Writings*, edited by Isaac Kramnick, 3–152. Chicago: University of Chicago Press, 1972.

Bracken, James, and Joel Silver. "Samuel Richardson (London: 1721–1761)." In *The British Literary Book Trade, 1700–1820*, vol. 154, edited by James K. Bracken and Joel Silver, 229–36. Farmington Hills, MI: Gale, 1995.

Braudel, Fernand. *On History*. Translated by Sarah Matthews. Chicago: University of Chicago Press, 1982.

Broich, Ulrich. "Alexander Pope, the Ideal of the Hero, Ovid, and Menippean Satire." *Studies in the Literary Imagination* 38, no. 1 (Spring 2005): 179–96.

Brown, John. *An Essay on Satire: Occasion'd by the Death of Mr. Pope*. London: Printed for R. Dodsley at Tully's Head in Pall-Mall, 1745.

Bullard, Paddy. "Digital Editing and the Eighteenth-Century Text: Works, Archives, and Miscellanies." *Eighteenth-Century Life* 36, no. 3 (Fall 2012): 57–80.

Carper, Thomas. "Gray's Personal Elegy." *Studies in English Literature* 17, no. 3 (Summer 1977): 451–62.

Caruth, Cathy. *Unclaimed Experience: Trauma, Narrative, and History*. Baltimore, MD: Johns Hopkins University Press, 1996.

Castle, Terry. *Clarissa's Cyphers: Meaning and Disruption in Richardson's Clarissa*. Ithaca, NY: Cornell University Press, 1982.

Cole, Lucinda. "The Contradictions of 'Community': Elegy or Manifesto?" *Eighteenth Century: Theory and Interpretation* 36, no. 3 (Autumn 1995): 195–202.

Colley, Linda. *Britons: Forging the Nation, 1707–1837*. New Haven, CT: Yale University Press, 2005.

Collier, Mary. "The Woman's Labour." In *The Broadview Anthology of British Literature: The Restoration and the Eighteenth Century*, 2nd ed., edited by Joseph Black, Leonard Conolly, Kate Flint, Isobel Grundy, Don LePan, Roy Liuzza, and Jerome J. McGann et al., 894–897. Ontario: Broadview, 2018.

Cowper, William. "The Task." In *The Norton Anthology of English Literature: The Restoration and the Eighteenth Century*, 7th ed., edited by M. H. Abrams and Stephen Greenblatt, 2875–880. New York: W. W. Norton, 2000.

Curran, Louise. "'Into Whosoever Hands Our Letters Might Fall': Samuel Richardson's Correspondence and 'the Public Eye.'" *Eighteenth-Century Life* 35, no. 1 (Winter 2011): 51–64.

———. "'A Man Obscurely Situated': Samuel Richardson, Autobiography and 'The History of Mrs. Beaumont.'" *Journal for Eighteenth-Century Studies* 36, no. 2 (June 2013): 279–95.

Doerksen, Teri. "Richardson, Celebrity, and Editorial Mediation in Anna Meades's *Sir William Harrington*." *Eighteenth-Century Fiction* 29, no. 2 (Winter 2016–17): 221–40.

Doody, Margaret Anne. "Samuel Richardson (July 1689–4 July 1761)." In *British Novelists, 1660–1800*, vol. 39, edited by Martin C. Battestin, 377–409. Farmington Hills, MI: Gale, 1985.

Dray, W. H. "David Hume on History." *Queen's Quarterly* 90, no. 3 (1983): 735–45.

Dryden, John. "Astraea Redux." In *Selected Poems*, edited by Steven N. Zwicker, 11–19. New York: Penguin, 2001.

———. "A Discourse Concerning the Original and Progress of Satire." In *The Norton Anthology of English Literature*, 7th ed., edited by M. H. Abrams, 2120–21. New York: W. W. Norton, 2000.

Duck, Stephen. "The Thresher's Labour." In *The Broadview Anthology of British Literature: The Restoration and the Eighteenth Century*, 2nd ed., edited by Joseph Black, Leonard Conolly, Kate Flint, Isobel Grundy, Don LePan, Roy Liuzza, and Jerome J. McGann et al., 891–93. Peterborough: Broadview, 2018.

Eagleton, Terry. *The Rape of Clarissa: Writing, Sexuality and Class Struggle in Samuel Richardson*. Minneapolis: University of Minnesota Press, 1982.

Edgecombe, Rodney Stenning. "A Source for the 'Village-Hampden' Stanza in Gray's 'Elegy.'" *Notes and Queries* 20, no. 1 (Winter 2007): 36–37.

Eisenstein, Elizabeth L. *The Printing Press as an Agent of Change: Communications and Cultural Transformations in Early Modern Europe.* Cambridge: Cambridge University Press, 1979.

Eron, Sarah. *Mind over Matter: Memory Fiction from Daniel Defoe to Jane Austen.* Charlottesville: University of Virginia Press, 2021.

Erskine-Hill, Howard. "Pope and the Poetry of Opposition." In *The Cambridge Companion to Alexander Pope*, edited by Pat Rogers, 134–49. Cambridge: Cambridge University Press, 2007.

Fairer, David. David Fairier: *English Poetry of the Eighteenth Century, 1700–1789.* London: Routledge, 2003.

———. "Thomas Warton, Thomas Gray, and the Recovery of the Past." *Thomas Gray: Contemporary Essays*, edited by W. B. Hutchings, 146–70. Liverpool: Liverpool University Press, 1993.

Foxon, David, and McLaverty, James. *Pope and the Early Eighteenth-Century Book Trade.* Oxford: Clarendon, 1991.

Gallagher, Catherine. *Nobody's Story: The Vanishing Acts of Women Writers in the Marketplace 1670–1820.* Berkeley: University of California Press, 1994.

Gay, John. *The Beggar's Opera.* Edited by Bryan Loughrey and T. O. Treadwell. New York: Penguin, 1986.

Goodridge, John. *Rural Life in Eighteenth-Century English Poetry.* Cambridge: Cambridge University Press, 1995.

Grant, Sarabeth. "Historical Representation, Commemoration, and the Pastoral: Writing History in Thomas Gray's 'Elegy Written in a Country Churchyard.'" *Clio: A Journal of Literature, History, and the Philosophy of History*, 45, no. 2 (Spring 2016): 137–57.

———. "Returning to Eton: Writing History and Temporality in Thomas Gray's 'Ode on a Distant Prospect of Eton College.'" *Papers on Language and Literature* 53, no. 2 (Spring 2017): 132–65.

Gray, Thomas. *The Bard.* Chester: Printed by Poole, Barker, 1775.

———. "Elegy Written in a Country Churchyard." In *The Norton Anthology of English Literature: The Restoration and the Eighteenth Century*, edited by M. H. Abrams and Stephen Greenblatt, 2826–28. New York: W. W. Norton, 2000.

———. "Epitaph on Mrs. Clarke." In *The Poetical Works of Thomas Gray, with the Life of the Author.* London: Printed under the Direction of J. Bell, British Library, Strand, 1788.

———. "Hymn to Ignorance." In *The Poems of Mr. Gray. To Which Are Prefixed Memoirs of His Life and Writings by W. Mason.* London: Printed by A. Ward and Sold by J. Dodsley, Pall-Mall, 1775.

———. "Ode Written on a Distant Prospect of Eton College." In *The Norton Anthology of English Literature: The Restoration and the Eighteenth Century*,

7th ed., edited by M. H. Abrams and Stephen Greenblatt, 2826–28. New York: W. W. Norton, 2000.

Griffin, Robert J. *Wordsworth's Pope: A Study in Literary Historiography*. Cambridge: Cambridge University Press, 1995.

Haggerty, George. "Desire and Mourning: The Ideology of the Elegy." In *Ideology and Form in Eighteenth-Century Literature*, edited by David H. Richter, 185–206. Lubbock: Texas Tech University Press, 1999.

Halbawchs, Maurice. *On Collective Memory*. Edited by Lewis Coser. Chicago: University of Chicago Press, 1992.

Hammerschmidt, Sören. "Print, Proximity, and the Marketing of Richard Phillips: Mediating Richardson." *Eighteenth-Century Fiction* 29, no. 2 (Winter 2016–17): 277–316.

Hammond, Brean. *Professional Imaginative Writing in England, 1670–1740, "Hackney for Bread."* Oxford: Clarendon, 1997.

Hawley, Judith. "Grub Street in Albion: or, Scriberlian Satire in the Romantic Metropolis." *Romanticism* 14, no. 2 (2008): 81–93.

Hay, Denys. "The Historiographers Royal in England and Scotland." *Scottish Historical Review* 30, no. 109 (April 1951): 15–29.

Hinnant, Charles H. "Changing Perspectives on the Past: The Reception of Thomas Gray's *The Bard*." *Clio: A Journal of Literature, History, and the Philosophy of History* 3, no. 3 (1974): 315–29.

Hughes, Helen Sard. "More Popeana: Items from an Unpublished Correspondence." *PMLA* 44, no. 4 (December 1929): 1090–98.

Hultquist, Aleksondra. "Matriarchs, Murderesses, and Coquettes: Investigations in Long-Eighteenth-Century Femininities." *Eighteenth Century* 53, no. 1 (2012): 119–25.

Hunter, J. Paul. *Before Novels: The Cultural Contexts of Eighteenth-Century English Fiction*. New York: W. W. Norton, 1990.

Jackson, Wallace. "Thomas Gray (26 December 1716–30 July 1771)." In *Eighteenth-Century British Poets: Second Series*, vol. 109, edited by John E. Sitter, 168–82. Farmington Hills, MI: Gale, 1991.

———. *Vision and Re-Vision in Alexander Pope*. Detroit, MI: Wayne State University Press, 1983.

Jameson, Frederic. *The Political Unconscious: Narrative as a Socially Symbolic Act*. Ithaca, NY: Cornell University Press, 1981.

Johnson, Samuel. *Rambler* 2, no. 60 (1752): n.p.

———. "The Vanity of Human Wishes." In *The Broadview Anthology of British Literature: The Restoration and the Eighteenth Century*, 2nd ed., edited by Joseph Black, Leonard Conolly, Kate Flint, Isobel Grundy, Don LePan, Roy Liuzza, and Jerome J. McGann et al., 761–65. Ontario: Broadview, 2018.

Jones, Steven E. "Shelley's Fragment of 'A Satire upon Satire': A Complete Transcription of the Text with Commentary." *Keats-Shelley Journal* 37 (1988): 136–63.

Kalter, Barrett. *Modern Antiques: The Material Past in England, 1660–1780.* Lanham, MD: Bucknell University Press, 2012.

Kaul, Suvir. *Thomas Gray and Literary Authority: A Study in Ideology and Poetics.* Stanford, CA: Stanford University Press, 1992.

Kernan, Alvin. *Printing Technology, Letters, and Samuel Johnson.* Princeton, NJ: Princeton University Press, 1987.

Keymer, Tom. *Richardson's Clarissa and the Eighteenth-Century Reader.* Cambridge: Cambridge University Press, 1992.

Kibbie, Ann Louise. "The Estate, the Corpse, and the Letter: Posthumous Possession in *Clarissa*." *ELH* 74, no. 1 (2007): 117–43.

King, Thomas A. *The Gendering of Men, 1600–1750, Vol. 2: Queer Articulations.* Madison: University of Wisconsin Press, 2008.

Krutch, Joseph Wood. *The Selected Letters of Thomas Gray.* New York: Farrar, Straus & Giroux, 1952.

Kumar, Krishan. *The Making of English National Identity.* Cambridge: Cambridge University Press, 2003.

Kurtz, J. Roger. *Trauma and Literature.* Cambridge: Cambridge University Press, 2018.

Lewis, Jayne Elizabeth. "*Clarissa*'s Cruelty: Modern Fables of Moral Authority in *The History of a Young Lady*." In *Clarissa and Her Readers: New Essays for the Clarissa Project*, edited by Carol Flynn and Edward Copeland, 45–68. New York: AMS, 1999.

Lockwood, Thomas. "On the Relationship of Satire and Poetry after Pope." *Studies in English Literature, 1500–1900* 14, no. 3 (Summer 1974): 387–402.

Looser, Devoney. *British Women Writers and the Writers of History, 1670–1820.* Baltimore, MD: Johns Hopkins University Press, 2000.

Lynch, Deidre. *The Economy of Character: Novels, Market Culture, and the Business of Inner Meaning.* Chicago: University of Chicago Press, 1998.

Mack, Maynard. *Alexander Pope: A Life.* New York: W. W. Norton, 1985.

Mack, Robert. *Thomas Gray: A Life.* New Haven, CT: Yale University Press, 2000.

Mack, Ruth. *Literary Historicity: Literature and Historical Experience in Eighteenth-Century Britain.* Stanford, CA: Stanford University Press, 2009.

Macpherson, Sandra. *Harm's Way: Tragic Responsibility and the Novel.* Baltimore, MD: Johns Hopkins University Press, 2010.

McLaverty, James. "Naming and Shaming in the Poetry of Pope and Swift, 1726–1745." In *Swift's Travels: Eighteenth-Century British Satire and Its Legacy*, edited by Nicholas Hudson, 160–76. Cambridge: Cambridge University Press, 2008.

Milton, John. "Lycidas." In *Poems upon Several Occasions*, 1–35. London: Printed for James Dodsley, 1785.

———. *Paradise Lost*. Edited by Christopher Ricks. New York: Penguin, 1968.

Newman, Gerald, and Leslie Ellen Brown. *Britain in the Hanoverian Age, 1714–1837: An Encyclopedia*. New York: Routledge, 1997.

Nicholson, Colin. "Illusion on the Town: Figuring Out Credit in *The Dunciad*." *Literature and History* 12, no. 2 (Autumn 1986): 181–94.

Nokes, David. *Raillery and Rage: A Study of Eighteenth-Century Satire*. New York: St Martin's, 1987.

O'Brien, Karen. "English Enlightenment Histories, 1750–c. 1815." In *The Oxford History of Historical Writing, Vol. 3: 1400–1800*, edited by Jose Rabasa, Masayuki Sato, Edoardo Tortarolo, and Daniel Woolf, 518–35. Oxford: Oxford University Press, 2012.

Odney, Paul. "Thomas Gray's 'Daring Spirit': Forging the Poetics of an Alternative Nationalism." *Clio: A Journal of Literature, History, and the Philosophy of History* 28, no. 3 (Spring 1999): 245–60.

Oliver, Kathleen. "'With My Hair in Crystal': Mourning Clarissa." *Eighteenth-Century Fiction* 23, no. 1 (2010): 35–60.

Parisot, Eric. "Piety, Poetry, and the Funeral Sermon: Reading Graveyard Poetry in the Eighteenth Century." *English Studies* 92, no 2 (April 2011): 174–92.

Phillips, Mark Salber. *Society and Sentiment: Genres of Historical Writing in Britain, 1740–1820*. Princeton, NJ: Princeton University Press, 2000.

Pope, Alexander. "A Discourse on Pastoral Poetry." In *The Poems of Alexander Pope, A Reduced Version of the Twickenham Text*, edited by John Butt, 119–23. New Haven, CT: Yale University Press, 1963.

———. *The Dunciad*. In *The Dunciad in Four Books*, edited by Valerie Rumbold. New York: Longman, 1999.

———. "Elegy to the Memory of an Unfortunate Lady." In *The Poems of Alexander Pope, A Reduced Version of the Twickenham Text*, edited by John Butt, 262–64. New Haven, CT: Yale University Press, 1963.

———. "An Essay on Criticism." In *The Poems of Alexander Pope, A Reduced Version of the Twickenham Text*, edited by John Butt, 143–68. New Haven, CT: Yale University Press, 1963.

———. "Epilogue to the Satires: Dialogue II." In *Alexander Pope: The Major Works*, edited by Pat Rogers, 400–407. Oxford: Oxford University Press, 1993.

———. "Epistle to Dr. Arbuthnot." In *The Poems of Alexander Pope, A Reduced Version of the Twickenham Text*, edited by John Butt, 597–612. New Haven, CT: Yale University Press, 1963.

———. "The Preface of 1717." In *The Poems of Alexander Pope, A Reduced Version of the Twickenham Text*, edited by John Butt, xxv–ix. New Haven, CT: Yale University Press, 1963.

Prescott, Sarah. "'Gray's Pale Spectre': Evan Evans, Thomas Gray, and the Rise of Welsh Bardic Nationalism." *Modern Philology* 104, no. 1 (August 2006): 72–95.
Rabb, Melinda Alliker. *Satire and Secrecy in English Literature from 1650 to 1750*. New York: Palgrave Macmillan, 2008.
Reed, Amy Louise. *The Background of Gray's "Elegy": A Study in the Taste for Melancholy Poetry, 1700–1751*. New York: Russell & Russell, 1924.
Richardson, Samuel. *The Apprentice's Vade Mecum; or, Young Man's Pocket-Companion*. Dublin: Printed by S. Powell, 1734.
———. *Clarissa, or, The History of a Young Lady*. Edited by Angus Ross. New York: Penguin, 1985.
———. *Letters Written to and for Particular Friends, on the Most Important Occasions*. London: Printed for C. Rivington in St. Paul's Church-Yard, 1741.
———. *Pamela; or, Virtue Rewarded*. London: Printed for C. Rivington in St. Paul's Church-Yard, 1741.
Rogers, Pat. *Alexander Pope: Selected Poetry*. Edited by Pat Rogers. Oxford: Oxford University Press, 1998.
Roxburgh, Natalie. "Rethinking Gender and Virtue through Richardson's Domestic Accounting." *Eighteenth-Century Fiction* 24, no. 3 (2012): 404–29.
Rumbold, Valerie. *Alexander Pope: The Dunciad in Four Books*. New York: Pearson Education, 1999.
Runge, Laura. "Gendered Strategies in the Criticism of Early Fiction." *Eighteenth-Century Studies* 28, no. 4 (Summer 1995): 363–78.
Runia, Eelco. "Burying the Dead, Creating the Past." *History and Theory* 46 (October 2007): 313–25.
Rushworth, John. *Historical Collections Private Passages of State*. London: George Thomason, [ca. 1659].
Sabor, Peter. "Rewriting *Clarissa*: Alternative Endings by Lady Echlin, Lady Bradshaigh, and Samuel Richardson." *Eighteenth-Century Fiction* 29, no. 2 (Winter 2016–17): 131–50.
Said, Edward. *Orientalism*. New York: Pantheon, 1978.
Seidel, Michael. *Satiric Inheritance: Rabelais to Sterne*. Princeton, NJ: Princeton University Press, 1979.
Sharp, Michele Turner. "Elegy unto Epitaph: Print Culture and Commemorative Practice in Gray's 'Elegy Written in a Country Churchyard.'" *PLL* 38, no. 1 (Winter 2002): 3–28.
Sherburn, George. "*The Dunciad*, Book IV." *Studies in English* (1945): 174–90.
Siebert, Donald T. "Hume's *History of England*." In *The Oxford Handbook of Hume*, 546–68. New York: Oxford University Press, 2016.
Sitter, John. *Literary Loneliness in Mid-Eighteenth-Century England*. Ithaca, NY: Cornell University Press, 1982.
Slater, Graeme. "Hume's Revisions of the 'History of England.'" *Studies in Bibliography* 45 (1992): 130–57.

Snead, Jennifer. "Epic for an Information Age: Pope's 1743 *Dunciad in Four Books* and the Theater Licensing Act." *ELH* 77, no. 1 (Spring 2010): 195–216.
Starr, Herbert. *Twentieth-Century Interpretations of Gray's "Elegy."* Englewood Cliffs, NJ: Prentice-Hall, 1968.
Steele, Kathryn. "*Clarissa*'s Silence." *Eighteenth-Century Fiction* 23, no. 1 (2010): 1–34.
Swift, Jonathan. "Verses on the Death of Dr. Swift." In *The Norton Anthology of English Literature: The Restoration and the Eighteenth Century*, edited by M. H. Abrams and Stephen Greenblatt, 2301–12. New York: W. W. Norton, 2000.
Thomas, Claudia. "Pope and His *Dunciad* Adversaries." In *Cutting Edges: Postmodern Critical Essays on Eighteenth-Century Satire*, edited by James E. Gill, 275–300. Knoxville: University of Tennessee Press, 1995.
Thompson, Peggy. "Abuse and Atonement: The Passion of Clarissa Harlowe." *Eighteenth-Century Fiction* 11, no. 3 (April 1999): 255–70.
Thomson, James. "Winter." In *The Broadview Anthology of British Literature: The Restoration and the Eighteenth Century*, 2nd ed., edited by Joseph Black, Leonard Conolly, Kate Flint, Isobel Grundy, Don LePan, Roy Liuzza, and Jerome J. McGann et al., 709–14. Ontario: Broadview, 2018.
Thorpe, Peter. *18th-Century English Poetry*. Chicago: Nelson-Hall, 1975.
Todd, Dennis. "The 'Blunted Arms' of Dulness: The Problem of Power in *The Dunciad*." *Studies in Philology* 79, no. 2 (Spring 1982): 177–204, 527.
Tonson, R. *The Works of Alexander Pope, Esq., in Nine Volumes*. London: Printed for A. Millar, J. & R. Tonson, and Others, 1776.
Watt, Ian. *The Rise of the Novel: Studies in Defoe, Richardson, and Fielding*. Berkeley: University of California Press, 1957.
Weber, Caroline. "Dreams of Stone: Femininity in the Eighteenth-Century Sculptural Imagination." *Studies in Eighteenth-Century Culture* 33 (2004): 125–51.
Weber, Harold. "The 'Garbage Heap' of Memory: At Play in Pope's Archives of Dulness." *Eighteenth-Century Studies* 33, no. 1 (1999): 1–19.
Weinbrot, Howard. "Gray's 'Elegy': A Poem of Moral Choice and Resolution." *SEL* 18 (1978): 537–51.
———. "The Pattern of Formal Verse Satire in the Restoration and the Eighteenth Century." *PMLA* 80, no. 4 (September 1965): 394–401.
Weinfield, Henry. *The Poet without a Name: Gray's Elegy and the Problem of History*. Carbondale: Southern Illinois University Press, 1991.
Weinsheimer, Joel. "Writing about Literature, and through It." *Boundary 2: A Journal of Postmodern Literature and Culture* 10, no. 3 (Spring 1982): 69–91.
West-Pavlov, Russell. *Temporalities*. New York: Routledge, 2013.
Wilkinson, Andrew M. "The Decline of English Verse Satire in the Middle Years of the Eighteenth Century." *Review of English Studies* 3, no. 11 (July 1952): 222–33.

Williams, Aubrey. "Literary Backgrounds to Book Four of *The Dunciad*." *PMLA* 68, no. 4 (September 1953): 806–13.

Williams, Raymond. *The Country and the City*. New York: Oxford University Press, 1973.

———. *Marxism and Literature*. Oxford: Oxford University Press, 1977.

Wilson, Jennifer. "*Clarissa*: The Nation Misrul'd." *Eighteenth-Century Novel* 3 (2003): 65–96.

Woolf, Daniel. "Historical Writing in Britain from the Late Middle Ages to the Eve of Enlightenment." In *The Oxford History of Historical Writing, Vol. 3: 1400–1800*, edited by Jose Rabasa, Masayuki Sato, Edoardo Tortarolo, and Daniel Woolf, 473–96. Oxford: Oxford University Press, 2012.

Wordsworth, William. "Lines Composed a Few Miles above Tintern Abbey." In *Selected Poetry of William Wordsworth*, edited by Mark Van Doren, 99–103. New York: Modern Library Classics, 2001.

———. "Preface." In *Wordsworth and Coleridge Lyrical Ballads, 1798 and 1802*, edited by Fiona Stafford, 95–116. Oxford: Oxford University Press, 2013.

INDEX

Abrams, M. H., 23, 82–83, 93
academy, academic institution. *See* archive
access, accessibility, 5–6, 7, 15–16, 26–27, 38–39, 53, 65–66, 76–77, 89–90, 114–15, 121–22, 160–61, 168, 185–86, 193–94, 217–18
accountability, 31–32, 49–50, 84–85
accumulation, 67–68, 85–86
action: and exemplarity, 4, 11, 20, 36–37, 45, 76–77, 127, 159–64, 167–69, 183–85, 201–2, 210; and history, vii–viii, 76–77, 86–87, 95, 127, 168, 170–71, 183–84, 186–87, 201–2; and interiority, 170, 172–74; and morality, 167, 170–72; outward, 152–53; and recompense, 166–67, 184–85; and trauma, 181–83, 196–97. *See also* agency
Act of Union (1707), 16, 222n24
Addison, Joseph, 7–8, 37
adjudication, 10–11, 50, 95, 222n15
Aeneid (Virgil), 21–22, 57–58, 63–64
aesthetics: and commemoration, 53; contemporary expectations of, 19, 23, 53, 55; of Englishness, ix–x, 9, 15–16; and history, 23, 114–15, 119, 136–37, 141; and recompense, 9, 143–44. *See also* genre; literature; poetry, poetics
agency: emotive, 92–93, 99, 102, 148–49; historical, 5, 73, 76, 78–79, 86–87, 89–90, 158, 192, 209–10; individual, 93, 95, 168, 197–98; and reading, 159–60. *See also* action
alienation, 50, 96, 107; and genre, 97–98; and history, 114–16, 121–22; of self, 9, 95–100, 107, 117, 120–21, 133–35, 209, 214–15
allegory, 83
Alpers, Paul, 99–103, 111, 129–30, 132, 136–37, 168, 233n93
ancients: and exemplarity, 21–22, 37; and imitation, 20, 54–57; versus moderns, 37, 42, 55–56, 59, 227n63; and present, 59
Anglo-Saxon. *See* England

Anne, Queen, 7, 225n11
anonymity, 11–12, 14, 118–19, 127, 130–31, 141–42; and exemplarity, 52; and readers, 15, 90, 148–49, 150, 156, 190–91, 200–201, 218–19
antiquarianism, 70–72. *See also* archive
antiquity. *See* ancients
apocalypse, apocalypticism, viii–ix, 28, 36–37, 68, 74–76, 87, 147, 150. *See also under* Pope, Alexander
Arbuthnot, John, 7, 40–41, 48. *See also* Pope, Alexander
archive, 64–65, 68; and burial, 68–69; and community, 108; as diversion, 72; and epistolary, 150–51; and history, 65–68, 72–73, 95–96, 203–4; and nation, 95–96; and objects, 64–65, 73; satiric, 69; and value, 65–66, 69–71
Aristotle, *The Art of Rhetoric*, 2–3
Arnold, Matthew, 92
audience, 13, 15–16, 25–27, 43–44, 88–90, 138; diversity of, 156–57; and domesticity, 160–61; and elegy, 131–34; and history, 218–19; and moral instruction, 155–56; and national identity, 143–44, 150–51. *See also* anonymity: and readers
Austen, Jane, *Mansfield Park*, 210–11

Bacon, Francis, 8–9
Benjamin, Walter, 12; "angel of history," 216–18; "moments of danger," 209; "On the Concept of History," 55, 111, 124–25, 183–84
Binhammer, Katherine, 162, 176, 182, 205
biography, 4, 91–93
Black, Jeremy, 44–45
Blair, Robert, 92
Bloom, Harold, 21
body: and authority, 185–86; and commemoration, 186–87; and death, 197–98; and discourse, 191. *See also* burial, burial practices; death

251

Bogel, Fredric, 59
Bolingbroke, Lord Henry St. John, viii, 1–4, 17, 37, 70–71, 212–13, 221n5; and historical knowledge, 1–2; *Letters on the Study and Use of History*, viii, 1–3
Boswell, James, 210
Bracken, James, 157–58
Bradshaigh, Lady, viii, 25–26, 195, 215–16, 234n2
breakage, 12–16, 74–77, 82, 114–15, 141, 164–65, 181–82. *See also* Caruth, Cathy; trauma
Brown, John, *Essay on Satire, Occasion'd by the Death of Mr. Pope*, 36
Brown, Leslie Ellen, 16
Bullard, Paddy, 66–67
burial, burial practices, 15, 68–69, 72, 88–90, 93–94, 103, 108, 111–12, 126; and class, 109–14; and collective, 207–8; and commemoration, 128–29, 138, 213–16; and history, 119, 217–18; and recompense, 210. *See also* death
Butler, Judith, 27
Butt, John, 39–40

canon, 6–8
capitalism, 109–10. *See also* class
Carper, Thomas, 133
Caruth, Cathy, 12, 74–75, 114–15, 141, 181–82, 196–97. *See also* trauma
Castle, Terry, 151, 161–62, 170, 172–74, 176–77, 180, 183–85, 203–4, 234n2, 235n36
Catholicism, 6–7, 58–59, 71–72, 87. *See also* Pope, Alexander
causality, 10, 37, 48–49, 81–82, 111, 125, 148, 150, 154–55, 181–84, 188, 192–93. *See also* history, historiography; linearity; recompense; time, temporality
Cave, Edward, *The Gentleman's Magazine*, 65
celebrity, 9, 26–27, 32, 42–43, 91–93, 210–12
Chambers, Ephraim, *Cyclopaedia*, 65
character. *See under* novel

Charles I, 7, 202, 229n94
Charles II, 7, 80–81
chronology. *See* history, historiography; time, temporality
Cibber, Colley, 60–64, 67–68, 76–77, 79–84, 142, 227n48; *Apology for the Life of Colley Cibber*, 41–42, 226n48
citizen, citizenship, viii, 2–6, 16, 84–85, 154. *See also* nation, nationalism
civic: and exemplarity, 3, 45, 221n4; and history, 4–5; and nation, 38–39, 80, 127, 154–55; virtue, 2, 21–22, 154–55
Clarissa (Richardson), viii–ix, 5–6, 8–9; and action, 181–83; and agency, 197–98; as archive, 203–4; and authority, 184–89, 191–96, 198–203; and commemoration, 182–91, 197–99, 206–7; and death, 184–92, 196–201; and deception, 27; and exemplarity, 150–53, 158–69, 181–85, 187–91, 199–202, 205–6; and gender, 160, 162, 235n31; and genre, 150–51, 153–54, 158, 168, 193–94; and history, 150–52, 154–55, 158–64, 166–68, 180–87, 190–92, 195–97, 199, 201–3; and intentionality, 170–72; and interiority, 164, 166–70, 172–73, 192; and language, 182–83; and law, 192–97; and letter writing, 159–60, 162–68, 170–72, 183–84; and linearity, 154–55; and morality, 163, 166–73, 199, 204; multivocal method of, 172, 174; and naming, 174–79, 204–6; narrative framework of, 202–7; and nation, 150–51, 154–55; and objects, 188–90; and public exposure, 160–62; radical element of, 162; and rape, 179–84, 186–87, 192–93, 195–97; and reader, 150–51, 234n2; and recompense, 14–15, 165–67, 192–93, 196, 206–7; and revenge, 198–99; and selfhood, 200–201; and silence, 162–64, 168; and succession, 190; and temporality, 187–88, 195–96; and violence, 168; and visibility, 194–97, 199. *See also* epistolary; Richardson, Samuel

class: and community, 113–14; and conflict, 21, 108–10; and death, 113–14; and elitism, 71–72, 108–12, 123–24, 134, 140–42, 181, 205–6; and exemplarity, 79, 81–82, 86–87, 181; and gender, 105–6, 238n91; growing middle, 71–72; and history, 107; and labor, 105–6; and law, 14–15; and memorialization, 14; and nonelite writers, 7; and recompense, 131; and remembrance, 118–20; and sexuality, 81–82; and visibility, 134

closure. *See* endings

Cole, Lucinda, 113–14, 116–17, 119

collective: and commemoration, 197–98; fractured, 64; and history, 28, 55, 64–66, 72–74, 118–19, 186–87, 204–5, 223n25; and individual, 72–74, 104, 108, 128–29, 145; and nation, 17, 38, 58–59, 62–64, 138–39, 204–5, 207–8; and personal, 204–5; and recompense, 10–14, 165; survival of, 104–5. *See also* community; individuals, individuality

Colley, Linda, 16, 222n24

Collier, Mary, "The Woman's Labour: An Epistle to Mr. Stephen Duck," 105–6

Collins, William, 93; "Ode on the Poetical Character," 23

comedy, 76–77, 195. *See also* satire

commemoration, viii; and exemplarity, 3–6, 48, 80, 100–101, 104, 118–19, 126, 130–32, 183; and history, 38, 52–53, 72–73, 75–76, 78–80, 90, 100–101, 123, 126–27, 136–37, 164, 187, 217–18; and nation, 15, 23, 53, 85, 120–21, 127, 143–44, 217–18; and ownership, 197–98; and recompense, 12–13, 15, 88, 143–45; and selfhood, 127–30, 134–35, 182–91, 193–94, 199, 206–7. *See also under* individual titles

commerce, commercialism, 35–36, 42–43, 55–56, 71, 83–84, 88–89

commodities, 109–10, 131–32

community, 103; continuity of, 125–26; and difference, 113, 116–17; and history, 94, 99, 104, 113–14, 126–27, 137–38; and lack, 116, 119; and literature, 8–9; and loss, 108; and rupture, 113–14; survival of, 108. *See also* audience; "Elegy Written in a Country Churchyard"; nation, nationalism

consciousness: collective, 104, 138; and experience of time, 12–13, 74; as historical, viii, 5–6, 23, 28, 76, 82, 90, 95–97, 101, 103–4, 111, 115–16, 129, 133–39, 141, 145–46, 150, 153, 166, 183–84, 199, 218–19; individual, 13–14, 165; and interiority, 30, 129, 164, 166; national, 13–14, 31–32, 84–85, 138–39. *See also* subjectivity

continuity, 21–22, 70–71, 154–55; and community, 102–8, 126–27, 132; and history, 28, 38–39, 63, 74, 106–7, 117–18, 120–21, 126–27, 209–11; and literature, 136–37; and recompense, 15–16. *See also* history, historiography; linearity; time, temporality

Cowper, William, *The Task*, 39

crime, 10–11, 222n15; moral, 15; and origins, 14–15. *See also* injury; recompense

Cromwell, Oliver, 119–21

curation, 66–67. *See also* archive

Curran, Louise, 25–26, 215–16

death, 108; and body, 197–98; commemoration, 128–29; and history, 119, 184–86; and individuality, 126; and memory, 146–47; and mourning, 126; and pain, 148; and poverty, 113–14; and temporality, 148, 188. *See also* burial, burial practices

democracy, democratic, ix–x, 138–39, 205–6

desire, desirability, viii–ix, 10–11, 17, 23, 25–26, 49–53, 62–63, 70–72, 81–82, 86–90, 95, 98, 122–23, 126, 128–32, 140, 145, 162–65, 170–71, 174, 176, 182–85, 187, 189, 196–98, 206–7, 217, 238n96

detail, 1–2, 24–26, 45, 110–12, 131, 192–93, 211

didacticism. *See* morality, moral didacticism

difference, 61; eradication of, 67–71; and history, 59, 90, 113, 233n93; narration of, 75–76; and nation, 16, 64, 87, 138–39, 222n24

disability, 6–7, 18–19, 88, 154–55. *See also* Pope, Alexander

discontinuity, ix–x, 11–12, 28, 108–9, 111, 114–18, 207, 233n93

disenfranchisement. *See* enfranchisement, disenfranchisement

Doerksen, Teri, 26–27

domesticity, 4, 7, 19, 104–5; connection between private and public, 4; and femininity, 186, 234n103, 238n91; and history, 202; and labor, 105–7; and mourning, 126; and public events, 160–61; ruptured, 145–46. *See also* gender

Doody, Margaret, 153, 155–56, 207, 235n20, 235n22

Dryden, John, 7, 42; *Absalom and Achitophel*, 58–59, 63, 76–77; *Astraea Redux*, 80; biblical and classical typologies of, 63; Catholicism of, 58–59; *A Discourse Concerning the Original and Progress of Satire*, 44–45, 47, 167–68; *MacFlecknoe*, 58–59; translations of French histories, 211–12

Duck, Stephen, "The Thresher's Labour," 105–6

Dunciad, The (Pope), vii, 5–6, 8–9, 15, 57–58, 227n54; and *The Aeneid*, 57–58; archival strategy of, 64–70, 72–73; and barbarians, 61–62; and burial, 88–89; and commercialism, 42–43; and contemporary, 84–87; and exemplarity, 35–39, 43, 52, 76, 79–84, 87–88; and exposure of secrets, 45–46, 48–49; and history, 19–20, 31, 36–39, 50–55, 57–58, 63–64, 66–67, 76–87, 140–41; and hostility, 45, 53; and injury, 49–50; and introspection, 74–76; and literary history, 58–59; and naming, 65; and nation, viii–ix, 87, 142; and *Paradise Lost*, 60–61; publication history, 82–86; and recompense, 15, 64, 82–85, 88–89; scatological language of, 58–59, 61–62, 72–73; and sexuality, 81–82; and time, 48–49; and trauma, 74–76, 88; and verse satire, 38–39, 41–45, 74, 77–79. *See also* Pope, Alexander; satire

Eagleton, Terry, 204–5, 237n88

Echlin, Lady, 25–26, 234n2

economy, 5, 37, 94–95, 107, 114–16, 122–23, 175–76. *See also* class

Edward I, 21–22

eiron (figure), 60–61

Eisenstein, Elizabeth, 64–65

elegy, 92–93; and audience, 131–32; and class, 134; and death, 103; and exemplarity, 104, 109–11; genre conventions of, 12–15, 104, 135–39, 144–45, 157–58; and history, 102, 124–25, 134, 135–39, 157–58; and isolation, 132; and memorial, 127–28; pastoral, ix, 99–100, 102; and poet, 128; and recompense, 12–13, 15; and satire, 110–11; subject of, 98, 130–31, 134. *See also* graveyard (or churchyard) school; Gray, Thomas

"Elegy Written in a Country Churchyard" (Gray), viii, 5–6, 8–9, 104; and alienation, 98–100, 114, 117, 120–22, 127–28, 132–33; and class, 108–14, 117–20, 131; and commemoration, 118–19, 121–23, 125–31, 138, 144; and community, 116–19, 126–27, 133, 137–38; composition of, 144–45; and death, 100–104, 108–12, 119, 126, 128–29; and empathy, 131–32; and exemplarity, 22, 95–96, 104, 108–9, 114, 120–21, 126–27, 131, 144–45; and fantasy, 119–21; and genre, 95–96, 104, 115–16, 124–25, 132, 134–35; and geography, 125; and history, 95–104, 108–11, 114–21, 123–25, 135–38, 231n10; and individuality, 126–27; and introspection, 144–45; legacy of, 91–92, 231n8; and memory, 116–17; and nation, viii–ix, 137–39; and pastoralism, viii–ix, 98–102, 111, 114–17, 122–24, 126, 136; and readership, 144–45; and recompense, 14, 131, 133–35, 143–45; and religion, 97–98; and reproduction, 104–8; and rural life, 99–100, 107, 136; and self, 98–100, 129–30; and subjectivity, 127–29, 137; and suffering, 105–6; and temporality, 98; and trauma, 114–15, 134–35. *See also* Gray, Thomas

emotion, 15–16, 18, 21, 28, 74, 76, 82, 88–90, 92–95, 98, 102, 112–15, 123–24, 133–34, 145, 148–49, 158–60, 165–72, 198–99, 202

endings, 25–26, 31–32, 64, 79, 97–98, 103–4, 129–30, 132, 150–51, 154–55, 195, 202–6, 211–12, 215, 217–18, 225n60, 234n2. *See also* burial, burial practices; death

enfranchisement, disenfranchisement, ix–x, 5, 7, 14, 17, 31–32, 86–87, 109, 199

England, vii–ix, 5; anti-monarchicalism, 120–21; and authority, 71; degeneration of, 88; establishment of Great Britain, 16, 222n24; and exemplarity, 37–39, 87–88, 205–6, 209–10, 212–13, 219; expansiveness of, 9, 17; and history, 95–96, 121, 154–55, 209–12; and identity, ix–x, 16–17, 23, 58–59, 71–72, 88, 127, 136, 140–44, 150–51, 211–12; and interiority, 19; and literature, 210–11; and morality, 154–55; and nationalism, 61–62, 64, 137–38, 219; and pastoralism, 98–99, 136; and print trade, 207–8; and progress, 142–43; reading public, 50; Revolution of 1642, 120–21; and similitude, 87

Enlightenment, 69–71, 83, 117–18, 189, 205–6

epic, 56–59, 61, 158–59, 192–95, 228n73

epideictic (form), 2–3, 22

epistolary (genre), 25–27, 150–51; and agency, 159–60, 170, 172–74; and breakage, 164–65; and coherency, 167–68; efficacy of, 157–58, 183; and exemplarity, 159–60; and exposure, 160–62; and gender, 159–60; and history, 151–52, 154, 158–59, 168; and interiority, 164, 173–74; and moral didacticism, 155–58, 166–67, 171–72; as multivocal method, 158–59, 173–74; and readers, 170; and recompense, 165–66; and silence, 163–64, 168, 180; and visibility, 151, 170–71. *See also Clarissa*

epitaph, 15, 53, 82, 84, 88, 127–39, 142–47, 150, 184–85, 196–97, 200–201, 206–7, 218–19, 234n105. *See also* Gray, Thomas: "Epitaph on Mrs. Clarke"

Erskine-Hill, Howard, 58–59

estrangement, 50, 58, 90, 98, 149, 185. *See also* strangers

ethics, 10, 31, 101–2, 151, 153. *See also* examples, exemplars, exemplarity; morality, moral didacticism

events, viii–ix; and exemplarity, 4, 12, 22, 63, 80–82, 114–15, 172–73; and history, 19–21, 25–26, 35–39, 44–45, 52–53, 58–59, 63, 65–67, 72–73, 80–82, 85–88, 93–95, 109–11, 114–15, 126–27, 135, 152–54, 163–65, 172–73, 195–99; and nation, 17, 95; and origins, 10–11, 14, 84–85, 192–93; public, 80, 160–61, 170; and recompense, 10–11, 13–14, 165; and trauma, 74–76, 88, 114–15, 181, 186–88. *See also* history, historiography

examples, exemplars, exemplarity, 2–4; and action, 162–65, 183, 202; and anonymity, 52, 150; and archives, 68, 73; and audiences, 150–51, 159–60; and authority, 183–84; and class, 79, 81–82, 86–87, 108–11; and domesticity, 202; as exclusionary, 4, 6–9, 162, 177–78, 205–6; and gender, 151, 192–93; geography of, 95; and heroism, 87–88; and history, 1–12, 11, 20–22, 28, 35–37, 45, 58–59, 63–64, 69–70, 80–82, 87–88, 90, 93–95, 99–100, 120–21, 150–51, 160–63, 166–68, 213–14, 217–19, 221nn6–7, 222n9; and imitation, 31–32, 36, 52–53, 56–57, 165–66; inadequacies of, 6, 74, 88, 209–10, 212–13, 219; and individuals, 96, 126–27, 131, 139–40,

examples, exemplars, exemplarity (*continued*)
175; and interiority, 90, 152–53, 164, 192, 209–10; and linearity, 37; and morality, 151–52, 160–61, 167–68; and naming, 40–41, 48, 50–52; and nation, 207–10, 212–13, 221n4; and novel, 158–59; and past, 54–57, 61–62; and population, 39–40; public and private, 160–61; and recompense, 12–13, 144–45; and satire, 35–41, 45, 88; and succession, 80–82; and temporality, 37; and trauma, 181, 183; and value, 69–70; and visibility, 162–63. *See also* history, historiography
exposure. *See* names, naming; visibility

Fairer, David, 18–19
fantasy, vii–ix, 17; and history, 86–87, 89, 119–21. *See also* imagine, imagination, imaginary
fiction, fictive, 22, 25–27, 153, 176, 204–7, 227n51, 234n2. *See also* novel
Fielding, Henry, 3, 7–8, 153; *The Adventures of David Simple*, 154; *The History of Tom Jones, Foundling*, 154; *Shamela*, 173–74
Foxon, David, 85
futurity, ix–x, 5–6, 8–9, 15–16, 42–43, 58–59, 124–27, 143–44, 150–52; and community, 103; and death, 89–90, 133–35, 148–49, 197–98, 200–201; disavowal of, 74; and exemplarity, 37, 42–43, 63–64, 139–43, 167–68, 210, 221n7; and individuality, 139–42; and memory, 49; and nation, 136, 138, 205–8, 210–11; and temporality, 11–12, 20, 63–64, 70–77. *See also* history, historiography; time, temporality

Gallagher, Catherine, 175, 178–79, 226n51
Gay, John, 15; *The Beggar's Opera*, 31–33, 212–13
gender, 7–8, 235n31, 236n81; and authority, 191; and commemoration, 130–31; and domesticity, 186, 234n103, 238n91; and exemplarity, 151, 166, 181–82, 191–93; and femininity, 205–6, 236n66; and history, 77–78; and identity, 27; and interiority, 166; and labor, 105–6; and letter writing, 159–60; and morality, 151, 166–67, 169; and possession, ix, 191–92, 197–98; and recompense, 145–46; and spaces of public and private, 162, 199; and subjectivity, 191–92, 194; and suffering, 7, 154–55, 179–80, 199; and visibility, 199
genre, viii–ix, 91–92; and alienation, 98; and biographical criticism, 91–93; and convention, 8, 31–33, 58–59, 114, 136–37; and Englishness, 16; and exemplarity, 150–51; expansiveness of, 17; and history, ix, 31–32, 45–46, 52–53, 94, 99, 102, 157–58, 209; inadequacies of, 134–35, 209; and rupture, 115–16, 136–37; and violence, 168. *See also* elegy; epistolary; novel
Georges I and II, 11, 38
Gibbon, Edward, 1, 3–4, 211–12
Goodridge, John, 104–5
gothic (genre), 187–88
graveyard (or churchyard) school, 21, 23, 91–92, 100–101, 214–15, 230n5; and death, 101–2; and empathy, 131–32; and history, 92–94, 100; and nature, 117. *See also* "Elegy Written in a Country Churchyard"
Gray, Thomas, viii–x, 5–6; and alienation, 214–15; "The Bard," 21–22, 93–94, 232n62; and commemoration, 23, 214–16; "Epitaph on a Child," 145–49; "Epitaph on Mrs. Clarke," 145–49, 234n105; "Epitaph on Mrs. Mason," 145; "Epitaph on Sir William Williams," 145; Eton Manuscript, 144; and exemplarity, 139–40; and history, 18–19, 21–25, 92–95, 139–40; "Hymn to Ignorance," 215; and laborers, 7; legacy of, 91–93; and melancholy, 96; and nation, 139–43, 232n62; "Ode on a Distant Prospect of Eton College," 13,

23, 139–43, 224n46, 234n98; Pindaric odes, 21–22, 93–94, 214–15; poetic style, 93–94; and poverty, 150; "The Progress of Poesy," 21–22; and recompense, 143–44, 146–48; and retreat, 6–8, 18–19, 21, 95, 135–36; as self-reflective writer, 121; "Sonnet on the Death of Richard West," 23, 224n46; and temporality, 141, 147–48; and trauma, 147–48. *See also* "Elegy Written in a Country Churchyard"

great, greatness, Great Men. *See* examples, exemplars, exemplarity

Great Britain. *See* England

grief, 12–13, 89, 104, 108, 131–32, 137, 139, 145–48, 179–80, 189–90. *See also* elegy

Grub Street, 55–56, 65

guilt, 10–12, 46–51, 121, 196, 219. *See also* recompense

Haggerty, George, 132, 137
Halbawchs, Maurice, 49
Hammerschmidt, Sören, 26–27
Hammond, Brean S., 35–36, 55, 86–88, 153, 169, 230n138
Hanmer, Sir Thomas, 56–57
Hanoverians, 16, 20, 36–38, 79–80, 110. *See also* England
Hay, Denys, 211–12
Haywood, Eliza, 7–8
heroic couplet, vii, 223n29
heroism. *See* examples, exemplars, exemplarity
heterogeneity, 4. *See also* difference
Hill, Aaron, 36
Hinnant, Charles, 21–22, 232n62
history, historiography, vii–x, 1–5, 18–19, 52–53, 209–10, 221–22nn7–8; and aesthetics, 23; and agency, 95, 184–85; and breakage, 12, 76–77, 82, 115; and causality, 37, 48–49, 58–59, 111, 154–55; and change, 2–3, 5–6, 38, 64, 70–71, 73, 76–82, 140–41; and class, 7, 14, 107–9, 113–14; and closure, 202–4; collective, 204–5; and commemoration, 15, 38, 53, 72–73, 75–76, 90, 104, 108, 118–19, 125, 127, 130–31, 134–35, 138, 184–86, 188, 217–18; and context, 21; and continuity, 38–39, 63, 70–72, 106–8, 114, 117–18, 126–27, 154–55, 210–11; and death, 101–4; and degradation, 61–62, 64; and disciplinarity, 3–4; and domesticity, 4, 202; and exclusion, 162; and exemplarity, 1–4, 8–9, 20–22, 28, 35, 37–38, 45, 56, 68, 76–82, 87–88, 90, 95, 99, 121, 149–51, 162–63, 202, 209–10, 212–14, 217–19, 221n6, 222n9; and fantasy, 17, 86–87, 89, 119–20, 139; and gender, 195; and genre, 8, 31–33, 52–53, 91, 102, 124–25, 209; and geography, 100, 124–25; historical consciousness, 5–6, 76, 136–37, 152, 199, 218–19; and identity, 10–11; and individuals, individuality, 36–37, 50–52, 72–73, 126, 139–40, 183–84, 217; integrity of, 61–63, 79–80; and interiority, 167–68; knowledge of, 65–70, 94, 99, 102–3, 113–16, 123–24, 126–27, 138–39, 152, 158, 170–71; and linearity, 37–38, 120–21, 140, 154, 172–73, 181–82; and literature, 5, 21–22, 58–59; as longue durée, 94–95, 101–3, 108, 126–27; and loss, 55, 74, 114; misappropriation of, 1, 53–54; and morality, 32–33, 166–67; and narrative, ix, 6, 138–39; and nation, ix–x, 5–6, 21–23; and objects, 65, 189–90; and origins, 22, 49–50, 111–12; and past, 55–58, 66–67, 71, 124–25; and poetry, 23–24, 94, 101–2; and politics, 11; and progress, 142–43; public and private, 23–24, 155–56; and recompense, 143–44; and repetition, 74–75, 102–5, 216–17; and revision, 211–13; and rupture, 113–14, 120–21, 138; and satire, 52–53, 77–78; and sexuality, 81–82, 106–7; and subjectivity, 12–13, 17, 47–48, 56–59, 61, 75–76, 89–90, 119–20, 140, 164, 166–67, 186–87, 191–92; and trauma, 11–12, 74–76, 88, 195; and value, 68–69, 118–19, 126, 134, 138, 175–76;

history, historiography (*continued*)
and violence, 74, 111, 168, 179–80, 183–84; and visibility, 71, 79, 81, 90, 118–19, 134, 149, 192, 195, 209–10; writing of, 8–9, 11–12, 16, 22, 45–46, 48, 94–96, 123–25, 135, 137–39, 143, 152, 154, 166–68, 180, 202–4, 209–13, 238n5. *See also* events; examples, exemplars, exemplarity; recompense; time, temporality
hope, 17, 47, 61, 74–75, 88–90, 133–35, 139–42, 144, 187, 205–6, 217. *See also* futurity
Howell, James, 211–12
Hume, David, 1, 3–4, 202, 210–13, 221n4; *History of England*, 2–3, 82–83, 226n38, 238n5
Hunter, J. Paul, 42, 153, 158, 202–3

identity: and anonymity, 127; as cohesive, 129–30; collective, 10–11, 13–14, 116–17, 143–44; and crime, 14–15; and death, 90; disavowing, 51–52; and gender, 27; and history, 58–59; individual, 10–11, 13–14, 67–68, 143–44; and memory, 49; and names, 175–77; narratives of, 10–11; and nation, vii–x, 8–9, 15–16, 88, 127, 207–8; as open ended, 17; and subjectivity, 58–59; and trauma, 114–15; unique, 50–51
Iliad (Homer), 20, 58, 87–88
imagine, imagination, imaginary, vii–ix; aesthetic, 15–16; and alternatives, viii–ix, 8–9, 25–27, 47–48, 119–21, 152–53, 162–63, 168–69, 176–77, 185–86, 205–6, 210, 219; and audience, 13, 25–26, 200–201, 205–7; and collectivity, 28, 223n25; and death, 129–32, 138–39, 187, 196; and gender, 162, 168–69, 181–82; and history, viii–ix, 8–9, 23, 59, 88–90, 100–101, 103, 107, 119–21, 138–39, 142–43, 176–79, 181–82, 210; and nation, 17, 86–87, 121–22, 125, 144–45, 219; and recompense, 13–14, 47–48, 64. *See also* fantasy

imitation, 2, 20, 31–32, 36–38, 52–55. *See also* examples, exemplars, exemplarity
improvement. *See* progress
inaccessibility. *See* access, accessibility
individuals, individuality: and collective, 17, 64–66, 72–73, 104–5, 108, 126, 204–5; and exemplarity, 96, 126–27; and history, 209–10, 217; and naming, 175–76; and nation, 13–16, 88, 209–10; particular, 50–52; private, 2; and recognition, 126; and subjectivity, 175–76; and suffering, 139–41; and trauma, 75–76. *See also* identity; self; subjectivity
information, 64–65, 69–70. *See also* archive
injury, 10, 49–50; anonymity of, 11–12; and nation, 11, 13–14; and origins, 111–12; public, 84–85; and selfhood, 13. *See also* recompense
innovation. *See also* progress
institutions. *See* archive
intentionality. *See* action
interiority, 6, 52–53, 74, 88, 139–40; and action, 152–53, 166–67, 172–73; and exemplarity, 90; fictive, 153; and gender, 166; and historical consciousness, 129, 137, 164, 166; and individual, 93, 96; and nation, 144–45; and recompense, 166–67
internationalism, 71–72
interpretation, 5–6, 9–12, 50, 122–23, 147–48, 160, 162–63, 170, 194, 206–7, 216–17
introspection. *See* interiority
isolation, 18–19, 29, 59, 108–9, 117–18, 122–23, 125–26, 144–45, 163–64, 217–18

Jackson, Wallace, 214–15
Jameson, Fredric, 136–37, 233n93
Johnson, Samuel, 4, 25; "The Vanity of Human Wishes," 76–77, 110–11

Kaul, Suvir, 21, 91, 95, 135–36
Kernan, Alvin, 85–86

Keymer, Tom, 170–71
Kibbie, Ann Louise, 187–90, 195, 197–98, 200
King, Thomas A., 71–73, 229n94, 229n96
knowledge, 4, 10–11, 155, 182; and community, 103; and genre, 124–25; and history, ix, 1–2, 8, 37–39, 65–70, 94–96, 99, 102–3, 113–16, 123–24, 126–27, 138–39, 152, 158, 162, 170–71; and poverty, 121–22; public forms of, 194; and trauma, 114–15, 179–80, 187. *See also* history, historiography
Krutch, Joseph Wood, 24–25, 224nn48–49
Kumar, Krishan, 16

labor, laborers, 7, 103–7. *See also* class
Law, William, 25
Lennon, Charlotte, 7–8; *The Female Quixote; or, The Adventures of Arabella*, 154
letters. *See* epistolary
library. *See* archive
linearity, 10–11, 37–38, 49, 74; breakage of, 81–82; and history, 140–41; and morality, 172–73; and recompense, 98, 131, 165, 173–74, 196, 219; rejection of, 77–80; and succession, 80; and trauma, 181–82. *See also* causality
literature: and commerce, 55–56, 91; and exemplarity, 6; and genre, 91; and history writing, 5–6, 53; literary history, 21–22, 58–59; and nation, 210–11; and novel genre, 153; and revision, 8, 211; and scholarship, 83; and space, 104–5; and trauma, 222n17. *See also* canon
Lockwood, Thomas, 39, 41–42, 227n54
longue durée. *See under* history, historiography
loss, ix–x, 12–14, 55, 74, 76, 79, 90, 102, 108–10, 114, 128–29, 131–34, 137, 145–47, 155, 180, 190, 209. *See also* elegy; grief
Lydgate, John, 9

Macaulay, Catherine, 3–4, 210–12; *History of England*, 2–3
Mack, Robert, 88, 144, 146–47, 221n6, 230n138, 234n105
Maimbourg, Louis, *History of the League*, 211–12
Marie, Henrietta, 7
Mason, William, 104
McLaverty, James, 47–48, 85
Meades, Anna, *Sir William Harrington*, 26–27
melancholy, 18, 21, 23–24, 43, 74, 91–94, 96, 100–101, 108–9, 138–39. *See also* Gray, Thomas
memory, memorial, 13–15, 90, 104, 125, 134–35, 187, 189–90, 226n50; and archive, 64–65; belatedness of, 49; collective, 72–73; and death, 146–47; and history, 12–13, 53, 188; and remembrance, 116–20; and trauma, 74–76; and value, 126–27
Milton, John, 7, 119–21; *Lycidas*, 12–14, 104, 127–29; *Paradise Lost*, 3, 60–61
moderns, modernity, 2–3, 15–16, 21–22, 37, 55–56, 63–64, 74–75, 83–85, 228n6. *See also* ancients
Montagu, Lady Mary Wortley, 7–8
monument, x, 29, 197–98, 213–16
morality, moral didacticism, 2, 35–36, 39, 65–66, 73, 111–12, 154–56; and authority, 163; and certainty, 157–58, 167–69, 172–73; degeneration of, 15; and gender, 169; and intention, 171–72; lessons of, 3, 31–33. *See also* examples, exemplars, exemplarity
More, Hannah, 7–8
mourning, 12–13, 126, 143–44, 184–85, 188–90, 197–99. *See also* death; elegy; loss
museum. *See* archive

names, naming, 20, 35–36, 40–41, 43–52, 174–75, 236n48; and archives, 65; and authority, 175; and identity, 176–79; refusing, 51–53; value of, 175–76; and visibility, 56–57
narration, narrative, 6; and difference, 75–76; efficacy of, ix; and exemplarity,

narration, narrative (*continued*)
1–13, 17, 22, 26–28, 36–37, 43, 45, 48, 50, 54, 56, 69, 73, 76–77, 80–82, 87, 93–94, 100, 108, 122, 129–30, 134, 144–45, 150–54, 165–67, 181; and history, 6, 65–68, 70–71, 73, 97, 108, 123–25, 138–39, 143, 209–12; and nation, 61–64, 115–16, 138, 141–43, 209–10, 217–18; writing, 162, 164–65, 168, 173–74, 180, 184–88, 190–91, 195–98, 202–3, 206. *See also* examples, exemplars, exemplarity; history, historiography

nation, nationalism, vii–x, 2–3, 5–6, 8–9, 11–12; and antagonism, 16; and archive, 69; and class, 14; and collective, 138; and commemoration, 143–44, 217–18; and degeneration, 88; and difference, 138–39; and domesticity, 145–46, 160–61; and exemplarity, 38–39, 68–69, 150, 207–10; and fantasy, vii, 17; and geography, 135–36; and history, ix–x, 5, 21–22, 53; and identity, 15–16, 71–72, 88, 150–51, 154–55, 207–8, 210–11; and individual, vii–viii, 11, 13–16, 64–65, 73, 141–42, 209–10; and injury, 11–12; and introspection, 144–45; and literature, 15–16, 210–11; and membership, 16; and memory, 65–66; narrating, 138–39, 141–43, 206–7; and recompense, 11–12, 84–85, 148–49, 219; and rupture, 120–21; and trauma, 114–15; and unity, 87; and violence, 150. *See also* examples, exemplars, exemplarity; history, historiography

Newman, Gerald, 16
Nicholson, Colin, 36–37
Nokes, David, 47–48, 82–83
nostalgia, 15–16, 94–95, 107–8, 111, 117–18. *See also* pastoral, pastoralism
novel (genre), 42; and character, 158–59; and epistolary form, 154, 157–58; and history, 153–54; and limits of narrative, 206; theories of, 153. *See also Clarissa*; epistolary; narration, narrative

objects: accumulation of, 67–68; and past, 64–65; and value, 65–66, 72–73
O'Brien, Karen, 5–6
Odney, Paul, 22
Odyssey (Homer), 20–22, 77–78, 87–88
Oliver, Kathleen, 188, 202–3
opera (genre), 31–32
originality, 65–66, 70–71, 111, 209
origins, originating, 5–6, 10–15, 22, 49–50, 84–85, 95, 112–13, 121, 124–27, 144, 154, 157, 192–93, 196–97, 210–11, 217, 219. *See also* history, historiography; recompense

Parisot, Eric, 92, 101–2, 126, 131–32, 230n5
particularity, 10–11, 13–14, 37, 45–47, 50–52, 63, 109–10, 122, 131, 135, 175. *See also* individuals, individuality
pastoral, pastoralism, ix, 20, 94, 98–99; and class, 107, 113–14, 122–24; and commonality, 102; and death, 101–2; and exemplarity, 122; and history, 99–102, 114–15, 123, 125; and ideal, 122–23, 132; inadequacy of, 115, 122–23; and reproduction, 104–5; and violence, 111. *See also* "Elegy Written in a Country Churchyard"; Gray, Thomas
patriotism. *See* nation, nationalism
patronage, 7, 57–58, 71
performance, performativity, 27, 31–33, 76, 114, 170–71
poetry, poetics: and commemoration, 145–46; and exemplarity, 22; and history, 19, 23–25, 53, 92–94, 100–102, 116, 223n27; and nation, 53; and poet, 128; primacy of, 85–86; and trauma, 129–30; and violence, 139–40. *See also* elegy; pastoral, pastoralism
Pope, Alexander, vii–x, 5–8, 15, 82, 221n2, 224n34, 235n25; and ancients, 56–57, 227n63, 228n73; apocalyptic vision of, 36–37, 68, 74–75, 87, 150; and audience, 7, 43–44, 50, 88–89; Catholicism of, 6–7, 58–59; and commemoration, 53, 213–16; and commercialism, 55–56;

A Discourse on Pastoral Poetry, 54–55, 98–99, 101–2; *An Essay on Criticism*, 1–2; *Elegy to the Memory of an Unfortunate Lady*, 111–12, 130–31, 133–34, 148–49; "Eloisa to Abelard," 88–90; *Epilogue to the Satires*, 39–40, 46–47; *Epistle to Dr. Arbuthnot*, 40–41, 214; and exemplarity, 42, 83–88, 133–34, 213–14; and friendship, 48–50, 85, 225n11, 230n125, 230n127; and history, vii–viii, 18–19, 37, 65, 82–87, 213–14; and imitation, 20, 54–55; legacy of, 91, 223n29; "Martinus Scriblerus of the Poem," 55–57; and nation, 61–62, 88; and nonelite writers, 7; personal grievances, 48–50, 225n9; and satire, 18–20, 35–36, 40–44, 47–48, 54–55, 74; and style, vii; translations, 87–88; and trauma, 74–75; *Works* (1717), 54–55, 213–14. See also *Dunciad, The*
populace, population. *See* public, publicity
Poussin, Nicolas, *Et in Arcadia ego*, 14, 113–14, 122–23, 125
poverty, 14, 113–14, 121–22. See also class
Priestley, Joseph, *Lectures on History and General Policy*, 212–13
print, 35–37, 55–56
private, privacy, 2, 4, 10–13, 23–28, 45–48, 71–72, 81–82, 84–87, 90, 104, 114–15, 126–39, 141–42, 151, 160–62, 165–68, 170, 184–85, 191–202, 206–7, 214, 217–19, 238n97. *See also* public, publicity; tort law
progress, 10–11, 22–24, 62, 74–76, 91–92, 114–15, 117–18, 120–21, 125–26, 135, 140–43, 164–65, 167–68, 177–78, 180–81, 188, 216–17. *See also* causality; history, historiography; linearity
Protestantism, 71–72
public, publicity, 2, 39–40; and exclusion, 162; and history, 8–9; and nation, 11; and personal, 160–62; reading, 8–9, 13, 15–16, 50, 238n97; and self, 71–72; and visibility, 44–45, 194. *See also* private, privacy

race, ix–x, 4–8, 29–30, 140–41, 151, 154–55, 177–78, 181, 205–6, 209–10
Raleigh, Walter, 8–9
Rambler, 4. *See also* Johnson, Samuel
rape, ix, 14–15, 68–69, 152, 179–87, 191–202. *See also Clarissa*; trauma; violence
readers. *See* audience; *and under* public, publicity
reception. *See individual titles*
recompense, 9, 11–12, 14; causality of, 48–51; and collective, 85; and crime, 14–15; and epistolary exchange, 165–66; ethics of, 10; and exemplarity, 12–13; and genre, 104; and history, 53–54, 88–89, 143–44; and individual, 13–14; and interiority, 13–14, 166–67; and law, 192–93; and linearity, 55, 98, 104, 115–16, 131, 165, 173–74, 196, 219; and nation, 15–17, 84–85, 219; and origins, 84–85, 192–93; and punishment, 47–48; and satire, 15, 37; timespan of, 95; trajectory of, 10–11; and trauma, 12. *See also* tort law
Reed, Amy Louise, 21, 92
reference, referentiality, 3, 20–21, 28–29, 50–52, 55, 60–62, 64–65, 95, 120–22, 136–39, 175–77, 179, 196, 227n51, 236n48
repair, reparation. *See* recompense
repetition, 37, 52–54, 70–71, 75–76, 102–5, 180–82, 197, 202–3, 206–7, 216–17. *See also* imitation
representation, 5–7, 16, 32–33, 135, 227n51, 236n66; and exemplarity, 88, 116, 227n63; failures of, 74, 77–78, 180; and history, 58–59, 120–21, 152–58, 166–67; and self, 185–86, 192, 196; and temporality, 70; and visibility, 44–47, 85
responsibility, 3, 22, 38–39, 50, 80, 112–13, 144–45, 165, 175–76, 191–92, 199–200
retreat, 18–19, 57, 106–7, 135–36, 144–45, 169, 192
revision, 8–9, 20, 26–27, 32, 82–88, 144, 203–6, 211–13, 226n38, 237n88

Richardson, Samuel, viii–x, 5–6, 235n20, 237n88; *The Apprentice's Vade Mecum*, 155, 169, 190–91, 207–8, 215–16; burial of, 207–8; and commemoration, 215–16; *Correspondence of Samuel Richardson*, 26–27; and domesticity, 7; and epistolary novel, 157–58, 173–74; and exemplarity, 153, 156–57, 169, 173–74, 207–8; and experimentation, 25–27; and gender, 169; and happy endings, 204; and history, viii, 25, 27–28, 158, 167–68; *Letters Written to and for Particular Friends (Familiar Letters)*, 155–57, 206; and marginality, 6–8; as moral guide, 155–56; and names, 178, 236n48; and nation, 150–51, 154–55; *Pamela; or, Virtue Rewarded*, 154–55, 173–74, 178, 205–6; as printer, 6–7, 25, 207–8; private life of, 154–55, 157–58, 190; and prose novel, 153–55; public legacy of, 156–58, 235n36; and readers, 25–27, 150–51, 204–7; relationship with nephew, 190; and secrecy, 202–3
Richardson, Thomas Verren, 190
Romans, 4, 61–62, 118, 221n5. *See also* ancients; examples, exemplars, exemplarity
Romanticism, 8, 19, 23, 43, 55, 74
Rowe, Elizabeth, 19, 221n2
Roxburgh, Natalie, 159, 164, 192–93
Rumbold, Valerie, 43–44, 55–58, 65, 74–75, 81–83, 85–86, 227n63, 230n125, 230n127
Runge, Laura, 151, 186
Runia, Eelco, 72–73, 103, 129–30, 134–35, 138–39, 143, 184–85, 187, 190–91, 197–98, 206–7, 214, 217–18. *See also* commemoration
rupture. *See* breakage
rural, viii–ix, 7, 14, 21, 91–92, 99–100; and class, 108–9; and commemoration, 127; and cottage door image, 104–6; and gender, 105–6; and history, 100; and isolation, 106; and labor, 105–7. *See also* "Elegy Written in a Country Churchyard"; pastoral, pastoralism
Rushworth, John, *Historical Collections*, 211–12, 221n7

Sabor, Peter, 25–26
satire, vii, ix, 18–20, 226n37; and alteration, 52–53; and anxiety, 76–77; and archive, 69–70; and audience, 43–44; and commercial development, 42–43; and common, 76–77; decline of genre, 41–42; and disreputable, 45; and exemplarity, 35–37, 88; and history, 36–37, 53–55, 58–59, 76–79; identity crisis of, 39, 42–43; instructional use of, 35–36, 39–41, 47, 50, 69; and naming, 44–48, 51–52; and recompense, 15; and time, 54–55, 73, 77–78; and visibility, 45–46. *See also Dunciad, The*
scatology, 45, 58–59, 61–62, 72–73
seclusion, 6–7, 135–36. *See also* pastoral, pastoralism
secret history, 45–46
secrets, secrecy, 45–48, 145–46, 152–53, 202–3; and Catholicism, 71–72; and naming, 46–47; and visibility, 45–46
Seidel, Michael, 50–51, 67–68
self: and alienation, 9, 95, 97–99, 133–35, 209; and history, 12–13, 74, 137; and identity, 129–30; and individual, 73; and injury, 13; integrity of, 27, 44–45; and introspection, 52–53; and language, 170–71; and maturation, 13; and motivation, 28; and narrative, 10–11, 200–201, 206–7; and nation, 11; negation of, 74; and public, 71–72; and temporality, 141–42. *See also* individuals, individuality; subjectivity
sentimentality, 31–32, 43, 74, 95–96, 101–2, 196
1740s (decade): and decline of verse satire, 39, 41–42; and development of novel, 153; and Englishness, ix–x; and historical subjectivity, 47–48; as ideological

decade, 107; as privileged decade, 8. *See also* England
sexuality, 236n66; and class, 81; and continuity, 104–7; and linearity, 81–82, 194–95. *See also* gender
Sharp, Michele Turner, 12–13, 91–92, 98–99, 104, 119–20, 126–27, 131–32
Shelley, Percy Bysshe, *Satire upon Satire*, 53–54, 227n56
Siebert, Donald T., 202, 221n7
Silver, Joel, 157–58
similitude, 4, 70–71, 82, 87, 207–8. *See also* difference
Sitter, John, 21, 41–42, 92–94, 101–2, 135–37, 223n27
Slater, Graeme, 82–83, 210–13, 226n38, 238n5
Snead, Jennifer, 41–42
Spenser, Edmund, *The Faerie Queene*, 3
spirituality, 12–13, 18, 97–98, 133, 146–47, 183, 193–94
Starr, Herbert W., 24–25, 231n8
Steele, Kathryn, 162, 179–80, 206–7
Sterne, Laurence, *The Life and Opinions of Tristram Shandy, Gentleman*, 154
strangers, 50, 58, 90
"structures of feeling," 99. *See also* Williams, Raymond
subjectivity, ix–x, 6, 177–78; and continuity, 70–71; and gender, 191–92; and history, 12–13, 16–17, 47–48, 55–59, 61, 89–90, 96, 104, 119–20; and individuality, 175–76; and interiority, 129, 137, 164; loss of, 74; and multiplicity, 143–44; and nation, 16; and poet, 127–28; and satire, 52–53; and temporality, 12; and trauma, 141; universal, 143–44. *See also* interiority
succession, 79–82, 120–21, 190. *See also* examples, exemplars, exemplarity; history, historiography; linearity; sexuality
Swift, Jonathan, viii, 7, 85, 211–12, 227n63; and historical change, 48; "Verses on the Death of Dr. Swift," 47

Temple, Sir William, 211–12, 227n63
theater. *See* performance, performativity
Theater Licensing Act of 1737, 41–42
Theobald, Lewis, 43–44, 83–84
Thompson, Peggy, 151–52
Thomson, James, "Winter," 106
Thorpe, Peter, 45, 93–94
time, temporality, viii, 20; apocalyptic, 147; and archives, 70; and breakage, 12; and commemoration, 217–18; and connection, 59; and continuity, 11–12, 63–64, 73–74, 76–78, 117–18, 127; and death, 188; and history, 12–13, 42, 54–55; interweaving and overlapping of, 98, 124–25, 135, 141–42; and linearity, 37–38, 48–49, 74, 79–81, 195–96; mythic, 20; and nation, 5–6; and objects, 189; and recompense, 95; and rupture, 111–12, 148; and satire, 20; and sexuality, 81–82; and spirituality, 97–98; and stagnation, 74–76, 82; transcending, 89–90; and trauma, 141–42, 147, 181–82. *See also* history, historiography; linearity
Todd, Dennis, 87–88
tort law, 10–12, 14–15, 50, 84–85, 88–89, 165. *See also* recompense
tragedy, 76–77. *See also* history, historiography
transparency, 1–2, 22, 157–58, 170–72, 176, 206, 219. *See also* examples, exemplars, exemplarity
trauma, 11–12, 74–75, 179–80, 196–97, 222n17; and action, 181; and history, 88; and injury, 147–48; and knowledge, 114–15, 179–80; and nation, 84–85; personal and collective, 204–5; and poetry, 129–30; and progress, 75–76; and repetition, 181–82, 197; and subjectivity, 141; and temporality, 141, 147; visibility of, 195, 199. *See also* rape
typology, 59, 63–64, 74, 227n51. *See also* examples, exemplars, exemplarity

verifiability, vii–viii, 17–19, 25–26, 73–75, 80, 86–87, 93–94, 112–13, 138–39, 153, 159–60, 175, 178–79, 183–84, 226n48
verse. *See* poetry, poetics; satire
violence, 10–11; and community, 114; cyclical, 74; national, 150; and originality, 111; and poetry, 139–40; of rape, 180; repetition of, 74–75. *See also* trauma
virtue. *See* examples, exemplars, exemplarity
virtuosos, 69–73, 229n96. *See also* antiquarianism; archives
visibility, 90; and class, 79, 81, 86–87, 118–19, 134; and epistolary, 151; and exemplarity, 149, 162–63; and gender, 199; and naming, 56–57; refusal of, 192; and representation, 44–47, 50–51; and secrecy, 45–46; and value, 55–56. *See also* names, naming

Walpole, Robert, 11
Warburton, William, 69–71, 85, 230n125, 230n127
Warton, Thomas, 91–92, 230n3
Warwick, Sir Philip, 211–12

Watt, Ian, 158–59
Watts, Mary, 25–26
Weber, Harold, 67–68, 85–86
Weinbrot, Howard, 97–98, 115–16, 133, 146–47
Weinfield, Henry, 21, 95–96, 101–2, 107, 109–10, 113–14, 116–22, 136–37
West, Benjamin, *The Death of General Wolfe* (c. 1770), 3
West, Richard, viii
West-Pavlov, Russell, 37, 70–71
Wilkinson, Andrew M., 35–36, 39, 41–42, 54–55
Williams, Aubrey, 57–58
Williams, Raymond, 94, 98–99, 117–18, 122–23, 135, 233n90
Wilson, Jennifer, 161–62, 236n48, 236n65
Wolfe, James, 3
Woolf, Daniel, 45–46, 211–12
Wordsworth, William, 23, 224n46; "Lines Written a Few Miles above Tintern Abbey," 13–14
wound. *See* injury

Young, Edward, *Night Thoughts*, 23, 224n44

www.ingramcontent.com/pod-product-compliance
Lightning Source LLC
Chambersburg PA
CBHW021658230426
43668CB00008B/661